Practicing Organization Development

The Change Agent Series for Groups and Organizations

MISSION STATEMENT

The books in this series are intended to be cutting-edge, state-of-the-art, and innovative approaches to participative change in organizational settings. They are written for, and written by, organization development (OD) practitioners interested in new approaches to facilitating participative change. They are geared to providing both theory and advice on practical application.

Finding Your Way in the Consulting Jungle

A Guidebook for Organization Development Practitioners

Arthur M. Freedman

Richard E. Zackrison

Foreword by Richard Beckhard

JOSSEY-BASS/PFEIFFER
A Wiley Company
San Francisco

Practicing
Organization
Development

Library of Congress Cataloging-in-Publication Data

Freedman, Arthur M., 1937-
  Finding your way in the consulting jungle : a guidebook for
organization development practitioners / Arthur M. Freedman, Richard E.
Zackrison; foreword by Richard Beckhard.
    p. cm.
  Includes bibliographical references and index.
  ISBN 0-7879-5300-8 (acid-free paper)
  1. Business consultants. I. Zackrison, Richard E. II. Title.
HD69.C6 F737 2001
001'.068—dc21

                                                                00-010812

Printed in the United States of America.

Published by

JOSSEY-BASS/PFEIFFER
A Wiley Company
350 Sansome Street, 5th Floor
San Francisco, CA 94104-1342
415.433.1740; Fax 415.433.0499
800.274.4434; Fax 800.569.0443

www.pfeiffer.com

Acquiring Editor: Matthew Holt	Senior Production Editor: Dawn Kilgore
Director of Development: Kathleen Dolan Davies	Manufacturing Manager: Becky Carreño
Developmental Editor: Susan Rachmeler	Interior and Cover Design: Bruce Lundquist
Editor: Rebecca Taff	Illustrations: Richard Sheppard

Printing   10 9 8 7 6 5 4 3 2 1

Contents

Dedication

As we were writing this book, we received the sad news that one of the founders of the field of organization development had died. Richard Beckhard was one of our mentors. He was a gracious and giving person. We drew upon many of his concepts and methods, especially for Chapter 8, Management of Change. He was one of the giants upon whose shoulders we stand. We will miss him. We dedicate this book to him.

Foreword
to the Series

ON **1967,** Warren Bennis, Ed Schein, and I were faculty members of the Sloan School of Management at MIT. We decided to produce a series of paperback books that collectively would describe the state of the field of organization development (OD). Organization development as a field had been named by myself and several others from our pioneer change effort at General Mills in Minneapolis, Minnesota, some ten years earlier.

Today I define OD as "a systemic and systematic change effort, using behavioral science knowledge and skill, to transform the organization to a new state."

In any case, several books and many articles had been written, but there was no consensus on whether OD was a field of practice, an area of study, or a profession. We had not even established OD as a theory or even as a practice.

We decided that there was a need for something that would describe the state of OD. Our intention was to each write a book and also to recruit three other authors. After some searching, we found a young editor who had just joined the small publishing house of Addison-Wesley. We made contact, and the series was born. Our audience was to be human resource professionals who spent their time consulting with managers in their development through various small-group activities, such as team building. More than thirty books have been published in that series, and the series has had a life of its own. We just celebrated its thirtieth anniversary.

At last year's National OD Network Conference, I said that it was time for the OD profession to change and transform itself. Is that not what we change agents tell our clients to do? This new Jossey-Bass/Pfeiffer series will do just that. It can be seen as:

- A documentation of the re-invention of OD;

- An effort that will take us to the next level; and

- A practical effort to transfer to the world the theory and practice of leading-edge practitioners and theorists.

The books in this new series will thus prove to be valuable resources for change agents to keep current with the new and leading-edge ideas and practices.

May this very exciting change agent series be most creative and innovative. May it give our field a renewed burst of energy and awareness.

Richard Beckhard
Written on Labor Day weekend 1999 from my summer cabin near Bethel, Maine

Introduction to the Series

"We must become the change we want to see."

—*Mahatma Gandhi*

"We live in a moment of history where change is so speeded up that we begin to see the present only when it is already disappearing."

—*R. D. Laing*

WE CAN EXPECT MORE CHANGE to occur in our lifetimes than has occurred since the beginning of civilization over ten thousand years ago. *Practicing Organization Development: The Change Agent Series for Groups and Organizations* is a new series of books being launched to help those who must cope with or create change in organizational settings. That includes almost everyone.

The Current State of Organization Development

Our view of OD in this series is an optimistic one. We believe that OD is gaining favor as decision makers realize that a balance *must* be struck between the drivers of change and the people involved in it and affected by it. Although OD does have

its disadvantages at a time characterized by quantum leap change, it remains preferable to such alternative approaches to change as coercion, persuasion, leadership
change, and debate.[1] Organization development practitioners are reinventing their
approaches, based on certain foundational roots of the field, in combination with
emerging principles to ensure that OD will increasingly be recognized as a viable,
important, and inherently participative approach to help people in organizations
facilitate, anticipate, and manage change.

A Brief History of the Genesis of the OD Series

A few years ago, and as a direct result of the success of *Practicing Organization Development: A Guide for Practitioners* by Rothwell, Sullivan, and McLean, the publisher—
feeling that OD was experiencing a rebirth of interest in the United States and in
other nations—wanted to launch a new OD series. The goal of this new series was
not to replace, or even compete directly with, the well-established Addison-Wesley
OD Series (edited by Edgar Schein). Instead, as the editors saw it, this series would
provide a means by which the most promising authors in OD whose voices had not
previously been heard could share their ideas. The publisher enlisted the support
of Bill Rothwell, Roland Sullivan, and Kristine Quade to turn the dream of a series
into a reality.

This series was long in the making. After sharing many discussions with the
publisher and circulating among themselves several draft descriptions of the series
editorial guidelines, the editors were guests of Bob Tannenbaum, one of the field's
founders, in Carmel, California, in February 1999 to discuss the series with a group
of well-known OD practitioners interested in authoring books. Several especially
supportive publisher representatives, including Matt Holt and Josh Blatter, were
also present at that weekend-long meeting. It was an opportunity for diverse OD
practitioners, representing many philosophical viewpoints, to come together to
share their vision for a new book series. In a sense, this series represents an OD intervention in the OD field in that it is geared to bringing change to the field most closely
associated with change management and facilitation.

---

[1]W. Rothwell, R. Sullivan, & G. McLean. (1995). Introduction (pp. 3–46). In W. Rothwell, R. Sullivan, &
G. McLean, *Practicing Organization Development: A Guide for Consultants*. San Francisco, CA: Jossey-Bass/
Pfeiffer.

What Distinguishes the Books in this Series

The books in this series are meant to be cutting-edge and state-of-the-art in their approach to OD. The goal of the series is to provide an outlet for proven authorities in OD who have not put their ideas into print or for up-and-coming writers in OD who have new, sometimes unorthodox, approaches that are stimulating and exciting. Some of the books in this series describe inspirational concepts that can lead to actionable change and purvey ideas so new that they are not fully developed.

Unique to this series is the cutting-edge emphasis, the immediate applicability, and the ease of transferability of the concepts. The aim of this series is nothing less than to reinvent, re-energize, and reinvigorate OD. In each book, we have also recommended that the author(s) provide:

- A research base of some kind, meaning new information derived from practice and/or systematic investigation and
- Practical tools, worksheets, case studies and other ready-to-go approaches that help the authors drag "theory" to "practice" to make these new, cutting-edge approaches more concrete.

Subject Matter That Will (and Will Not) Be Covered

The books in this series are varied in their approach, but they are united by their focus. All share an emphasis on organization development (OD). Hence, books in this series are about participative change efforts. They are not about such other popular topics as leadership, management development, consulting, group dynamics—unless those topics are treated in new, cutting-edge ways and are geared to OD practitioners.

This Book

There is a need in the OD consulting world to optimize the effectiveness of engagements and to assure a match between the consultant's unique competencies and the needs and preferences of the client system. *Finding Your Way in the Consulting Jungle* presents the information and guidance OD consultants need to understand their own place in the consulting network, to differentiate themselves from other types of consultants, and to work with both clients and colleagues to make sure everyone's needs are met. This book covers such topics as how to market oneself; consulting types, philosophies, and competencies; how to interview prospective clients;

how to write proposals; who is responsible for what during a change process; and ethical considerations. You will find this book to be an invaluable tool as you work your way through "the consulting jungle."

Series Website

For further information and resources about the books in this series and about the current and future practice of organization development, we encourage readers to visit the series website at *www.PracticingOD.com.*

William J. Rothwell
University Park, PA

Roland Sullivan
Deephaven, MN

Kristine Quade
Minnetonka, MN

Statement
of the Board

IT IS OUR PLEASURE TO PARTICIPATE in and influence the start up of *Practicing Organization Development: The Change Agent Series for Groups and Organizations.* The purpose of the series is to stimulate the profession and influence how OD is defined and practiced. This statement is intended to set the context for the series by addressing three important questions: (1) What is OD? (2) Is the OD profession at a crossroads? and (3) What is the purpose of this series?

What Is Organization Development?

We offer the following definition of OD to stimulate debate:

> Organization development is a system-wide and values-based collaborative process of applying behavioral science knowledge to the adaptive development, improvement, and reinforcement of such organizational features as the strategies, structures, processes, people, and cultures that lead to organization effectiveness.

The definition suggests that OD can be understood in terms of its several foci:

First, *OD is a system-wide process.* It works with whole systems. In the past, the bias has been toward working at the individual and group levels. More recently, the focus has shifted to organizations and multi-organization systems. We support that trend in general but honor and acknowledge the fact that the traditional focus on smaller systems is both legitimate and necessary.

Second, *OD is values-based.* Traditionally, OD has attempted to distinguish itself from other forms of planned change and applied behavioral science by promoting a set of humanistic values and by emphasizing the importance of personal growth as a key to its practice. Today, that focus is blurred and there is much debate about the value base underlying the practice of OD. We support a more formal and direct conversation about what these values are and how the field is related to them.

Third, *OD is collaborative.* Our first value commitment as OD practitioners is to bring about an inclusive, diverse workforce with a focus of integrating differences into a world-wide culture mentality.

Fourth, *OD is based on behavioral science knowledge.* Organization development should incorporate and apply knowledge from sociology, psychology, anthropology, technology, and economics toward the end of making systems more effective. We support the continued emphasis in OD on behavioral science knowledge and believe that OD practitioners should be widely read and comfortable with several of the disciplines.

Fifth, *OD is concerned with the adaptive development, improvement, and reinforcement of strategies, structures, processes, people, culture, and other features of organizational life.* This statement not only describes the organizational elements that are the target of change, but also describes the process by which effectiveness is increased. That is, OD works in a variety of areas, and it is focused on improving these areas. We believe that such a statement of process and content strongly implies that a key feature of OD is the transference of knowledge and skill to the system so that it is more able to handle and manage change in the future.

Sixth and finally, *OD is about improving organization effectiveness.* It is not just about making people happy; it is also concerned with meeting financial goals, improving productivity, and addressing stakeholder satisfaction. We believe that OD's future is closely tied to the incorporation of this value in its purpose and the demonstration of this objective in its practice.

Is the OD Profession at a Crossroads?

For years, OD professionals have said that OD is at a crossroads. From our perspective at the beginning of the new millennium, the field of organization development can be characterized by the following statements:

1. Practitioners today are torn. The professional organizations representing OD practitioners, including the OD Network, the OD Institute, the International OD Association, and the Academy of Management's OD and Change Division, are experiencing tremendous uncertainties in their purposes, practices, and relationships.

2. There are increasing calls for regulation/certification.

3. Many respected practitioners have suggested that people who profess to manage change are behind those who are creating it. Organization development practitioners should lead through influence rather than follow the lead of those who are sometimes coercive in their approach to change.

4. The field is defined by techniques.

5. The values that guide the field are unclear and ill-defined.

6. Too many people are practicing OD without any training in the field.

7. Practitioners are having difficulty figuring out how to market their services.

The situation suggests the following provocative questions:

- How can OD practitioners help formulate strategy, shape the strategy development process, contribute to the content of strategy, and drive how strategy will be implemented?

- How can OD practitioners encourage an open examination of the ways organizations are conceived and managed?

- How can OD focus on the drivers of change external to individuals, such as the external environment, business strategy, organization change, and culture change, as well as on the drivers of change internal to individuals, such as individual interpretations of culture, behavior, style, and mind-set?

- How much should OD be part of the competencies of all leaders and how much should it be the sole domain of professionally trained, career-oriented OD practitioners?

What Is the Purpose of This Series?

This series is intended to provide current thinking about OD as a field and to provide practical approaches based on sound theory and research. It is targeted for full-time external or internal OD practitioners; top executives in charge of enterprise-wide change; and managers, HR practitioners, training and development professionals, and others who have responsibility for change in organizational and trans-organizational settings. At the same time, these books will be directed toward cutting-edge thinking and state-of-the-art approaches. In some cases, the ideas, approaches, or techniques described are still evolving, so the books are intended to open up dialogue.

We know that the books in this series will provide a leading forum for thought-provoking dialogue within the OD field.

About the Board Members

David Bradford is senior lecturer in organizational behavior at the Graduate School of Business, Stanford University, Palo Alto, California. He is co-author (with Allan R. Cohen) of *Managing for Excellence, Influence Without Authority*, and *POWER UP: Transforming Organizations Through Shared Leadership*.

W. Warner Burke is professor of psychology and education and chair of the Department of Organization and Leadership at Teachers College, Columbia University, New York, New York. His most recent publication is *Business Profiles of Climate Shifts: Profiles of Change Makers*, (with William Trahant and Richard Koonce).

Edith Whitfield Seashore is organization consultant and co-founder (with Morley Segal) of AUNTL Masters Program in Organization Development. She is co-author of *What Did You Say?* and *The Art of Giving and Receiving Feedback* and co-editor of *The Promise of Diversity*.

Robert Tannenbaum is emeritus professor of development of human systems, Graduate School of Management, University of California, Los Angeles; recipient of Lifetime Achievement Award by the National OD Network. He has published numerous books, including *Human Systems Development* with Newton Margulies and Fred Massarik.

Christopher G. Worley is director, MSOD Program, Pepperdine University, Malibu, California. He is co-author of *Organization Development and Change* (7th ed.), with Tom Cummings, and of *Integrated Strategic Change*, with David Hitchin and Walter Ross.

Shaolin Zhang is senior manager of organization development for Motorola (China) Electronics Ltd. He received his master's degree in American Studies from Beijing Foreign Studies University, Beijing, China, and holds a Ph.D. in sociology from York University, Toronto, Canada.

Acknowledgments

WE ARE IMMENSELY GRATEFUL to Robert Tannenbaum, the series advisors, W. Warner Burke, the late Richard Beckhard, and the editors of Jossey-Bass/Pfeiffer's series of books on organization development—Kristine Quade, William J. Rothwell, and Roland Sullivan—for their recommendations. They helped us to gain perspective and clarity. We are most appreciative for the assistance and patience of Susan Rachmeler, Pfeiffer's developmental editor, who must have gone over this manuscript as frequently as we did.

We also want to express our appreciation to a number of people who have reviewed our earlier efforts and helped us to clarify what we have been trying to communicate: Ken Green, Kristine Newman, and Frank Friedlander.

Introduction

Ⓜ️ANY YEARS AGO one of the authors saw an advertisement in a business daily for a two-day course in "Consultant Training." Out of curiosity, he registered for the course. In return for a $350 fee, he was told that to be a successful consultant all he needed was a power wardrobe, embossed business cards, a leather attaché case, and someone with a sensual female voice to answer the telephone. Oh, yes . . . it was also important to seek assignments at least five hundred miles away from your residence—the problem of being a prophet in one's own land and all that! Today, a similar two-day course costs nearly $1,300!

It is no wonder that so many executives distrust those who call themselves "consultants" these days. Because there are no regulatory, legal constraints or financial barriers to entering the field, virtually anyone can claim to be a "consultant."

Qualified, experienced, ethical organization development (OD) practitioners and management consultants are justifiably concerned with what we call "the consulting jungle," a landscape filled with many *ersatz-consultants* who lack the requisite competencies—conceptual perspective, experience, skills, and/or ethical standards—to deliver professional OD consulting services effectively and with

1

integrity. Such individuals and their firms have become adept at feeding off of unsuspecting, naïve, and/or desperate client organizations.

Charting Our Path Through the Jungle

Based on our sixty years of combined experience in training and mentoring OD consultants, the authors have concluded that the most practical perspective for studying effective consultant behavior is to follow the natural flow of a typical OD consulting assignment, that is, from the initial stage of marketing one's services to the final stage of evaluating the results of the consulting effort.

The reward for effectively surviving each stage of the OD consultant's trek through the consulting jungle is the opportunity to embark on the next leg of the journey.

Contacts with Potential Client Systems. Many highly skilled consultants fail before they have a chance to talk face-to-face with representatives or agents of potential client systems. In most cases this failure is caused by a nonexistent, inadequate, or inappropriate marketing strategy. In Chapter 1 we examine how all kinds and types of consultants and agents typically connect with each other—including our perceptions of the strengths and weaknesses of various marketing approaches.

Does the Organization Need a Consultant? Consultants whose marketing strategies are successful will gain at least one exploratory meeting with agents. In Chapter 2 we consider the question of whether or not the prospective client system really needs consultation. We also consider a number of organizational contingencies that either increase or decrease the probability that consulting assistance is required.

Types of Consultants. Survival in any jungle is highly dependent on a thorough familiarity with the other beasts that surround you. In Chapter 3 we focus on the various types of consultants with whom OD consultants may compete or collaborate. We include a discussion of which types of consultant are best suited for different consulting assignments.

Consulting Philosophy and Consultant Competencies. Even clever amateurs can bluff their way far enough into the consulting jungle to obtain interviews with agents. In Chapters 4 and 5 we examine the critical qualities, attributes, and characteristics that differentiate OD consultants from other types of consultants—those factors that are essential for OD consultants' long-term effectiveness and survival.

The Selection Interview. Many otherwise skilled consultants fail to negotiate the pitfalls and snares that lie along the twisting, turning paths that emerge during selection interviews. In Chapter 6 we discuss selection interviews, including specific suggestions for preparing for them, surviving them, and learning from them. We also try to help competent and ethical OD consultants to assist agents to select the most competent consultants and to match the type of consultant with the organization's specific requirements.

Consulting Proposals and Contracts. After OD consultants survive a selection interview, they are given an opportunity to submit a proposal. The rewards for impressive proposals are contracts. Chapter 7 specifies the information and skills that OD consultants need to write winning proposals and viable contracts that significantly reduce implementation problems.

Management of Change. Although the preceding steps consume a lot of the consultant's time and energy, they are merely the prelude to the real journey. In Chapter 8 we examine the dynamics and processes that OD consultants need to know to facilitate complex systems change initiatives, including the management of resistance to change. We provide practical tips and tools to help OD consultants help leaders and members to comprehend and manage large and small changes in their own organizations.

Consultant Ethics. Effective consultants, in our minds, are invited to *return* to the consulting jungle when they demonstrate their ability to negotiate its traps, pitfalls, and denizens in a professional, ethical manner. In Chapter 9 we present what we consider to be the minimal acceptable ethics for OD consultants.

We have written this book for OD practitioners and other kinds and types of consultants who, caught up in the confusing, competitive maelstrom, may be unclear about their place or may have lost their sense of *who* they are, *what* they do, and *why* they do it. This is particularly relevant for OD consultants, leaders, and agents with limited experience in finding their way, unescorted, in the consulting jungle. We hope this book is also useful for those leaders and managers who recognize that it is in their enlightened self-interest to add and integrate OD concepts, methods, and skills into their repertoire of leadership styles and management practices.

Throughout this book, we have emphasized the perspectives of leaders and agents in order to challenge OD consultants—students, novices, and old pros—to climb into the leaders' shoes and seriously question their own assumptions, strategies, and practices.

Framing the Book

Who Is the "Client"? We consider the proper *client* of OD consultants to be *the entire organization,* not just the agent who selects and negotiates contracts with consultants or the organization's leadership. Neither do we think of any particular population of employees as the client: We think of the agents, leaders, managers, and populations of employees as parts of the client system.

Terminology: To avoid tedium and for the sake of brevity, we use several terms throughout this book. Specifically, we use the term "agent" to refer to a representative of a prospective or current client system. An agent may be a designee or a leader. The term "leader" refers to the formally designated senior manager of an entire organization, a major or minor subsystem, or a committee, team, or task force. The term "client system" refers to the organizational entity with which we contract to provide our OD services. It could be an entire organization, a major or minor subsystem, or a committee, team, or task force. We trust that you will not be confused by our terminology.

The Virtual Setting: Imagine that the two of us are sitting with you in your classroom, office, or conference room. We are discussing your intent to market and deliver your OD consultation services in a volatile market—either as an internal or external OD practitioner. We hope to address many of your doubts, concerns, and reservations about this confusing, complex, and uncertain environment.

So, without further preliminary discussion, let us pack our gear and prepare to begin our journey. Welcome to the consulting jungle.

① Contacts with Potential Client Systems

MARKETING IS A FUNDAMENTAL SURVIVAL SKILL. No successful consultant can do without it. Both internal and external consultants should be continually, consciously, considering the question, "Where will my next (or first) contract come from?" You must have a flow of inquiries from reliable agents to satisfy both your personal and financial needs.

You must rely on yourself. Even though you have had long-term engagements in the past, once your current contracts are completed, revenues can easily fall to zero. Even worse, your current contracts could be cancelled midstream.

When we work independently, we cannot afford to become complacent or comfortable with our current engagements. This is also prudent advice for "permanent" internal OD consultants.

In your ideal world, potential client systems would already know about you. Ideally, they would also know a lot about the OD consulting discipline, that is, what you do, how you do it, your strategies and methods, and your values and philosophies. However, because none of us live in that ideal world, you cannot count on any of the above.

The truth is that consultants inevitably find themselves in a position of having to market and—heaven forbid—*sell* themselves and their services to rather naïve, skeptical, or cynical agents and executives. Paradoxically, these people are *gatekeepers,* who act for the very organizations that usually need and can benefit most from our OD consulting services!

Promotional and Marketing Options

Not all consultants actively promote or market themselves and their services. Some rely on their consulting firms' senior partners to function as rainmakers. But most of us do not have that luxury.

Many marketing options are available. We typically employ some combination of the following methods, some of which we may find compatible with our personal values, beliefs, and preferences, and others we may not. You will have to decide which ones are compatible with your own values, beliefs, and preferences. In no particular order, the most popular methods are:

1. Direct mail, such as brochures, white papers, and other marketing materials.

2. Booths and/or receptions in hospitality suites at industry and professional association conferences and exhibitions.

3. Presentations at trade and professional association conferences or meetings.

4. Cold calls, that is, engaging in personal selling by making unsolicited appointments to visit and talk with senior managers of target organizations.

5. Networking efforts with influential individuals or firms that are in a position to open doors and establish contacts.

6. Published articles on "hot" topics in trade or business journals that agents and their organizational leaders are likely to read.

7. Published books on hot topics.

8. Responses to hot issues that are reported in the business media.

9. Interactive websites.

10. Partnerships with other consultants (or firms) who have complementary capabilities, relationships with clients, and synergistic potential.

11. Telemarketing.

12. Responses to requests for proposals (RFPs) and requests for quotations (RFQs).

13. Headhunters, executive and specialist recruiters.

14. Referrals and endorsements from satisfied leaders of former client organizations.

15. Public relations (PR) campaigns utilizing press releases on hot issues.

Direct Mail Marketing

Most senior managers are inundated by an ever-increasing number and variety of sophisticated brochures from consulting firms of all types. Because it is virtually impossible to distinguish competent, qualified consultants from hucksters on the basis of these brochures, they usually receive little or no attention.

Prospective clients may keep a file of brochures that most interest them, that is, those that indicate that the consultant or firm has a coherent consulting philosophy, substantial experience, and functional competencies that might "fit" the organization's needs at some time in the future.

Less interesting brochures say little about the consulting firm's principals, philosophy, experience, or capabilities. Instead, they list the Fortune 1000, 500, 200, 100, or 50 organizations that have supposedly "benefited" from their services. Seldom do the consultants specify what they have done for these organizations or how they may have benefited. Such lists are worthless as a measure of a consultant's effectiveness.

Exhibitions and Receptions at Conferences

Trade and professional association and business conferences with exhibitions can provide excellent opportunities for you to connect with agents of prospective client systems. However, the costs of setting up display booths or hospitality suites are prohibitive for independent consultants or smaller, "boutique" consulting firms.

On the other hand, you might want to attend these conferences as a participant to learn about emerging business issues and get a bright idea or two about new services that you might offer. You may also find yourself sitting beside or enjoying a coffee break with a senior executive whose organization may be a potential client system. Or perhaps that executive may provide you with a hot lead or referral.

One warning about conferences. Many executives have learned to be wary of consultants who are more interested in finding clients than in the content of the workshop they are attending. Truly competent consultants will focus on learning as much as possible from the workshop, not selling themselves or their firms to other participants. So if agents perceive you selling more than listening and learning, they are likely to perceive you as tuna-seeking sharks and tune you out.

Presentations at Trade and Professional Associations

You can increase the odds of a welcoming response when you first make contact with agents who know your name and have a positive impression of what you do and what you stand for. Presentations at trade and professional associations may be the most effective means of gaining that name recognition, assuming you are a talented presenter with truly compelling material.

If you are interested in making presentations, a first step is to determine which conferences attract the kinds of people who are concerned about the kinds of issues with which you might be of assistance. These people are also gatekeepers for their organizations. Next, obtain the name and phone number or e-mail address for the chairperson of the program committee for the next conference to find out both the themes (if any) of the next conferences and how you can get on the program. Program committee chairs are concerned with the relevance of presentations to their members—the more topical the better. When you find a match between the association's interests and your capabilities, you will have to design a high-impact presentation that is backed up with some colorful, drop-dead PowerPoint® slides. You can print out and duplicate your PowerPoint slides to distribute as handouts that can be effective, takeaway marketing devices.

We engage in lots of conversations following our presentations. A few audience members tell us a lot about how our presentations fit their organizations' current concerns. They also educate us about issues that we should look into. They give us their business cards. We can make and maintain contact with these new members of our marketing networks at some time after the conference.

Cold Calls

Cold call selling can be an effective means for consultants to establish initial contact with prospective client systems' agents. Consultants who use this direct approach will usually reveal their true consultation style during the first two minutes. Some are most interested in selling themselves and in impressing agents, so they use the call to talk about who they know, where they have been, and what they have done to help other client organizations to accomplish their objectives. Other consultants are more interested in the agents and their organizations' current situations. They ask questions about the organization's current issues, how these issues impact the organization's mission or business plan, and what the organization is doing or plans to do about dealing with the issues. Then, they listen to the agent's answers while adopting an attitude of intense interest, curiosity, and understanding. When they hear an opportunity to offer relevant services, they say so. Guess which one we would hire to work with us!

In choosing the cold calling option, understand that the more you know about the organization before you call, the easier it will be to know what questions are most pertinent. Be sure to do some in-depth homework so you will be conversant with significant aspects of your prospective client system before trying to make an appointment. Internet searches of the company in the business media are very useful in learning what might be occurring within or external to a particular company that would qualify it as a potential client system. For example, you can search the online archives of *Fortune* or *Business Week* for stories about many major global companies. You can find out a lot about a prospect's business, senior officers, competitive position, and financial condition by searching out the Form 10-Ks that they must file with the U.S. Securities and Exchange Commission.

Networking

Networking seems to be the most effective and reliable means of obtaining new OD consulting contracts, through two major categories of network members: colleagues and influential client system members. This is a viable approach for both internal and external OD consultants.

Many consultants of any kind or type seem to find it easier to market themselves to people in their own field. As OD consultants, many of our marketing "targets" are *external* OD consultants, who already have contracts that are too large for them to service by themselves. Other targets are *internal* OD consultants or internal HR generalists, who occasionally require the services of external OD consultants.

Of course, internal or external OD colleagues generally are one or two steps removed from the leaders of the organizational subsystems with whom you would ultimately like to work. It is highly desirable for you to include leaders of potential client organizations and/or their major subsystems in your network. This is *essential* for internal OD consultants. For externals, participating in and presenting at trade and professional associations, as we discussed earlier, is an effective way to connect with organizational and subsystem leaders.

An obvious but frequently neglected point about networking is that once you choose to consider influential persons as part of your network, you must *stay in contact* with them, consistently and frequently. Call them at least once a month. Ask how they and their organizations are doing. Tell them about what you have been doing. Send them relevant (but short) articles (by you or others) on subjects of interest. Reprints of published articles are most impressive and effective. Staple your business card to the article along with a personal FYI note. If you are in the neighborhood, get together for coffee, drinks, or dinner. Send birthday or holiday cards. In other words, maintain and nurture these relationships! The members of your network must feel that they are gaining something from a continuing relationship with you. If they feel you are engaged only in a long-term effort to extract some business from or through them, they are likely to rebuff your efforts to maintain contact.

Published Articles

If you are an academician, there are career-enhancing reasons to publish books, as well as articles in professional journals. However, as OD consultants, there are more practical reasons.

The first step, of course, is to target your intended audience of leaders and agents. The second step is to show how the services you offer are "solutions" to the specific issues with which organizations are confronted. Third, you must publish your articles in the kinds of publications that are likely to be read by influential members of your prospective client systems. These will probably not be your own professional publications; rather, they will be business magazines, trade association journals and newsletters, and professional journals published by other disciplines' associations.

The intent is for you to gain name recognition. You also want to show influential members of prospective client systems both that you understand their issues and that you have relevant, practical services to offer them—services that can add value to their organizational performance and results.

Published Books

The logic for writing and publishing books to advertise your consulting services is essentially identical to the logic for making presentations at conferences and for publishing books and articles. Obviously, with a book, you have more space to make your point.

When publishing books, you have two options: Self-publishing or contracting with established publishers. It is difficult for an author without an established reputation to attract the attention of most publishing houses. However, the benefits of persistence are often worth the trouble. Once you have a contract, publishers offer assistance with formatting, editing, and graphics. They manage printing, some advertising, and distribution. You will have to do some research to make sure that their distribution channels target the markets you want to reach. You will have to agree to participate actively in marketing the book. That should be fine, because that is precisely what you want to do.

Self-publishing is far more labor-intensive and time-consuming. You will have to learn or secure the resources required to perform all the editing, printing, advertising, and distributing tasks that publishing houses typically do for their authors.

Of course, you can use the so-called "vanity press" services, for which you foot the bills for all the expenses that these publishers incur in producing your book. Vanity presses do not merchandise or distribute for you, but you can have a nicely packaged vehicle for marketing your services that you can send to or leave on the desks of agents of your targeted prospective client systems.

Scanning for Hot Issues

Consultants—and especially consulting firms—must be continually alert for changes in the relevant environments of their prospective client systems. Sudden, dramatic changes in their market environments are the "hot" issues. These may include domestic and foreign governmental legislation and regulations, customers' needs and preferences, competition, geopolitics, economics, productivity-enhancing technology, workforce and market demographics, innovative organizational theory, and the like.

Although we cannot predetermine what information will emerge from which source or when, vigilance requires us to invest some of our discretionary time in staying current with and in anticipating emerging events and developments. We think of this as maintaining a very broad, multidimensional "radar screen."

So we read a lot of newspapers, business publications, popular and specialized journals and books, and, increasingly, the Internet. We watch CNN. We attend business conferences and association meetings to listen for what is attracting the attention of the various audiences. We listen to the sponsors and participants in our public workshops, in-house training/educational seminars, and OD consultations.

Informed and competent OD consultants can produce credible information that describes how they can apply their OD competencies to the issues that organizational leaders feel are critical for their personal, professional, and organizational well-being.

Interactive Websites

This is a rather passive initiative that can pay off in generating agents' interest in your services. There are a couple of difficulties to cope with. First, you must make several decisions: What to put on your website, how complex and interactive to make it, and how to get it up and running. Many consultants use their websites to display brief papers on current, hot organizational issues and how their services can help client systems to deal with them. You will probably have to select an IT specialist who can help you to do it or serve as your webmaster. You will also have to contract with an Internet service provider (ISP) to serve as the host for your web page. All of this can be expensive.

Second, you have to determine how to inform agents that they should surf the net and log on to your website. We suggest that you emulate other B2B (business-to-business) companies that advertise their websites in their print and broadcast advertising and on their business cards.

Partnerships with Other Consultants or Firms

You can fill empty space in your calendar if you can hook up with other OD consultants who are managing large OD initiatives. In essence, you would serve as a subcontractor to colleagues who serve as project leaders. It should be common sense that colleagues who bring you onto their projects will expect you to reciprocate sooner or later. If you cannot reciprocate, for example, if your engagements are too small or too specialized, keep these very special colleagues very well-informed of your future activities on an ongoing basis. Otherwise, you may gain an unearned reputation as an ungrateful colleague and you may be excluded from other OD consulting teams in which these persons are involved.

Another kind of partnership is far more significant these days. It is becoming increasingly essential for OD consultants to become respected and credible members of multidisciplinary consulting teams. We foresee a decline in pure OD consulting assignments. With so many techno-structural change efforts being implemented these days, even stand-alone OD consulting contracts operate interdependently with a variety of techspert consultants, extra-pairs-of-hands, and training/educational specialists.

We believe a great deal of potential synergy is lost when separate contracts are written for many types of consultants and for many disciplines that are properly involved in the same complex systems change initiatives. Often, this is because each single-discipline consultation is managed by different system managers, who are inattentive to how the implementation of one consultant's contract in one subsystem impacts other interdependent subsystems and other consultants' work in other parts of the organization. In other words, the client system neglects to assign a single person or mechanism to provide the essential integration, coordination of effort, and monitoring for progress and secondary side effects.

Telemarketing

Telemarketing is not an option that we, personally, recommend. However, we include it because we have recently been targeted by several training/educational specialist firms that probably hired telemarketing firms to use commercially available lists of potential customers to generate some sales. We find this annoying and offensive. However, if prospects bother to listen to the call-center operators, we suppose they might find something of value.

RFPs and RFQs

Requests for proposals (RFPs) and requests for quotes (RFQs) are most often used by governmental, grant-giving institutes, or funding agencies that are obliged to open the bidding for a piece of work to all competitors and then accept the low bid. The most qualified bidders who do the best work are not necessarily considered.

We have also discovered, through disappointing experience, that many agencies get help from favored consulting firms or vendors when writing the RFPs and RFQs. The requests are constructed so that only the preferred vendors have a realistic chance to meet the criteria and receive a contract. In some cases, we have suggested innovative strategies and interventions in our proposals. We did not receive the contracts but found out later that the preferred firms used our ideas.

If you choose to use the RFP/RFQ option, you will want to subscribe to governmental publications that list and briefly describe all current RFPs and RFQs and/or apply to put yourself on the agencies' lists of qualified bidders. It is also useful to have a friend inside the agency that issues the RFP/RFQ who can tell you whether or not the contract is "wired."

Headhunters

Search firms, known also as "headhunters" or executive and specialist recruiters, can be useful intermediaries if you seek a position as an external OD consultant in a consulting firm or as an internal OD consultant within a host organization. Many of these search firms specialize in recruiting human resource management (HRM) specialists and OD consultants.

Search firms identify which positions are available in consulting firms and host organizations. Then they call or send e-mail to members of relevant associations—such as the American Society for Training and Development (ASTD), the OD Network, or the OD Institute. They typically ask questions such as, "Would you or anyone you know be interested in thus-and-such a position with this-or-that kind of an organization?" For obvious reasons, they try to conceal the identity of the organization that is hiring.

Recruiting is lucrative. Search firms often collect around 30 percent of the first-year salaries for successfully placed candidates.

Referrals

The most effective consultants we know do not market themselves at all. These consultants often rely on "word-of-mouth" advertising from satisfied senior managers in previous client systems. Referrals from satisfied customers are, beyond any doubt, the most effective way for agents to find consultants who are likely to meet their organizational needs.

As an OD consultant, your job is to influence executives who can influence leaders and agents in other companies who are now or may soon be looking for consultative assistance.

We are never reluctant to ask our satisfied current client systems' leaders to recommend or endorse us when we are looking for new business. Of course, we also include these folks in our networks and we maintain constant, consistent contact with them, even though we are not and may never again work directly with them or their organizations.

Public Relations Campaigns

Let's assume that you are in the habit of tracking current and emerging trends and hot topics, as we previously suggested. The question is, "How can you convert that information into potent marketing initiatives that will yield appointments with agents of potential client systems?"

Public relations campaigns can make this information work for you. You may choose to do it yourself or hire a consultant or firm specializing in public relations and communications to do it for you.

Remember that PR campaigns are intended to bring you to the attention of qualified agents. You want them to know enough about you to call and discuss possible consulting engagements. So you have to find ways to associate your name and service capabilities with related, current or emerging issues that your target audiences consider to be important.

You have to consider what media your intended audience is most likely to read, watch, or hear and then put your message in front of them. Public relations firms should be capable of packaging your message into attractive, compelling press releases and then placing these messages with reporters, columnists, and the editorial staff for the print and broadcast business media. Leaders and agents who receive and respond to these messages may then consider your messages, compare what you have to say with their perceptions of what is going on in their companies, and reach for their phones.

A Strategy for Marketing Your Services

You may find the Marketing Strategy Worksheet in Exhibit 1.1 useful to clarify your thinking about which of the fifteen options presented you are able and willing to implement.

Exhibit 1.1. Marketing Strategy Worksheet

Strategy	Able?	Willing?	Do More	Continue	Do Less	Specific Actions
1. Use Direct Marketing						
2. Rent Booth at Association Conferences						
3. Present at Association Conferences						
4. Make Cold Calls						
5. Network						
6. Publish Journal Articles						
7. Publish Books						
8. Scan for, Respond to Hot Issues						
9. Set Up a Website						
10. Establish Partnerships						
11. Telemarket						
12. Respond to RFPs and FRQs						
13. Utilize Headhunters						
14. Solicit Referrals						
15. Mount a Public Relations Campaign						

Review each of the fifteen options on the exhibit. Ask yourself whether or not you are (1) *able* to implement this strategy on your own and (2) *willing* to implement this strategy. Focus on those strategies for which you answer "yes" to both questions. Compare these strategies with what you have been doing over the past year. For each strategy for which you are able, but not willing, answer the following questions and fill in the boxes on the exhibit:

1. If you have been doing too little of this strategy, then you may want to check "Do This More."

2. If you have been using a strategy too much (without desired results), check "Do This Less."

3. If you think that you have been doing a strategy just enough, you may simply want to check "Continue."

Now focus on those strategies for which you assessed yourselves as "not able" but "willing." Here is where you consider bringing in various kinds of specialized consultants to assist you or to do it for you. Consider your resources and constraints and compare each strategy against your assessment of how effective it is likely to be in enabling you to reach your marketing goals. The major constraint may be an inadequate budget. If so, ask yourself, "Can I afford *not* to do this?" Disregard, at least for now, any strategy for which you think you are neither "capable" nor "willing." Write up some specific actions you will take for strategies for which you are going to take action of some kind.

What's in a Name?

We offer one last but important caveat. We are sadly aware that many client organizations select their consultants following a scenario similar to that described in the following case.

▶ CASE IN POINT

The director of a large public agency decided it was time to "take the temperature" of his organization. He asked around and found that Acme Consulting, Inc., was the largest, most prestigious consulting firm in his area. So he contacted Acme Consulting and arranged for a visit by one of the firm's senior consulting partners.

Acme Consulting's senior consulting partner called on the director and presented an extremely competent and confident image. It did not take long before the director agreed to engage the firm to conduct a complete assessment of the organization's strengths and weaknesses, with an emphasis on the management development needs of the organization's senior staff.

The assessment process took approximately one month. During that time the senior consulting partner was noticeably absent. The assessment itself was conducted by a staff of "junior consultants," most of whom were newly minted MBAs with little or no real-world experience. ◄

The director in the above case made a major mistake. He relied on the prestigious *image* of the consulting firm and the impressive senior partner who represented it. He was unaware of the "bait-and-switch" tactics that are used by many consulting firms. He did not realize that a major element of senior consulting partners is to be a rainmaker to generate contracts for their firms and billable work for their junior consultants. The director did not explore such vital questions as: "Who will actually do the work involved in this contract?" "Will you [the senior partner] be actively leading this intervention?" If not, "Who will be leading this effort? What are their qualifications?"

As they explore the consulting jungle, agents should ask themselves: "What am I trying to accomplish? What are my personal interests in selecting consultants? Am I more concerned about what the consultants can do for me and my organization or am I more concerned about impressing my associates at the club when I tell them I just engaged a prestigious consultant or consulting firm?"

As an ethical OD consultant, you must be totally up-front with your agents about who will do the work that you are marketing. Bait-and-switch tactics are totally unethical and, sooner or later, will damage your reputation.

Summary

Organization development consultants inevitably have to market themselves and their services to naïve yet skeptical or cynical agents and leaders in a proactive manner. Promotional and sales efforts are essential aspects of the consulting business.

Fifteen distinct options for marketing your services as either an internal or external OD consultant were described in this chapter. We have distinguished between those options that we endorse and those we dislike—specifically making cold calls, telemarketing, and responding to RFPs or RFQs. Further, we presented a method for you to assess and lay the groundwork for developing your own multidimensional marketing strategy.

We hope that your implementation of your marketing strategy will result in a successful initial meeting with agents or leaders.

Does the Organization Need a Consultant?

ON THIS CHAPTER, we shall consider the question that dominates initial meetings between OD consultants and agents: Does the organization really need a consultant? Then we shall consider a number of contingent factors that may contribute to the answer. We have a lot more to say about conducting yourself during these initial meetings in Chapter Six.

Imagine that you are an internal or external OD consultant. You have an appointment with an agent of an organization that you hope will become your next client system.

Let's say you are making your final preparations to meet the agent. Your aim is to achieve four goals during this initial contact:

1. To determine whether or not the prospective client system really needs consultation of any sort.

2. To understand fully the agent's perceptions of the organization's current situation or condition, including both the issues and the organization's internal resources.

3. To assess the organization's readiness and willingness to make proper use of consultants.

4. To determine whether or not the organization needs OD consultation.

To obtain this information, you will have to establish rapport with the agents and help them to feel comfortable enough to open up and tell you the truth—as they understand the truth. They will not have all of the answers to your questions. Much of the information they do have is likely to be biased and incomplete. They may also feel embarrassed or threatened by your questions. It is not easy for agents to answer questions about sensitive organizational information.

You will have only a limited amount of time during the meeting. Therefore, consider the issues raised in Exhibit 2.1. Answer as many questions as you can in advance of your meeting, using information that is already available to you. This process will also reveal any additional information that you should obtain during your meeting. Pay particular attention to the second and third questions. They ask you to consider whether or not you may encounter value conflicts with the prospective client system. If so, you may want to cancel the meeting in order to maintain your integrity.

Exhibit 2.1. Planning Sheet for an Initial Meeting with a Potential Client

Issues	Comments
1. What do you know about the organiza-tion? What else do you need to know?	
2. Are you willing to consult with this organization? Do you have any doubts, concerns, or reservations about what it does or how it operates?	
3. Are your personal and professional val-ues compatible with those of the organi-zation? If not, what is different?	
4. What do the agents and leaders know about you? What else do you want them to know?	
5. What do the agents and leaders know about your department or firm? What else do they need to know?	

Exhibit 2.1. Planning Sheet for an Initial Meeting with a Potential Client, Cont'd

Issues	Comments
6. What assumptions do the agents and leaders have about you? About your department or firm?	
7. If you don't know what assumptions the agents are making, how can you find out?	
8. What can you do to clarify and correct the agents' inaccurate or negative assumptions?	
9. What are your specific goals for this meeting? How will you know when you have reached those goals?	
10. What are the agents' and leaders' goals for this meeting? If you don't know, how can you find out?	
11. What are the organizational norms regarding formality versus casualness of business relationships, personal dress, appearance, and the like?	
12. Who is likely to attend this meeting? What effect will this have on you and/or on your behavior?	
13. What are the worst things that could happen during this meeting? What can you do to handle them effectively?	
14. What is the physical setting for the meeting? How can you use this to your best advantage?	
15. What is the client likely to ask you? How can you prepare in advance to answer these questions?	
16. What questions should you ask the client? How can you best phrase these questions?	
17. What type of consulting style and/or behavior will work best for this meeting?	
18. What materials should you bring with you to the meeting?	

Does the Organization Really Need a Consultant?

You can gain considerable credibility by guiding agents through a reality-testing process that clearly results in an informed, high-quality decision that the prospective client system or subsystem either does or does not need consultants. Ordinarily, some kind of consultation is needed when all three of the following criteria are met:

- The system's leaders are committed to deal with their persistent and significant organizational issues;

- The system lacks—and chooses *not* to develop—its own internal, fully qualified resources; and

- Avoiding the issues will, ultimately, cost more than the expense of bringing in consultants to help deal with them.

If all three criteria are satisfied, you may conclude that the organization is *qualified* as a prospective client system. That is, it is *ready* and probably *willing*, but *not able* to deal with its issues without consulting assistance. If one or more of these criteria are not satisfied, most consultants will *not* be appropriate or relevant! Specifically, consultants may be needed if:

- The critical or persistent issue is highly *technical*. It cannot be ignored or tolerated, but it is *non-recurring*. There is no compelling need for permanent employees to gain proficiency in applying the skill sets that technical specialists use to deal with such issues.

- Permanent employees are capable of dealing with the issue but must be redeployed to do so, leaving their routine work responsibilities unattended. Therefore, qualified contract employees must fill their temporarily vacant positions.

- Existing employees are competent enough, but their routine responsibilities are too critical to redeploy them, so specialized consultants must be brought in to deal with the issue.

By discussing these three contingencies with agents, you can help them clarify their need for consultants. You should encourage agents and their leaders to consider job enlargement and development of some of their permanent employees if the issues recur frequently enough. As a side effect, they would become less dependent on costly external consulting services.

Everybody wins if you help agents and leaders to clarify why they do or do not need consultants. The corollary is: Everyone *loses* if hiring consultants turns out to have been unnecessary or they hire the wrong kind of consultants.

What Are the Agents' Perceptions of the Organization's Current Situation?

Many consultants approach their first meeting with agents with a single objective foremost in their minds—to obtain a contract! We prefer to build authentic relationships with agents that enable us to have transparent discussions and meaningful exchanges of pertinent information. Our first concern is to understand fully the issues that the agent's organization is currently facing or anticipates. Then we may ascertain whether the organization has the internal resources it needs to deal with these issues. If not, we can consider what types of consultants the organization requires to help it to deal with the issues.

In our experience, internal or external OD consultants who are prospecting for work rarely leave their initial meetings with a consulting contract. But that is OK. You may be more effective over the long haul if you do not even *try* for a consulting engagement right away. When you see your initial task as beginning a campaign to develop an enduring relationship with agents and their organizations, if and when they need some kind of consultation you could be the first person they call.

An important aspect of establishing your credibility is to demonstrate how you will work with them if they select you as their consultant. Therefore, you should treat the initial interview as if it were a mini-consultation.

If the agents asked you to come in to talk with them, let *them* take the lead. There will probably be some anxiety-reducing small talk as you feel each other out. (Pay attention! There may be some metaphoric significance in the topics.) Listen and respond briefly, when appropriate, but do not introduce new topics. Silence puts pressure on agents and gives them plenty of air time to tell you what they have been thinking about. If they hold back, ask them directly, "What's on your minds?" After all, they didn't invite you over for a cup of coffee and idle chatter. Don't waste their time, or yours. Your job is to make it as easy as possible for them to talk openly with you. This is vital. At this point, they are the only ones who can provide pertinent information about organizational conditions that may enhance or obstruct the effective utilization of any type of consultants.

Remember that you need to know what issues the organization is confronting and what kinds of *internal* resources they can apply in dealing with these issues. However, you are likely to run into some of the following difficulties.

A Question of Reliable Information. Agents often sound quite authoritative when they describe current organizational conditions. Particularly if you initiated the meeting and they merely agreed to it, they are also likely to sound noncritical and optimistic. Organization development consultants who are prospecting for work might ask agents and leaders, "How do you know that things are really as good (or as bad) as you think they are?" Of course, you do not want to sound like a prosecuting attorney. You are trying to elicit the agent's perceptions of organizational indicators of either systemic health or dysfunction—or both.

Agents may exhibit some defensiveness by telling you, with considerable confidence, about their fail-safe mechanisms or the reliability of their management information system in keeping them well-informed. To push the envelope, ask them how they know, with certainty, that these mechanisms and systems are *really* reliable and/or comprehensive (remember "garbage in/garbage out"). Such a direct confrontation may evoke more defensiveness (Argyris, 1990). It is most productive to use respectful but probing questions to keep them talking. Sooner or later, they just may open up to you. Remember that they probably would not be sitting with you this long if they were actually not interested in your services or if they were totally satisfied with and unconcerned about their operation.

Who Owns the Issue? Whether you have been invited in for a specific purpose or you are prospecting, you may hear about an issue that has been *disowned*, that is, an issue for which no one accepts ownership. Many agents speak of issues as if they materialized out of thin air or have been caused by external events or by unknown forces outside their subsystem but within the total organization.

Agents often present their organizations or subsystems or leaders as hapless victims of impersonal forces that are beyond their comprehension, control, or influence. They may feel that, because they did not *cause* it, they should not have to deal with it. So the issue persists—like the dead elephant decaying in the front yard. Agents often reflect their leaders' attitudes. If they do not feel any sense of ownership for the problem, how will their leaders deal with it? Very often, they won't.

Increasing Ownership of Issues. Agents and leaders can easily justify their belief that an issue does not exist or that it exists but is too trivial to invest much time with. For example, agents and their leaders may say they feel overwhelmed by an excessive number and variety of unrelated issues. So they can easily justify putting a number of significant issues on the back burner, hoping they will disappear by themselves. This indicates they are *implicitly* and *expediently* establishing priorities. You can learn a great deal about the current climate and the underlying culture of your prospective client system by inquiring about the ways in which issues are placed on the back burner or become orphans. You may not get much useful information until you have established rapport and developed a sense of mutual trust. However, this is a good time to begin to show you have empathy for and are concerned with these matters.

Managers may be avoiding the challenging task of using hard-nosed criteria to establish priorities among all of their issues in order to reduce them to a manageable few. Or organizational politics and their desire to avoid unpleasant confrontations may play a role. Agents and leaders probably know they must deal with such sensitive issues, but may not know how to do it without threatening or embarrassing someone. Take note of these dilemmas. You may want to push the issue by challenging agents to consider whether their organizations are more likely to suffer if issues are confronted or if key persons are protected from threats or embarrassment.

You can demonstrate your value as an OD consultant by helping agents and leaders to develop a healthy sense of ownership for their high-priority issues. Otherwise, they will continue to avoid or ignore them.

You can enhance their ownership by using the initial interview as a mini-consultation. You can guide them through a simple process that helps them create a sense of order and determine which issues they own and which ones belong to others. Through their active participation in the process, it is almost certain that their investment in the results will increase.

You can use the following criteria to help them decide whether or not they own an issue. Even if you have only one participant in this process, that is OK as long as this person understands that you should repeat this process with the organization's leaders. An issue is theirs if:

- It is something about which they feel dissatisfied, disappointed, frustrated, and/or fearful;
- It has significant negative implications for their costs, revenues, profitability, productivity, quality, morale, innovations, and anything else that has meaning for them;
- It is something over which they have control or, at least, something that is within their sphere of influence;
- They do not have control over the issue, but they do have sufficient discretion to determine how to *respond to* and *deal with* it; and/or
- It is something for which they are willing to sacrifice the opportunity to do other things.

Use Exhibit 2.2 to assess agents' ownership for any given organizational issue. This process should result in a provisional distinction between owned and not owned issues. Often, it is an emotionally loaded step to raise the next question: "If you do not own this issue, to whom does it rightfully belong?" Agents can make educated guesses about the proper owners of issues. (Of course, you will remind the agents that their leaders should also participate in this process.)

Exhibit 2.2. Whose Issue Is It?

Instructions: Use a separate copy of this questionnaire for each issue that emerges during your initial meetings with agents. First, ask agents what they, personally, believe or feel in answer to each point below.

ISSUE:

This issue	*Yes*	*No*
1. Is a source of dissatisfaction, disappointment, frustration, or fearfulness.		
2. Has significant negative implications for revenues, profitability, costs, productivity, quality, innovations, customer satisfaction and/or employee morale.		
3. Is one that we can control or influence.		
4. Is one they cannot control, but they do have sufficient discretion to determine how to respond and deal with it.		
5. Has enough value to justify sacrificing the opportunity to do other things.		

Second, ask agents how they think their organizational leaders would think or feel about each issue.

This issue	*Yes*	*No*
1. Is a source of dissatisfaction, disappointment, frustration, or fearfulness.		
2. Has significant negative implications for revenues, profitability, costs, productivity, quality, innovations, customer satisfaction, and/or employee morale.		
3. Is one that we can control or influence.		
4. Has enough value to justify sacrificing the opportunity to do other things.		

Even if the agents and leaders with whom you are now engaged are not responsible for causing these issues, they are responsible for dealing with them. You can help them to clarify what is, very often, a very confusing situation.

Confusing "Symptoms" with "Root Causes." Agents and leaders may or may not have distinguished between *symptoms* and their underlying *root causes*. You should be prepared for the very real probability that agents will have made their own diagnosis. However, they may not have distinguished between the *symptoms* of an issue and its *root cause* (or, more likely, multiple root causes). This ambiguity is particularly likely if they feel overwhelmed and stressed by work overload and/or the emergence of recurring issues that force them to redirect their attention from routine operations.

Some pernicious symptoms have several root causes. Further, many symptoms can be generated by a single root cause. Frequently, root causes are obscured by symptoms. It is, therefore, more effective to identify and address the root causes. Many symptoms simply go away when the organization recognizes and deals with one or more relevant root causes. You can demonstrate the value of your OD consultation skills by assisting agents to focus on the few critical root causes of a vast number of symptoms.

What do we mean by "root cause"? Consider this metaphor: A high fever is an obvious symptom of an undetermined medical problem. You may get quick, temporary relief by placing an icepack on your forehead, but when you remove the icepack the fever returns. To cure a serious fever, its underlying root causes must be identified and treated. This can be complex, costly, and time-consuming.

Many people settle for the immediate, temporary relief they get by treating their symptoms. We guess they are betting that the fever is not a sign of anything particularly serious. If they can endure it and it goes away, they've saved time and money.

You can establish a valued position for yourself by helping agents and leaders to specify and think through the tangible advantages and disadvantages of their options and make an informed choice to either search for and treat the underlying root causes or to seek symptomatic relief. If the organization chooses to ignore or avoid the root causes of the issues, the danger is that people will come to accept and tolerate them as "normal." Without adequate attention, secondary issues quietly fester over time and—to everyone's surprise—grow to become new, critical issues.

▶ CASE ɪɴ POINT

The COO of a large manufacturing firm was concerned because his product development (PD) staff was becoming increasingly dissatisfied. He brought in an external consultant who was an "expert" in employee compensation. The consultant's assigned objective was to "increase the satisfaction levels of PD staff members."

The expert consultant began by studying wage and benefits programs for PD staff in other companies in the area and compared these with the program offered by his client firm. He then recommended higher wages and better fringe benefits. Several months after the consultant's plan was implemented, PD staff dissatisfaction continued to grow and several key technicians left the firm.

The COO brought in a new consultant, an OD practitioner, who asked permission to begin her assignment by interviewing the firm's PD staff. She quickly found that their dissatisfaction had nothing to do with compensation and benefits. Rather, they were extremely dissatisfied with having to work at facilities located a half mile from the main plant area, with no opportunity to get together informally with other employees. They felt isolated and ignored.

Satisfaction levels increased drastically as soon as the PD department was moved into new quarters in the main plant. This enabled them to interact frequently with both marketing and production personnel. This increased the PD staff members' feelings of being a important part of the larger organization. ◀

Each consultant relied on a very different strategy to deal with the PD staff's dissatisfaction. The first focused on eliminating what he *believed* were the causes (lower compensation and benefits than other companies in the area) of the symptoms (staff dissatisfaction); the second focused on identifying the root causes (feelings of isolation and perceptions of their reduced importance). These different approaches led to two very different recommendations for dealing with the issue.

During initial discussions, you must help agents accept the notion that OD interventions will yield *enduring* results only if the root causes are identified and addressed. This can be tricky.

The leaders' informal, intuitive organizational diagnoses *may* be accurate and comprehensive or not. In either event, it is their diagnosis. They put their energy into it. They own it! Now, you come along and tell them that their diagnosis may be flawed or biased. You may be correct, but they will not enjoy hearing that. You want them to accept the fact that, without an *accurate, independent,* and *comprehensive* diagnosis and analysis of the root causes of their issues, their preferred interventions may be irrelevant or ineffective (at best) or dysfunctional (at worst). To accept this fundamental principle, agents and leaders have to *repudiate* their own diagnoses and prescriptions and suspend their disbelief that these are other, more accurate cause-effect relationships. This requires courage.

Agents often prefer to select consultants who offer quick, inexpensive "cures" for organizational symptoms based on plausible, but often inaccurate, hunches about the specific root causes.

Naturally, you will want to start your OD consultation with an independent organizational diagnosis, but remember that your agents may think they have already diagnosed the situation. Your job is not to debate your agents' diagnosis, but to induce them to test its validity.

Getting to the Root Causes. To get to the root causes, you must act like the second consultant in our case, who left her options open and was unencumbered by any predispositions. To find root causes you must explore the following open-ended questions with a variety of respondents from different parts and levels of the client system, each of whom can address the issues from a different perspective.

1. Tell me specifically what issues you are concerned with right now? (List these issues on a flip chart so respondents can see and validate or challenge what you are recording.)

2. Describe the first of these issues as you first saw it. How do you see it right now? (Repeat Questions 2 through 9 for each identified issue.)

3. How did you first become aware of this? What information first brought this to your attention? Who brought this information to you?

4. Why is this important for you?

5. What has happened between the time these issues emerged and the present?

6. What do you suppose would happen if you tolerated or ignored these issues? What would it cost you or your organization? Can you afford these costs?

7. What happened when you tried to deal with these issues?

8. What do you see as the causes of these issues? What do you think caused that? And what caused *that?*

9. What is it about your organization that allowed this issue to become critical?

Again, your job is to induce the agents' active involvement by asking nonjudgmental questions and by listening and probing. These questions will stimulate agents to rethink their assumptions and conclusions and see the need for additional information. They may then appreciate the value of your independent, comprehensive OD diagnosis.

The Potential Client System's Internal Resources

We are referring to internal OD consultants, HR generalists, and/or other technical specialists who could play useful roles. There are three reasons to be concerned with a prospective client system's internal resources. First, if you aren't, you may unintentionally trigger a territorial battle. Second, they may be extremely useful allies. Third, assuming that you are committed to the ultimate goal of OD consulting—to work yourself out of a job—responsible organizational members must gain proficiency and sufficient visibility and credibility to be allowed to use the competencies that you want to transfer to them.

You have to find out whether these resources exist, who they are, and how you can gain access to them. Exhibit 2.3 lists questions that you should begin to ask during your initial meetings with the agents. They may not have the answers, but they should get the message that you are trying to enable the organization to become self-reliant and to avoid unnecessary consulting costs.

Exhibit 2.3. Internal Resources Checklist

The following checklist enables you to help agents and leaders of your prospective client systems determine the degree to which they should rely on their own internal resources or bring in some kind of an external consultant.

Yes	**No**	1. Existing employees can gather and organize the data they need to comprehend the issues fully and assess the effects they may have on the organization's efforts to achieve its goals and objectives.
Yes	**No**	2. Existing employees can organize and thoroughly analyze the above data and distinguish between symptoms and their root causes.
Yes	**No**	3. Existing employees can identify obstacles (technical, structural, procedural, political, interpersonal, and cultural) that might interfere with efforts to deal with the issue at hand.
Yes	**No**	4. Existing employees can mobilize and involve representatives of relevant groups and subsystems and help them to develop realistic and effective action or implementation plans for managing the issue.

Exhibit 2.3. Internal Resources Checklist, Cont'd

Yes	**No**	5. Existing employees can mobilize and involve representatives of relevant groups and subsystems and help them to develop effective strategies for achieving the organization's desired future state.
		6. Existing employees can manage the education of the implementation plan, including:
Yes	**No**	a. Managing the change process;
Yes	**No**	b. Coordinating and integrating the efforts of all people involved;
Yes	**No**	c. Monitoring reactions and responses from significant individuals and groups that are likely to be impacted;
Yes	**No**	d. Scanning for emerging, unpredicted side effects; and
Yes	**No**	e. Identifying the need for and making necessary adjustments to the action plan.
Yes	**No**	7. Existing employees can perform and manage tasks objectively, without being unduly affected by their own biases and vested interests.
Yes	**No**	8. Existing employees will say what they truly think and feel about issues without fear of upsetting their superiors, peers, and subordinates.
Yes	**No**	9. Existing employees have sufficient status and credibility to be accepted by executives and informal organizational opinion leaders.
Yes	**No**	10. Utilizing existing employees will not significantly interfere with or disrupt normal operational responsibilities, or routine responsibilities can be transferred to others without a significant drop in organizational performance.
Yes	**No**	11. Management is prepared to recognize and properly reward people for their contributions in dealing with the issue.
Yes	**No**	12. If the answer to *any* of the questions, 1 through 6, is "No," does the organization have the resources necessary to enable existing employees to *develop* their potential so they can perform any or all of these responsibilities?
Yes	**No**	13. If the answer to *any* of the questions, 7 through 11, is "No," is the organization *willing* and *able* to do whatever is necessary to convert all the "No" answers to "Yes"?

A "No" in response to *either* Question 12 or Question 13 suggests that agents of your prospective client system will need to bring in some kinds and types of external consulting assistance.

You must also determine leadership's willingness to authorize internal/external collaboration and the use of multidisciplinary consulting teams.

Combining Internal and External Consulting Resources. Assume that the leaders are interested in developing the competence and credibility of their internal consulting resources. We believe that the most effective means of dealing with many complex organizational issues is to create a multidisciplinary intervention team composed of both internal and external resources with skills in OD and other relevant disciplines.

▶ CASE IN POINT

The management of a large organization decided it was time for radical changes in current managerial and supervisory skills, practices, attitudes, and behaviors. They also decided that the organization's internal HR training function lacked the numbers, skills, and credibility needed to design and implement a program to train fifteen hundred managers and supervisors effectively. It was also clear that total reliance on external resources to design and implement the program would be inordinately expensive.

An internal "management development team" was convened. The team members were drawn from all levels and major subsystems and included several HR generalists. Executive management contracted with a reputable consulting firm to design and conduct a program to increase the team members' abilities to design, implement, manage, and evaluate change efforts within their own organization. The goal was to enable the team to take responsibility for and conduct as many change activities as possible.

The consulting firm's lead consultant assumed the role of "senior consultant" to the internal development team. She worked closely with the internal development team:

- To enhance the skills, knowledge, pride, dignity, and self-respect of organizational leaders and members;
- To identify and develop additional internal resources that could be used to deal with similar issues in the future;
- To reduce the costs of complex systems change significantly;
- To reduce the resistance that managers and members often feel toward imported (imposed) programs; and
- To develop change initiatives that were compatible with the organization's unique culture, traditions, practices, and so forth. ◀

Assessing Organizational Readiness

Let us assume that it is clearly understood that the prospective client system does need some kind of consultation. In addition to understanding its issues and the nature and numbers of accessible internal resources, you must appreciate the probability that your efforts will constitute a palpable threat to the status quo and, therefore, to the prestige, privileges, and prerogatives of many influential organizational members. It is unlikely that you and your practices will be universally accepted and appreciated. Of course, many of the adverse responses with which you will have to cope are related to individual efforts of people who believe they have to protect themselves. Some opposition may be a function of organizational politics.

However, we think that your greatest challenges will derive from the organizational context. Culture and climate will determine whether or not your prospective client system is ready to authorize any type of consultation.

Organizational Context: Culture and Climate

During your initial contacts with agents, you must be vigilant, continuously assessing their perceptions of their organizational context, that is, the enduring *culture* and current *emotional climate.* This determines what agents and leaders understand about their organizations and their issues. Culture and climate also influence what kinds and types of consultative assistance the agents will seek out and what the leaders will accept as "appropriate." Context also influences what interventions will be accepted and adopted by members and which will be rejected.

Organizational Culture. Organizational culture can be described as "the way we do things around here." Of course, this is an oversimplification. Organizations that have survived and been "successful" in the past tend to institutionalize their historical assumptions and belief systems (mental models), norms for acceptable behavior, and practices (Schein, 1999). Thus, a new enterprise may begin its existence as an aggressive, focused, innovative, profitable, and family-oriented entity but, over time, may become sluggish, complacent, bureaucratic, and unresponsive to volatile changes in its market environment. The organization continues to operate as it has always operated, assuming that what worked in the past is the template for future success.

It is, therefore, not surprising that the leaders of organizations that are in the greatest need of renewal and revitalization tend to be the most *conservative.* They prefer stability, predictability, and certainty rather than risk taking, exploration, and discovery. As their prospective OD consultant, you can expect that they will prefer to stay with their traditional managerial practices, even when their current issues are discontinuous with their historical experiences and their traditional practices exacerbate the problems they are experiencing as they try to deal with their current issues. If, on the other hand, there is an issue that they can no longer endure or ignore, they will be very anxious for you to offer them a technical, procedural, or structural fix that is quick, inexpensive, and nondisruptive.

So you should not be surprised to discover that the guiding principle used by many agents is, "Don't fix it if it isn't broken!" Of course, this principle ignores the probability that many organizational elements and practices work only as long as conditions remain constant; as soon as some critical conditions change, those elements and practices will become dysfunctional and break. Further, you know that it will be far more costly for the leaders to fix things *after* they are broken than it would be to *prevent* them from breaking in the first place.

When considering a prospective client system's culture, we like to discuss three questions in depth with agents and leaders—and we like to have these discussions frequently:

1. What kinds of action are considered to be "heroic"? To what extent are managers recognized and rewarded for quick *solutions* for critical issues, in contrast to the conscientious *prevention* of such issues?

2. To what extent is this organization focused on maximizing profits by improving the *efficiency* of its traditional business, in contrast to anticipating and preparing for a *discontinuous future* (Morrison, 1996).

3. Is there an effective mechanism in place that actively scans and assesses the organization's internal and external environments in order to seek and respond to emerging issues before they become critical?

You should be particularly attentive to cues from agents and leaders that indicate how they deal with these questions. If they are ignored or if their responses support the perpetuation of historical assumptions and practices, prepare yourself to examine the prospective client system's culture.

Current Emotional Climate. Usually, for OD consultants, the critical dimension of the organization's current emotional climate is the crisis versus steady state continuum. You may be dealing with agents to whom responsibility has been delegated to find and hire someone to douse their fire. If this hypothesis is valid, the agent will be facing an urgent, if not a crisis, situation. Leaders will want a quick, yet permanent fix. They will be anxious and fearful about the potential negative consequences of either the perpetuation of the current, unsatisfactory situation or the disruptive side effects of corrective interventions—or both. They will have intensely ambivalent feelings about you. They will respond best if you listen a lot and come across as empathetic, as sharing their sense of urgency, and as both reassuring and confident in the presence of an organizational conflagration.

Dysfunctional Culture-Based Assumptions

You should scan and explore the organization for cultural assumptions or beliefs that induce caution, skepticism, conservatism, or complacency. There are three assumptions that we think are quite common.

Issues Are Seen As Weaknesses. Executives and managers may be reluctant to admit that there are serious issues in their areas of responsibility. They may fear that such an admission will be interpreted as a sign of weakness. So they hide their "weaknesses" from their superiors, peers, subordinates (suppression) and, frequently, even from themselves (repression).

Suppression, because it is a conscious act, is a major stumbling block for OD consultants. *Repression,* because it is a nonconscious act, is an even more troublesome impediment. It will be up to you to create an atmosphere that is safe enough for people to express their true thoughts and feelings. If they feel it is safe, they may open up and talk about sensitive issues and tell you what they really think is going on within their organizations. A tactic that we use is to reflect what we think may be going on in the agents' minds. So we talk about how hard it is for us to talk openly about sensitive issues with strangers. We talk about how courageous it is to take the risk of unpleasant repercussions for talking about those sensitive issues. Agents may agree, disagree, or simply not respond.

Issues Are Suppressed. Many senior executives are shielded from unpleasant realities by subordinates who function as self-appointed "mind-guards" (Janis, 1982).

Leaders will need solid, verifiable evidence that this is happening—and that it is dysfunctional. Once convinced, they might ask for help to explore this phenomenon and remove the factors that sustain it.

Issues Are Muffled. Some senior managers are unaware of the existence of issues in their organizations because some of their subordinate managers provide carefully crafted *mis*information or *dis*information.

▶ CASE in POINT

Over a two-year period, a plant manager received a great deal of praise and recognition from senior management because his plant had consistently exceeded production quotas. It was only after he had moved on to a more senior position with a competitor that corporate headquarters discovered that their favorite plant manager had consciously suppressed two significant facts in his reports. First, he neglected to mention that there was growing labor unrest throughout his plant caused by his unresponsive, autocratic management style. Second, he failed to inform headquarters that his production equipment was in critical need of costly maintenance and repairs because he had systematically deferred essential preventative maintenance in order to minimize his operating costs and exaggerate his unusually high production levels. ◀

Framing How the Organization Can Use an OD Consultant

Just as your agents and leaders probably diagnosed their own issues, they may also have developed their own prescriptions or preferred methods for dealing with them. The specific interventions that they prescribe for themselves will determine the types of consultants they look for. You may have a problem if you disagree with their self-prescription. However, if you were successful in helping them to reconsider their diagnosis, you may also induce them to reconsider their preferred interventions.

Five Types of Interventions

Do not simply accept leaders' self-prescriptions. Offer to help them to make informed choices from among five basic types of interventions: Strategic, preventive, early-warning, corrective, and intensive care or terminal.

1. *Strategic* interventions involve assisting leaders to formulate compelling visions and missions for a compelling and meaningful future. If effective, these will "pull" (as opposed to "push") organizational members in that direction. You may also assist leaders to develop goals, strategies and action plans for reaching that desirable future state. In addition, you may also help them to identify and manage the critical success factors that are necessary to reach the desired state—and to reduce or eliminate factors that hinder the strategic effort.

2. *Preventive* interventions focus on maintaining the organization's long-term survivability and growth. Preventive interventions are focused on two areas (Ruma, 1974): (1) the area of organizational health, organizational elements that are working well now and seem likely to continue to be functional going forward, for example, a flat structure composed of a network of high-performing teams, and (2) the stop-gap measures in which organizational elements are functioning adequately under current conditions but, when these conditions change, the organization would be vulnerable.

3. *Early-warning* interventions focus on mechanisms that identify and address emerging issues before they become acute by continually scanning the external and internal environments for early indications of trends that may benefit or threaten the organization. Sociotechnical processes such as "open-systems planning" (Jayaram, 1976) are appropriate here.

4. *Corrective* interventions involve helping members to develop solutions to current critical issues. Something is broken and the organization both wants and needs it to be fixed pronto! Such issues may be thought of as "natural targets" for change (Ruma, 1974). Rapid and accurate assessments are essential, and quick, decisive action is necessary to "stop the bleeding." Because the focus is usually on critical operational issues under crisis conditions, strategic issues may be neglected. As a result, a degenerative spiral can evolve quickly and virtually guarantees the need for crisis management.

5. *Intensive care* or *terminal* interventions are used when preventive and early-warning interventions are neglected, conditions deteriorate, and corrective interventions are "too little, too late." Under these conditions, all available energy is devoted to dealing with survival or, if that fails, developing an exit strategy. At such times, a board of directors is likely to seek turnaround specialists to take total control, hack and slash overhead, or divest themselves of unprofitable or "noncore" product lines. Organization development consultants may help to minimize the bloodshed and care for the wounded and also help the board of directors decide when it is time for the turnaround specialist to exit.

Any one or any combination of these types of interventions may be better suited for a given situation at a given time. If you strongly disagree with the leaders' choices, you may have reached another choice point. Should you stay engaged or gracefully withdraw?

You can ascertain the degree to which OD consultation is relevant depending on which set of interventions is selected. If OD is relevant, you can determine whether the agents and leaders understand the advantages and disadvantages of the OD approach. If so, they can make informed decisions. If not, you will have an educational challenge to deal with. If OD consultation is not needed, you can still assist agents to determine precisely which kinds and types of consultation are most relevant and appropriate. Even if you do not negotiate the largest contract, you will maintain your integrity and enhance your credibility with agents and leaders.

Summary

In this chapter, we have shown that, whether you are an internal or external OD consultant, you must understand and appreciate the role of organizational agents, the gatekeepers who determine which types of consultants are selected and deployed.

Organization development consultants can determine whether or not the prospective client system really needs consultation by eliciting and assessing agents' and leaders' perceptions of the organization's current situation though use of highly participative methods that help agents and leaders to develop a sense of ownership of their issues. These perceptions should include consideration of various cultural and climatic conditions that may either facilitate or obstruct the use of internal or external consultants. Explore the possible mutual advantages of developing partnerships with a prospective client system's internal resources. You should also assess the organization's readiness to make use of consultants, in general, and whether or not it needs OD consultation, in particular.

We are now ready to consider the various types of consultants with whom you may find it more effective—and profitable—to form partnerships, joint ventures, or strategic alliances rather than to compete.

Types of Consultants

AFTER LEADERS RECOGNIZE that they have significant issues for which they require some form of external assistance, they are about to step further into the depths of the consulting jungle! Now they must determine precisely what kind of consultative assistance is most appropriate to help address these issues.

A critical prerequisite to surviving the consulting jungle is the leader's ability to distinguish among the four distinct types of external resources who call themselves "consultants." We have elaborated on Peter Block's original set of three types (1981, 1999) and developed four consultant types. These are "extra-pair-of-hands," "training/educational specialist," "technical expert" (techspert), and "OD consultant." Because each of these four consultant types has unique, distinctive capabilities and tends to use different strategies and methods, each can be used most appropriately in different situations. If agents or leaders select a consultant with qualifications that do not fit the situation, all parties are likely to experience problems—the most obvious being that they may not achieve the intended results.

The Four Types of Consultants

A primary distinction among the four types of consultants is the focus of their activities and interventions. Table 3.1 provides an easy reference.

Table 3.1. Four Types of Consultants

	Extra-Pair-of-Hands	Training/Educational Specialist	Techspert	OD Consultant
Best Suited for	A temporary need for a competency that is normally available internally	A need to provide specific employees or groups of employees with specific information, knowledge, or skills	A short-term, non-recurring need for specific technical skills, knowledge, or information	Solving a problem and, simultaneously, developing people to deal with similar problems in the future or making system-wide changes in the organization
Primary Focus	Performing those responsibilities that are inherent in the position	Enhancing the knowledge, skills, and information of specific individuals (or populations of employees)	Providing expert solutions to specific, mostly technical problems	Improving the overall effectiveness of the entire organization or of a specific subsystem

We begin this chapter with comprehensive descriptions of each of these four basic types of consultants, followed by several questionnaires to enable you to help organizational agents to find the type of consultant best suited to deal with their issues.

Extra-Pair-of-Hands

An extra-pair-of-hands is an individual who fills a temporary void caused by the redeployment or extended illness of key employees, covers for people who are on vacation, or catches up on backlogs of work that may be caused by cyclical surges in demand for the organization's products.

Some extra-pairs-of-hands—particularly those who are very senior or extremely competent—may be paired with existing employees to serve as models, demonstrating the proper ways to perform specific responsibilities. In this instance, their usefulness ends when permanent employees return from other assignments, sick leave, or vacations, or when they acquire sufficient understanding, skill, and judgment to perform their roles proficiently.

The primary difference between an extra-pair-of-hands and one of the other three consultant types is that these consultants fit into the workforce, accepting routine tasks as assigned. They are supervised and evaluated just as are permanent employees in the same positions.

Although extra-pairs-of-hands may like to see themselves as "consultants" or even "management consultants," we believe the terms "temporary employee" or "independent contractor" are more appropriate to reduce confusion, misunderstandings, and inappropriate expectations of persons who are more properly called "consultants."

Training/Educational Specialist

Training/educational specialists assess the training and educational needs of organizational members. If the underlying root causes of critical issues are clearly traced to a lack of knowledge and/or skills that people need to perform current or future responsibilities effectively (Mager & Pipe, 1970), external specialists can design, test, develop, conduct, and/or evaluate the technical and behavioral skill-training programs, educational seminars, and hands-on workshops when internal resources are either not capable or not available to deliver the necessary training or education.

It is disturbing when participants are unable or unwilling to apply their newly acquired information, skills, and knowledge to their workplace settings. The potential benefits of their training or education are lost. More often than not, this disconnect occurs because organizational constraints prevent employees from, or even punish them for, trying to apply their newly learned skills (Fournies, 1988; Mager & Pipe, 1970; Robinson & Robinson, 1995). Such disconnects occur with frustrating frequency.

Participants frequently tell their trainers and seminar or workshop leaders when they think they will encounter obstacles in applying what they learn in their classrooms to their real-life workplaces. Training/educational specialists should not attribute such information to the participants' irrational resistance. Rather, they should take it seriously enough to alert leaders to the existence and effects of this dynamic and, when feasible, help them to consider how to develop some effective corrective or preventive measures (Robinson & Robinson, 1995).

Many training/educational specialists are trained as instructional designers. Many are enhancing their skills by becoming performance consultants (Robinson & Robinson, 1995) and adding OD consulting skills to their skill sets. With such cross-training and job expansion, the distinctions between types of consultants begin to blur.

Technical Expert (Techspert)

Technical experts (techsperts) typically possess in-depth information, knowledge, skill, and experience in their own relatively narrow, highly specialized technical areas. Some examples are lawyers, dentists, physicians, enterprise resource planning (ERP), customer relations management (CRM) software platform specialists, public relations experts, inspirational public speakers, econometric modeling specialists, industrial/organizational psychologists, and, of course, various kinds of both technical and managerial behavior training/educational specialists. Many techsperts develop their specialized skills before becoming consultants; many are generalists who have added marketable consulting skills. Many how-to books have been published to assist them in making these kinds of career shifts (Barcus & Wilkinson, 1995; Bray, 1991; Connor & Davidson, 1985; Greiner & Metzger, 1983; Jones, 1993; Salmon & Rosenblatt, 1995; Tobias, 1990; Tuller, 1992).

Large, complex organizations often employ techsperts on a permanent, full-time basis. A market for external techsperts exists because most client systems do not have sufficient work to keep such narrow-band specialists occupied on a full-time basis. So when a client system must achieve some specific results, external techsperts are hired on a temporary basis.

Techspert services are most appropriate when the issue is nonrecurring *and* technical or highly specialized. For example, in 1999 a great many techsperts were kept extremely busy helping client systems around the globe to fix their Y2K problems. Today, many European and African firms engage techsperts to help bring their production procedures in line with emerging ISO quality control standards.

The primary function of techsperts is to apply their specialized skills and methods to do the following:

- Analyze problems in order to recommend solutions;
- Implement their own or some other recommended solutions; or
- Both.

When assigned either or both of these functions, techsperts are usually given a relatively free hand from the time they accept the assignment until they present their conclusions and recommendations. After all, the techsperts' arcane competencies are usually not understood well by the client organizations' leaders, managers, and members. So they cannot very well supervise techsperts. Usually, techsperts are terminated once they have delivered their recommendations or completed their assignment.

Techsperts market themselves as "problem solvers" and "solution providers." Therein is a major paradox. The biggest disadvantage in using a techspert is that their elegant technical solutions frequently fail because they lack the active and enthusiastic commitment and support of a critical mass of organizational members. This support is often crucial for proper implementation of the recommendations. Members may feel that the techsperts' solutions were *imposed* on them in an arbitrary, insensitive manner. Therefore, members may withhold their support and resist the techspert's solutions.

Organization Development (OD) Consultants

Organization development consultants operate on the fundamental assumption that their client system's leaders and members already have the essential technical skills and content information they need to deal with their issues. Therefore, rather than solving client systems' problems, OD consultants strive to work collaboratively with the organization's leaders and members, helping them to identify, clarify, prioritize, and deal with complex organizational issues. Their services are most appropriate when management wants both to achieve a set of specific results and to enhance internal capabilities for dealing effectively with similar issues in the future.

Traditionally, OD consultants are seen as "process" experts, rather than as content experts. However, in those increasingly frequent situations in which client systems require assistance in both content and process, OD consultants are (or should be) partnering with trainer/educators and techsperts in providing integrated, multidisciplinary consultative services.

Because OD consultants are typically skilled in creating opportunities to involve organizational members actively, they are the best choice when the success of the consulting effort depends on those members' commitment to support the action plans. In addition, their highly interactive and didactic methods are essential in transferring their skills and knowledge to organizational members—thus empowering members while reducing their dependency on consultants.

Typical assignments for OD consultants include providing relevant information about current organizational and marketplace trends and issues and assisting client system leaders in the following ways:

- To anticipate unpredicted, emerging implementation issues and deal effectively with planning and implementing complex systemic changes (see, for example, Bennis & Mische, 1997; Champy, 1994, 1995; Cunningham, 1993; Freedman, 1997; Geisler, 1997; Hambrick, Tushman, & Nadler, 1997; Johann, 1995; Jones, 1993; Kanter, Stein, & Jick, 1992; McHugh, Merli, & Wheeler, 1997; Nadler, 1998; Nader & Merten, 1998; Nadler, Shaw, & Walton, 1994; Tenner, 1996; Tichy & Charan, 1998; Tichy & Sherman, 2000; Tushman & O'Reilly, 1996; Walton, 1989).

- To implement changes in an organization's culture, such as transforming from a technocratic or bureaucratic culture to one that is participative, team-based, and customer-oriented (see, for example, Cameron & Quinn, 1997; Davis, 1984; Frost, Moore, Louis, Lundberg, & Martin, 1985; Glidewell, 1989; Hall, 1976; Hofstede, 1984, 1991, 1994; Lawler, 1988; McLagan & Nel, 1995; Meyerson & Martin, 1987; Schein, 1992, 1999; Tichy & Devanna, 1997; Trompenaars, 1994).

- To formulate the creation of an organization's core mission and strategic plans so as to bring all elements and operations of the organization into alignment (see, for example, Ackoff, 1999; Barker, 1992; Coates & Jarratt, 1989; Finkelstein & Hambrick, 1996; Goodstein, Nolan, & Pfeiffer, 1993; Kaplan & Norton, 1996; Labovitz & Rosansky, 1997; Mintzberg, 1994; Montgomery & Porter, 1991; Nanus, 1992; Ohmae, 1990; Parker, 1990; Porter, 1990; Schoemaker, 1995; Scott, Jaffe, & Tobr, 1994; Tichy, 1990; Worley, Ross, & Hitchin, 1995).

- To redesign an organization's structure to enhance its effectiveness, for example, to flatten it, make it laterally oriented, or make it transparent and open to transactions for both internal and external suppliers and customers (see, for example, Ashkenas, Jick, Ulrich, & Paul-Chowdhury, 1999; Bennis & Mische, 1997; Clegg & Birch, 1998; Galbraith, 1977; Jaques, 1989; Miller, 1982; Mohrman, Cohen, & Mohrman, 1995; Mohrman, Galbraith, & Lawler, 1998; Morgan, 1997; Morgan, 1989b; Nadler, Gerstein, Shaw, & Associates, 1992; Nadler & Tushman, 1997; Nohria & Eccles, 1994; Pasmore, 1994; Pasternack & Viscio, 1998).

- To develop a strategy and process for accurately identifying and effectively deploying and utilizing scarce organizational resources (see, for example,

Adams & Hansen, 1992; Mohrman, Cohen, & Mohrman, 1995; Pfeffer, 1994a, 1998b; Schuster, Carpenter, & Kane, 1996; Spencer, 1989).

- To improve the level of cooperation and integration or reduce the level of dysfunctional conflicts between interdependent organizational subsystems and across vertical hierarchical levels (see, for example, Brown, 1983; Johnson, 1992; Kernberg, 1998; Labovitz & Rosansky, 1997; Morgan, 1997; Neuhauser, 1990; Parker, 2000; Pascale, 1990; Rothman, 1997).

- To design, install, and utilize mechanisms to accumulate, archive, manage, and disseminate the organization's collective "lessons learned," enabling the enterprise to become a "learning organization." A recent innovation is "action learning," which is a clever integration of action research, organizational learning, and leadership development that calls for a multidisciplinary team of OD consultants and training/educational specialists (see, for example, Argyris, 1993, 1999; Argyris & Schon, 1995; Brown & Duguid, 1991; Dotlich & Noel, 1998; Fiol & Lyles, 1985; Gasparski & Botham, 1998; Huber, 1991; Kline & Saunders, 1993; Marquardt, 1999; Rothwell, 1999; Senge, 1990, 1999; Senge, Roberts, Ross, Smith, & Kleiner, 1994).

- To coach and provide other pertinent developmental experiences for managers who must adapt their behaviors to bring them into alignment with and to support the purposes of their organizations' change initiatives. Action learning is pertinent here, also (see, for example, Argyris, 1993; Bennis, 1998, 1999; Bennis & Goldsmith, 1997; Bennis & Nanus, 1997; Bennis & Townsend, 1995; Black, Gregersen, & Mendenhall, 1992; Block, 1996; Collins, 1995; Collins & Porras, 1994; Goleman, 1998; Hardy & Schwartz, 1996; Kets de Vries, 1984, 1991; Kets de Vries & Miller, 1989; Kilburg, 1996; Levinson, 1994; McKenna, 1997; Merry & Brown, 1990; Miller & Brown, 1984; Morrisey, 1996; Nadler, 1998; Ohmae, 1982; Peterson & Hicks, 1996; Pfeffer, 1994b; Ritvo, Litwin, & Butler, 1995; Rothwell, 1999; Ryan & Oestreich 1991; Shula & Blanchard, 1995; Srivastva, 1983; Srivastva & Cooperrider, 1997; Tichy & Sherman, 2000; Tobias, 1990; Waldman & Atwater, 1998; Weisbord, 1987; Whitmore, 1994; Wind & Main, 1998).

- To deal with the human sides of mergers, acquisitions, and strategic alliances and their aftermath, including restructuring and downsizing, and helping management develop a sense of renewal among surviving employees (see, for example, Astrachan, 1990; Buono & Bowditch, 1989; Cartwright & Cooper, 1999; Clemente & Greenspan, 1998; Feldman & Spratt, 1999;

Knowdell, Branstead, & Moravec, 1994; Lajoux, 1998; Marks & Mirvis, 1998; Mirvis & Marks, 1992; Nahavandi & Malekzadeh, 1993; Noer, 1993; Pritchett, Robinson, & Clarkson, 1997).

- To recognize their organizations' core competencies and to design and use knowledge-based organizations (see, for example, Arbnor & Bjerke, 1996; Barchan, 1998; Bushko & Raynor, 1998; Drucker, 1999; Lynn, 1998; Myers, 1996; Sanchez & Heene, 1997; Sarvary, 1999).

- To use a total systems approach to operate and transform their organizations' businesses simultaneously (see, for example, Ackerman-Anderson, 1996; Adams, 1984; Blumenthal & Haspeslagh, 1994; Bridges, 1991; Bunker & Alban, 1997; Davidson, 1996; Davis, Maranville, & Obloj, 1997; Flamholtz & Randle, 1998; Gouillart & Kelly, 1995; Greenwood & Hinings, 1996; Greiner, 1972; Hambrick, Tushman, & Nadler, 1997; Kilmann & Covin, 1988; Lichtenstein, 1995; Mink, Mink, Owen, & Esterhuysen, 1993; Nadler, 1998; Newman & Nollen, 1998; Nolan & Croson, 1994; Nutt & Backoff, 1997; Owen, 1987, 1991; Quinn & Cameron, 1988; Romanelli & Tushman, 1994; Srivastva & Cooperrider, 1990; Weisbord, 1992).

- To learn from the metaphors provided by chaos and complexity theory (see, for example, Brown & Eisenhardt, 1997; Conner, 1998; Gleick, 1987; Masterpasqua & Perna, 1997; Price Waterhouse Change Integration Team, 1996; Sherman & Schultz, 1998; Stacey, 1996; Waldrop, 1992; Wheatley, 1992).

- To convene, deploy, and manage temporary project organizations effectively (see, for example, Demarco & Lister, 2000; Freedman, 1997, 2000; Lewis, 1998; Nicholas, 1990).

- To appreciate the need to develop effective leadership skills for a post-industrial, global organization operating in a volatile, discontinuous marketplace (see, for example, Bass, 1998; Block, 1988; Cohen & Bradford, 1990; Culbert, 1996; Gabarro, 1987; Kotter, 1996; Morgan, 1989a; Muirhead & Simon, 1998; Nadler, 1998; Nanus, 1992; O'Toole, 1995; Tichy, 1997).

- To enhance the appreciation of organizational agents, managers, and members for the challenges and implications of globalism (see, for example, Barnet & Cavanagh, 1994; Black, Gregersen, & Mendenhall, 1992; Cooperrider & Dutton, 1999; Drucker, 1993; Francesco & Gold, 1997; Hofstede, 1984, 1991, 1994; Huntington, 1996; Miller, 1982; Mohrman, Galbraith, & Lawler, 1998; Moynihan, 1993; Naisbitt, 1994; O'Hara-Devereaux, & Johansen, 1994;

Ohmae, 1990; Pucik, Tichy, & Barnett, 1993; Sorensen, et al., 1995; Stein, 1987; Tichy & Devanna, 1997; Tichy, McGill, & St. Clair, 1997; Trompenaars, 1994).

- To understand and apply theory and research appropriately in organizational behavior (see, for example, Bolman & Deal, 1987; Clegg, Hardy, & Nord, 1996; Cohen et al., 1988; Cook, Hunsaker, & Coffey, 1996; de Geus, 1997; Francesco & Gold, 1997; Gibson, Ivancevich, & Donnelly, 1998; Golembiewski, 1993; Greenberg & Baron, 1999; Handy, 1993; Hatch, 1997; Hellriegel, Slocum, & Woodman, 1997; Hersey & Blanchard, 1988; Hesselbein, Beckhard, & Goldsmith, 1998; Hunt, Schermerhorn, & Osborn, 1997; Ivancevich & Matteson, 1995; Johns, 1996; Katz & Kahn, 1990; Kolb, Rubin, & Osland, 1994; Luthans, 1997; Matteson & Ivancevich, 1998; Moorehead & Griffin, 1997; Morgan, 1994; Nahavandi & Malekzadeh, 1998; Natemeyer & Gilberg, 1990; Newstrom & Davis, 1996; Pepall, Norman, & Richards, 1998; Pfeffer, 1998b; Robbins, 1998, 1999; Schermerhorn, Hunt, & Osborn, 1996; Shani & Lau, 1999; Van Maanen, 1998; Woodward, 1994).

Disappointing past experiences that the leaders, managers, and members may have had with people who called themselves "consultants" may have led to so much skepticism that your marketing efforts and the effectiveness of your OD consulting will be adversely affected. Specifically, if executives and managers are used to working with techsperts, they may misunderstand attempts to involve and collaborate with them. For example, they may take proposals to apply OD processes and methods as indications that you (their OD consultant) think they lack competence or that you are attempting to avoid personal responsibility or extend the contract. If management is most familiar with extra-pair-of-hands consulting, they may see OD initiatives to stimulate high levels of participation by all involved parties as irrelevant at best or insubordination at worst. Leaders may confuse OD consultation with training/educational interventions and apply the reasonable but inaccurate expectation that OD consultants should achieve their goals by conducting a series of conveniently scheduled and budgeted workshops or seminars.

The fact that many OD consultants also refer to themselves as "facilitators" may create additional confusion, as many skilled training specialists also refer to themselves as "group facilitators." The major distinction between group facilitator/trainers and OD consultants is that the primary purpose of the former is to conduct classroom exercises with groups of students/participants who are individuals coming from many different, often unrelated, organizational subsystems. Organization development consultants, however, are more likely to work directly with organizational members in their natural work settings or in retreats, enabling members of intact teams to enhance the quality and effectiveness of their real-life meetings. Organization development consultants help team members to improve their participative problem-solving and decision-making skills so they can deal effectively with their specific team issues. Therefore, they must not only be competent trainers but must also be proficient in enabling team members to apply their skills properly.

The confusion and misunderstanding of the nature of OD consultation is perplexing yet interesting. Organization development is the most theorized, studied, and published of the four types of consultants (see, for example, Anderson, 1999; Argyris, 1990; Argyris, Putnam, & Smith, 1985; Beckhard 1969; Beckhard & Prichard, 1992; Bennis, 1969; Blake & Mouton, 1969; Burke, 1977, 1982, 1993, 1996; Conger, Lawler, & Spreitzer, 1998; Cummings & Worley, 1997; French & Bell, 1995; Golembiewski, 1993; Gouillart & Kelly, 1995; Kilmann, 1989; Lawrence & Lorsch, 1969; Lippitt & Lippitt, 1978; Massarik, 1990, 1993, 1995; Nevis, 1987; Nevis, Lancourt, & Vassallo, 1996; Pauchant & Mitroff, 1992; Rothwell, Sullivan, & McLean, 1995; Schein, 1992; Skibbins, 1974; Steele, 1973; Tannenbaum, Margulies, Massarik, & Associates, 1985). In addition, the field of OD is supported by a number of established journals, for example, the *Journal of Applied Behavioral Science,* the *OD Practitioner,* and the *OD Journal.*

Yet, although we have seen increased organizational awareness, jobs, and business for OD consultants over the past forty years, when we identify ourselves as OD consultants, we still run into blank stares from many prospective leaders and agents. This is disheartening. It indicates that too many agents and leaders are not making *informed* decisions when recruiting and selecting their consultants. We believe that consumer education is a critical activity for leaders in our field (see Zachrison & Freedman, 2000).

Which Type of Consultant Is Needed?

We have developed a series of simple questionnaires that you can use to enable agents and leaders to determine which of the four consultant types can best help them to deal with various issues within their organizations. It is important for you to help them to respond to these questionnaires in the sequence in which we present them. The first questionnaire (Exhibit 3.1) will help them determine whether the organization will be best served by an extra-pair-of-hands or by one of the remaining three consultant types. The second (Exhibit 3.2) narrows the choice down by helping them decide whether training/educational specialists are most relevant, or if one of the two remaining consultant types is most appropriate. The last questionnaire (Exhibit 3.3) will help them choose between techsperts or OD consultants.

Exhibit 3.1. Do You Need an Extra-Pair-of-Hands?

This questionnaire will help you and your associates to determine whether your organization needs an extra-pair-of-hands (contract employee) or another type of consultant.

Instructions: Think about the situation in your organization for which you are considering hiring some help from an external or internal consultant. Use the five-point scale below to rate how well each of the six statements describes the situation.

> 5 = This is an excellent description of our current situation.
> 4 = This is a good description of our current situation.
> 3 = This is a fairly accurate description of our current situation.
> 2 = This is a poor description of our current situation.
> 1 = This does not describe our current situation in any respect.

1. The consultant(s) are intended to be a strictly temporary   5 4 3 2 1
    addition to the existing workforce due to short-term
    demand for the skills and experience that they possess.

2. The consultants are expected to fit into the existing   5 4 3 2 1
    workforce and function as full-time or part-time but
    temporary "producers."

3. Permanent line managers will determine exactly *what* the   5 4 3 2 1
    consultants are expected to do and, to a large extent,
    how they are to do it.

4. Consultants are expected to accept the objectives and   5 4 3 2 1
    schedules given by the organization's permanent managers.

5. Line managers will actively supervise the consultants as   5 4 3 2 1
    they perform the tasks, activities, or functions for which
    they were engaged.

6. The consultant's performance will be evaluated against the   5 4 3 2 1
    same standards that are used to evaluate the performance
    of permanent employees occupying the same positions.

Total the points that you have given to each of the six statements above and write your total below.

Total Points:

If your points total 24 or more, this *clearly* indicates that you are seeking an extra-pair-of-hands consultant. A total of fewer than 24 indicates that the organization may be better served by one of the other three consultant types. See Exhibit 3.2 for the next questionnaire.

Exhibit 3.2. Do You Need a Training/Educational Specialist?

This questionnaire will help you to determine whether your organization needs the services of training/educational specialists.

Instructions: This questionnaire contains ten statements. As with the preceding questionnaire, use the five-point scale below to rate how well each statement describes the specific situation for which you are considering hiring a consultant.

5 = This is an excellent description of our current situation.
4 = This is a good description of our current situation.
3 = This is a fairly accurate description of our current situation.
2 = This is a poor description of our current situation.
1 = This does not describe our current situation in any respect.

1. The primary cause of the problem is a deficiency in essential information, conceptual knowledge, and/or behavioral or technical skills among employees. 5 4 3 2 1

2. The information, knowledge, and skills that our employees lack are needed on a *continual* basis, both now and in the future. 5 4 3 2 1

3. Individuals who will be trained are highly motivated and will respond positively to an opportunity to learn. 5 4 3 2 1

4. Individuals to be trained will have little difficulty in applying and making use of their new information, knowledge, and/or skills in performing their roles and responsibilities. 5 4 3 2 1

5. Executive management is prepared to take concrete, visible steps to support, reinforce, and reward individuals as they apply the knowledge and skills that they have gained from the training activity. 5 4 3 2 1

6. Executive management is prepared to identify and remove or minimize any obstacles that might interfere with applying the new information, knowledge, and/or skills in the work setting. 5 4 3 2 1

7. The training activity will have minimal disruptive effects on essential current activities, functions, or processes within the organization. 5 4 3 2 1

8. Organizational leaders have made a conscious decision that the training activity is worth any temporary disruptions that might occur. 5 4 3 2 1

Exhibit 3.2. Do You Need a Training/Educational Specialist?, Cont'd

9. Executive management believes the value of training   5 4 3 2 1
   individuals is greater than the costs.

10. Executive management believes there is a good probability   5 4 3 2 1
    that, over time, the costs or training will be recouped in the
    form of tangible increases in effectiveness.

Total the points that you have given to each of the ten statements and write the total below.

Total Points:

A total of 40 or above is a clear indication that you need a training/educational specialist type of consultant. Any other result indicates that the services of a different type of consultant are required.

However, it is possible that training/educational specialists may be the best choice if your total is from 32 to 39 points, if they are capable of helping participants and their managers to clarify and deal with the post-training issues, indicated by questions 3 through 10. If this is not the case, training/educational specialists should be supplemented with OD consultants.

For example, one reason for a lower point total may be your belief that the organization cannot, at present, provide sufficient support, reinforcement, or rewards to ensure the continued application of the knowledge and skills taught (item 5). Training/educational specialists could still be the best choice if they are qualified to help organizational leaders to develop effective support systems. Again, OD consultants may be brought in to assist in this effort.

Exhibit 3.3. Do You Need a Techspert or an OD Consultant?

If your responses to the preceding two questionnaires showed that extra-pairs-of-hands or training/educational specialists were *not* essential in your situation, you still have two options: techsperts or OD consultants.

Instructions: The following questionnaire differs in format from the previous two. It contains twelve sections, each of which has two possible responses. Your task is to distribute seven points between the two alternatives within each section.

Use the seven points to indicate your sense of the *relative* importance of each of the two options. For example, if you believe that option "B" is considerably more important than options "A," your response might look like this:

<u>2</u> A.

<u>5</u> B.

When evaluating each pair of responses, reflect on the specific assignment for which you are considering hiring a consultant. What do you want, need, and expect the consultant to do for your organization? Think about what is best for your organization in the short term *and* in the long run. What kind of a working relationship do you want or need between the members of your organization and your consultants?

1. The nature of the issue:

_____ A. We have a one-of-a-kind, nonrecurring problem. There is no advantage to our organization in acquiring the competencies necessary to deal with similar problems in the future. We expect consultants to recommend a solution or to solve the problem and achieve the results we need.

_____ B. The same or similar issues are likely to occur in the future. Therefore, we expect consultants to collaborate with our organization's managers and other members in dealing with the issue while *simultaneously* enhancing our organizational members' competence to deal with similar issues in the future.

2. Determination of goals and methods:

_____ A. Our organization's management will determine the *goals* to be achieved by our consultants; consultants will determine the best *methods* for reaching these goals.

_____ B. Management *and* consultants will jointly determine what goals are to be achieved through the consulting effort and what methods are to be used to achieve these goals.

Exhibit 3.3. Do You Need a Techspert or an OD Consultant?, Cont'd

3. **Consultant/client relationship:**

____ A. The relationship between management and consultants is not a significant factor, as long as management can trust consultants to provide viable solutions to the problems through the application of their specialized knowledge, skills, and procedures.

____ B. A high-trust, open relationship between management and the consultant is essential. All parties have to collaborate and exchange information in a transparent and timely manner throughout the consulting assignment.

4. **Reporting:**

____ A. Consultants will assume primary responsibility for the successful completion of all stages of the consulting assignment, but may call on organizational members from time to time to collect information and report progress.

____ B. Management and consultants will share *joint* responsibility for the successful completion of the consulting assignment and will maintain continual contact.

5. **Control:**

____ A. Consultants will have technical control over the project because they have more practical knowledge and experience in this area than organizational members. However, management will retain control over available resources, budgets, schedules, and logistics.

____ B. Management will share control with consultants by surfacing, discussing, and negotiating all issues that may emerge.

6. **Situation analysis:**

____ A. Consultants are expected to take full responsibility for analyzing the situation. They will decide what information will be required, the methods to be used to gather it, from whom, and how it will be organized, analyzed, and used.

____ B. Management and the consultant will make joint decisions about what data will be collected, from whom, and how it will be organized, analyzed, and used.

7. **Conclusions and recommendations:**

____ A. Consultants will derive conclusions from their analyses of the problems and will use these as the basis for personally formulating concrete recommendations for improving or correcting the situation.

____ B. Management, key members of the organization, and consultants will work together to draw conclusions from the data collected, to specify and prioritize issues, and to formulate recommended action plans to deal with the selected issues.

Exhibit 3.3. Do You Need a Techspert or an OD Consultant?, Cont'd

8. Implementation of solutions or action plans:

____ A. Consultants' responsibilities will end when they provide management with their recommendations for solving the problem(s) at hand or consultants may be responsible for implementing the technical solutions that they have recommended.

____ B. Although management will take primary responsibility for implementation, consultants will be actively involved in the process. Consultants' roles may vary from coaching from the sidelines ("shadow consultant") to project management. Whatever roles they take will be the result of open negotiations between management and consultants as they jointly develop the implementation plans.

9. Managing disagreements:

____ A. Consultant are experts in their fields and view any disagreements with organizational members as unjustified interference or as a lack of trust in their competence or professionalism.

____ B. Disagreements between organizational members and consultants are expected because of the differences in roles, responsibilities, backgrounds, and interests. Management and consultants see differences as sources of potential innovation.

10. Acceptance of the consultant's recommendations:

____ A. Consultants expect that their recommendations will be accepted quickly and implemented willingly by organizational members.

____ B. Consultants are expected to help management to gain acceptance, support, and commitment from organizational members who are relevant to implementing the problem solutions and the recommended (and accepted) action plans.

11. Evaluation of results:

____ A. Evaluation will take place at the conclusion of the consultation to determine whether consultants have delivered what they promised. Consultants may write periodic progress reports for senior management.

____ B. Evaluations will be conducted throughout the consultation to determine whether adjustments to recommended plans and strategies are necessary. These evaluations will cover such factors as (a) the progress being made, (b) the quality of the results being achieved, (c) identification of emerging issues and how they are handled, and (d) the effectiveness of the plan and the methods being used.

Exhibit 3.3. Do You Need a Techspert or an OD Consultant?, Cont'd

12. Evaluators:

_____ A. Management or someone assigned by management will evaluate the quality, relevance, and effectiveness of consultants' deliverables (results). Or consultants will evaluate their own work.

_____ B. Objective third parties who have no other involvement with either the client organization or consultants are hired to conduct objective evaluations. Alternatively, management and consultants may jointly evaluate the ongoing, emerging progress and results of the consultation.

Scoring

Copy the values from each of the twelve sections above to the appropriate columns below. Then total your points in each column.

Although it is unlikely that the total points in either of the two columns will be zero, you will probably give more points to one of the two consulting types than to the other. The results should tell you which of the two consultant types is more appropriate.

	Techspert	OD Consultant
1.	A. _____	B. _____
2.	A. _____	B. _____
3.	A. _____	B. _____
4.	A. _____	B. _____
5.	A. _____	B. _____
6.	A. _____	B. _____
7.	A. _____	B. _____
8.	A. _____	B. _____
9.	A. _____	B. _____
10.	A. _____	B. _____
11.	A. _____	B. _____
12.	A. _____	B. _____
Totals:	_____	_____

Interpretation

The greater the similarity between the total points given in the two columns, the more likely it is that the consultants you choose for this assignment must have sufficient competence and flexibility to function in *both* modes. For example, you may discover that you need primarily OD consultants who are also able to function as techsperts and/or training/educational specialists—or even, on occasion, as extra-pairs-of-hands. However, in such instances it is more functional to create a multidisciplinary consulting team.

Multidisciplinary Consulting Teams

The potential benefits of many consultation efforts are often undermined by dysfunctional competitive relationships between consultants of different kinds and types. Even when they work for the same consulting firm, consultants often compete for the same client system's limited time, attention, and budget. This is a counterproductive orientation that is often based on a severely restricted world view. Each type of consultant performs a useful purpose when properly matched with the needs of client system and aligned with one another. We believe that there are powerful but usually unrealized synergies to be achieved through combining the talents of various types of consultants within multidisciplinary consultation teams.

▶ CASE IN POINT

One of the authors was involved in the implementation of a $150-million, enterprise-wide resource planning software platform system project with a global engineering company. The project was scheduled for completion in three years and required well over one hundred twenty internal and external consultants. The cadre of consultants was composed of the following:

- Extra-pairs-of-hands were hired as temporary replacements for the eighty permanent employees who were redeployed to the project as content or business experts. The permanent employees were to participate in the project's essential feasibility tests, developing value propositions, design, configuration, integration, data cleansing and transfer, data migration, and implementation (deployment) planning. The extra-pairs-of-hands were to occupy the permanent employees' back-home positions and perform their role responsibilities until their parts in the project were completed.

- Training/educational specialists were brought in to design and supervise the essential technical training for the client organization's people who were to be responsible for operating one of the twelve different modules to be rolled out.

- Techsperts who were brought in included specialists in project management, ERP software and hardware technology, human resource management (recruiting, job descriptions, and compensation and incentives), communications and public relations, project office and facilities management, and project equipment. In addition, many of the client organization's own employees were brought into the project, in part because of their expertise with the company's business processes and the existing "legacy systems" that were to be replaced by the ERP software platform.

- Organization development consultants provided "change management" support. They were to (1) facilitate team development for design teams, the team of design team leaders, and project management teams; (2) facilitate inter-team and inter-group transactions within the project team and between the project group and the end-user subsystems, both nationally and globally; and (3) anticipate and prepare mechanisms and methods to identify and deal with emerging planning, involvement, and implementation issues. ◀

Matching Consultants with Purpose

When properly matched to an assignment, each of the four consultant types can serve legitimate and useful organizational purposes. However, for you to help agents and leaders create such a match, you must help them to become thoroughly familiar with each of the seven legitimate purposes that might be served by consultants. You must be able to explain or demonstrate how each consultant type is best suited to contribute to the realization of one or more of these seven purposes.

The seven distinct consulting purposes can be arranged in a hierarchical fashion (Turner, 1982). As shown in Figure 3.1., lower-order purposes must be achieved before engaging in efforts to realize the higher-order purposes, because a solid foundation is needed to support the realization of the higher-order purposes.

Figure 3.1. Hierarchy of Consulting Purpose

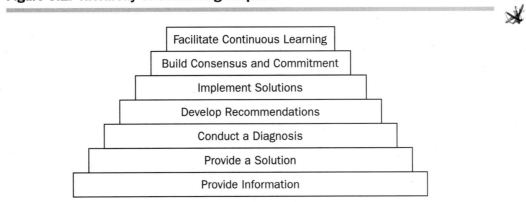

Facilitate Continuous Learning

Build Consensus and Commitment

Implement Solutions

Develop Recommendations

Conduct a Diagnosis

Provide a Solution

Provide Information

Adapted from Turner (1982).

As an ethical and practical OD consultant, it is in your enlightened self-interest to make sure that agents and leaders have realistic expectations for each of the four types of consultants. Be prepared to discuss which types of consultants are most likely to be able and willing to deliver each of the seven levels of services defined by Turner's pyramid, shown in Figure 3.1 and described in more detail below.

Provide Information

An extra-pair-of-hands is there to do a specific job. These consultants are expected to provide only minimal information—unless, of course, the position that they are temporarily filling involves providing information.

Training/educational specialists can provide information and related skill-development training in their specialized subject areas. They should also help decision makers by clarifying which alternative educational or training methods are most appropriate in a given situation, which content is necessary to best enable leaders and members to deal with their organizational issues.

For techsperts, providing information is one of their two primary functions. They should be able to tell the leaders of their client organizations such things as: "If you want such-and-such result, you will have to buy or build thus-and-such a system" or "If you are getting undesirable consequences or side effects from M and N, then you probably have to add such system elements as X and Y and eliminate element Z."

Techsperts can provide the technical characteristics, attributes, qualities, and requirements for various kinds of process systems (for example, computerized materials management, ERP and CRM software platforms, automated production or manufacturing systems, PR-driven corporate image campaigns, and employee compensation and incentive systems). Some specialized techsperts should be able to provide such information as current economic, political, market, social, demographic, or new technological trends and innovations in their areas of expertise.

Organization development consultants can provide quite a bit of relevant information, for example, about the probable consequences of maintaining the status quo versus changing existing interpersonal, inter-group, and organizational conditions. They can also conduct brief informational seminars for influential opinion leaders on various pertinent topics, such as strategic thinking, transformational leadership during systemic change efforts, the impacts of complex change on organizational dynamics, the human consequences of restructuring, or the predictable nature of resistance to organizational changes.

Provide a Solution

In some cases, the recruiting, screening, deploying, and managing of a cadre of extra-pairs-of-hands may, in itself, be a temporary solution for a purely temporary problem.

Training/educational specialists may claim that they provide training and educational solutions for their client systems' issues. Although this may be valid in some circumstances, we are extremely skeptical when training/educational specialists respond unquestioningly to an agent's description of an issue. For example, if an HR director tells training/educational specialists that there is a "communication problem" in the organization, many will accept that self-diagnosis and respond too quickly by recommending a communication skills training program as the remedy. The specialist offers the recommendation without taking the time to study the situation for root causes and discover whether the so-called "communications problem" is actually the result of members' lack of skill. It may be the result of unclear roles and vague expectations and/or persistent conflicts between key individuals or groups. These alternative root causes would require interventions *other* than—or in *addition* to—training in communications.

Providing solutions is the techsperts' second primary arena. Their forte is providing solutions in such functional areas as finance, engineering, IT systems, knowledge management, marketing, manufacturing, maintenance, and so forth. Because most of these specialties are undergoing continual change and innovation, leaders can benefit from the in-depth knowledge of a techspert, who can simply install the newest technology or provide turnkey solutions to technical problems. Alternatively, decision makers might ask techsperts for their recommendations. Ideally, there would be three parts to such recommendations: (1) at least three ways to fix the problem; (2) the advantages and disadvantages for each alternative; and (3) the alternative that the techspert believes is most appropriate and effective.

Organization development consultants usually insist on performing their own diagnosis to confirm, elaborate, or challenge the beliefs of the agents or leaders before recommending a process for developing an action plan to deal with the issue. However, some are prepared to make "best guess" recommendations without a diagnosis if the organization is in a crisis and immediate action is required. In emergencies, they "change hats" and take on some aspects of the techspert role (Freedman, 1995).

Conduct a Diagnosis

In our experience, only the extra-pair-of-hands is not actively concerned with conducting a diagnosis. The other three consultant types usually recommend assessment methods to identify and/or clarify the root causes of the issues that they have been asked to help manage. However, there are significant differences among how training/educational specialists, techspert consultants, and OD consultants view the diagnostic process.

Training/educational specialists most often recommend a training needs assessment. For example, if qualified specialists are given the task of delivering a course in "improving delegation skills" in an organization, they should begin by conducting an assessment of the individual members of the target population. They should focus on the prospective participants' current level of *knowledge* and compare that with their own and others' perceptions of their *competence* in actually delegating work to others. Unfortunately, some training/educational specialists honestly believe that they already know what skills and competencies must be provided in order to improve any group of employees' skills in their given area of specialization (communications, decision making, delegation, dispute resolution, and the like). Based on this belief, they see no need to conduct what seems to them to be a redundant assessment. Such arrogance may lead to a major error. The specialists' models for appropriate and effective skills may be incompatible with the culture of their trainees' organization. If so, the trainees are unlikely to apply their newly acquired skills if they are perceived to be competitive with traditional cultural norms that define the limits of acceptable behavior and practices.

Techspert consultants tend to limit the scope of their in-depth diagnoses to their own specific areas of expertise. Depending on their specialties, they may focus exclusively on a single organizational subsystem, for example, research and development, or on their specialized function as it threads its way along their client systems' delivery chains. That is, they act as if the targets of their diagnostic studies are isolated parts of the larger system. Thus, whatever occurs within the targeted department, function, group, system, process, or region is treated as if it will not impact other operational parts of the larger organization. As a result, organizational members—who usually know better—may disagree with or resist the techspert's diagnostic process, conclusions, and recommendations.

Organization development consultants treat the diagnostic process, in itself, as an intervention. They realize that, more likely than not, the act of searching for and gathering information sends a message and triggers a "ripple effect" throughout the client system's interdependent levels and subsystems. They anticipate that diagnostic interventions evoke a wide range of reactions from subsystem members. They also know that imposed diagnoses and derivative recommendations are usually resented, rejected, and resisted. So they design ways to involve intact work units and key individuals who will be affected by the execution of any implementation plans. They know that "buy in" or a sense of ownership of the diagnosis and conclusions is critical to assure that people will support plans to change the organization. They also take the mystery out of the diagnostic process by making it as transparent as possible by describing the entire process and explaining why they do what they do at each step.

Develop Recommendations

Extra-pairs-of-hands seldom make recommendations unless it is part of the role responsibilities that are inherent in the temporary positions that they fill.

Training/educational specialists often provide recommendations on the basis of their training needs assessments. Only recently, some training/educational specialists have begun to acknowledge that they must consider what happens when well-trained former participants return from the classroom to their respective workplaces. Far too often, the newly acquired information, knowledge, and behavioral skills are not applied, so a few training/educational specialists have begun to experiment by following their ex-participants into the workplace to conduct situational analyses. As mentioned earlier, they often discover powerful cultural forces being exerted by colleagues and supervisors that prevent ex-participants from applying what they have learned. In addition, they often discover that ex-participants would have to violate prevailing contradictory policies and practices in order to use what they have learned. We have had several experiences in which training/educational specialists recommended that OD consultants be brought in to help leaders deal with these formal and informal impediments to change.

Recommendations, supported by their findings and conclusions, are frequently the primary content of techsperts' final reports. These recommendations may include specific implementation plans, as well as instructions for how to execute those plans.

Organization development consultants are not likely to offer recommendations for *what* should be changed (the content). Rather, their recommendations typically focus on how organizational members might take the next steps (the *process*) that might be taken in developing solutions. Their usual approach is to organize the raw data that they collect to prepare for two or more data feedback meetings, first with the leaders, then with managers, and then, possibly, with members. During these meetings, OD consultants typically help the leaders do the following:

- Review and accept (or challenge) the data and the categories;
- Derive conclusions from the organized data;
- Acknowledge and specify the issues about which they are concerned;
- Explicate the criteria on which they will determine the relative importance of each of these issues;
- Use these criteria to establish priorities;
- Set change goals for the high-priority issues; and
- Develop implementation or action plans (which they may see as "solutions") to achieve the goals.

Organization development consultants know that this process is essential in creating compelling, meaningful opportunities for the leaders and members to cooperate in generating their own goals and action plans. As a result, leaders and members develop a shared sense of ownership of the results and are more likely to commit themselves to supporting the execution of those plans.

Implement Solutions

Extra-pairs-of-hands are often essential resources in implementing complex systems changes, especially when permanent employees are overloaded. Extra-pairs-of-hands can relieve the pressure by taking on and working off the overload. Some may execute selected parts of the implementation plan, leaving permanent employees to perform their routine jobs undisturbed. However, although this approach seems to be logical and expedient, there is a possible significant downside. Because permanent employees will not have had to sacrifice or invest extra time and energy in the implementation, they may not understand or accept the changes and will not develop a sense of ownership. Therefore, they may resist and withhold their support or not make proper use of the changes.

Many complex change efforts require leaders and members to acquire competence in applying new information, knowledge, and/or technical or behavioral skills. The most expedient approach often seems to be some sort of classroom-based education or technical and behavioral training. However, as we have pointed out, there may be formal and/or informal impediments to applying these kinds of learnings in their real-life workplaces. So training/educational specialists may also have to involve themselves during the implementation phase. However, we believe they should collaborate with OD consultants, who can serve as coaches to help newly trained leaders recognize and deal with the impediments and apply what they have learned. Organization development consultants can also help specify and deal with cultural and structural impediments.

Many techspert consultants consider their responsibilities to be fulfilled once they have submitted their conclusions and recommendations. The most frequent exception is when the solutions are so specialized that they require the techsperts' continued leadership and guidance during the implementation. For example, an organization may engage techsperts to design and install a CRM software system. In such cases, techsperts are not just involved in the implementation; more often than not, they are given the critical roles of project leaders and primary implementers.

Organization development consultants should be actively involved in the execution of implementation plans. However, their relevance is frequently overlooked until the change initiative runs into difficulty. To the extent that they are able to influence the scope and focus of their involvement, OD consultants abide by Saul Alinsky's Iron Law (1969, 1972): "Don't ever do nothing for nobody that they can do for themselves" (our paraphrase). That is, OD consultants should take on responsibilities to solve problems or make decisions *only* when organizational leaders and members lack the knowledge and skills they need to ensure the successful implementation of the planned changes. At times, they may function as techsperts; perhaps if they are also qualified clinical psychologists, they may recognize and deal with the occasional psychological crises that are precipitated by radical changes in organizations (Freedman & Levinson, 1998).

More frequently, OD consultants help leaders and members to acquire the skills for managing complex systems change that they will need in the future. This is a four-phase process, the first three of which are *guiding, escorting,* and *following* (Freedman, 1982). Organization development consultants may *guide* inexperienced project managers by modeling and explaining how to engage relevant stakeholders in joint issue identification, goal setting, problem analysis, aligning project goals with organizational missions and business plans, and action planning. Then, as project managers learn to perform such functions, OD consultants shift into *escort* roles as partners so that project managers gain essential hands-on practice in using the skills being modeled. As project managers increase their proficiencies further, OD consultants shift roles again, pulling back to serve as *followers,* that is, coaching and preparing project managers to perform some specific function, observing them, and debriefing and providing feedback. To do otherwise would be to deny organizational leaders and members important opportunities to learn to rely on themselves. At this point, OD consultants shift their roles for the fourth time: *They get out!*

Build Consensus and Commitment

For obvious reasons, extra-pairs-of-hands cannot be expected to aid in this function. Training/educational specialists may perform this function by inducing their seminar and workshop participants to commit themselves to applying what they have learned in the classroom to their respective real-life work situations. As we have discussed, this commitment may be naïve unless learners are members of intact work teams and the commitment is based on realistic assessments of the informal social pressure and formal structure and policies with which ex-participants will have to contend.

Techsperts seldom become involved in building consensus among those who must use or will be affected by their solutions. Nor do they ordinarily seek commitment to the solutions that they have recommended. They seem to assume that the elegance of the technical results of their work will be sufficiently compelling to win people over. They also seem to assume that once their technical innovations are installed, organizational members will have no choice other than to comply and adapt.

For OD consultants, building commitment is a primary process competency. They must be capable of designing a variety of engaging, relevant methods and processes to induce all involved parties to participate in the activities that are essential to moving the system forward with organizational change efforts. Active involvement and participation in pertinent problem-solving and decision-making processes will evoke commitment to supporting the decisions made and actions taken to achieve complex systems change.

Facilitate Continuous Learning

Arguably, only OD consultants and, to a lesser degree, training/educational specialists see this as an essential part of their jobs. Training/educational specialists often contribute to the kinds of continuous learning that OD consultants believe are most relevant by training managers in the use of participatory and strategic management philosophies, concepts, methods, and skills. Unfortunately, many specialists try to do precisely what OD consultants try to avoid. Acting as experts, they train organizational leaders and members to use *specific* solutions for particular situations, but often do not teach them how to learn from their own experiences. Only if they provide systems or mechanisms that further leaders and members to create knowledge and competencies by themselves can they perform this function.

One of the explicit functions of OD consultants, in fact, one of the defining purposes of our discipline, is enabling leaders, managers, and members to acquire sufficient competence, confidence, and comfort to learn enough from their collective experience to deal with similar issues, on their own, in the future. Organization development consultants actively encourage leaders and members to take the strategic view. They stand ready to assist in any efforts that contribute to their client systems' vitality and resilience in the face of continuous, volatile change and increasing complexity. In addition, they encourage leaders to make sure that their internal and external environments are continuously scanned for unprecedented events and circumstances with which they will have to cope or to which they will have to adjust—or anything that offers unexpected opportunities.

Table 3.2 summarizes our discussion of how each of the four types of consultants ideally contributes to each of Turner's seven consulting purposes (seen in Figure 3.1).

Table 3.2. Hierarchy of Consultant Purposes

Purposes	Extra-Pair-of-Hands	Training/ Educational Specialist	Techspert	OD Consultant
Facilitate Continuous Learning	seldom	seldom	seldom	primary function
Build Consensus and Commitment	seldom	as related to training offered	seldom	primary function
Implement Solutions	primary role	seldom	seldom (either do it themselves or leave)	only in cooperation with internal staff
Develop Recommendations	seldom	often, based on assessment of training needs	primary task	only in cooperation with internal staff
Conduct a Diagnosis	seldom	limited to training needs assessment	primary activity	primary activity
Provide a Solution	seldom	training programs as solutions	primary function	seldom
Provide Information	as part of assignment	seldom	primary task	on occasion

We believe that the lower levels of the hierarchy represent the "traditional" purposes of most types of consulting. It is these levels to which consultants dedicate most of their time and energy. The effects of the first five levels, by themselves, are temporary and frequently disappointing. It is only recently that building consensus and commitment and facilitating continuous learning have begun to be accepted as legitimate and essential consultative purposes. This is in sharp contrast to some critics' past beliefs that they were "unnecessary fluff."

Early in their careers, many older OD consultants were training/educational specialists and, in that capacity, served important supportive roles in organizational change efforts. Organization development consultants still endeavor to design and deliver high-quality training and education as part of a comprehensive set of interventions.

We have found Turner's hierarchy to be invaluable in our discussions with agents of prospective client systems in clarifying desired outcomes, discussing and negotiating the scope of prospective consultations, and making informed decisions about the substance of the contracts we negotiate. In particular, the hierarchy suggests the work for which leaders and members will assume responsibility after you leave.

Summary

We have described each of four different types of consultants whose specialized services your client systems may need. You may need to educate agents and leaders so they understand the capabilities and limitations of the various types of consultants. You can use any or all of the three questionnaires that we designed to help them to determine optimal matches between their organizations' needs and the respective strengths of various types of consultants.

We encourage you to consider the potential synergies that can be harvested by developing multidisciplinary consulting teams, in contrast with the prevailing, implicit model of the stand-alone consultant that, we believe, will result in the isolation of "independent" OD consultants and their replacement by the "change management specialists."

The task of matching different types of consultants with the seven purposes of consultation reveals that each is capable of serving some, but not all of these purposes. It also supports the argument favoring multidisciplinary consulting teams. You can use the matching process to help leaders and agents make high-quality, informed selection and deployment decisions.

4

Consulting Philosophy

ORGANIZATIONAL LEADERS SELDOM hire the first consultant or consulting firm that they interview, with the exception of those with whom they have already established a mutually satisfying relationship. Most agents interview several prospects before they make a decision.

Consultant candidates invariably profess to be highly competent. Most claim that their expertise exactly covers the particular area that seems to be of concern or interest. So agents have to distinguish among:

- *True Positives:* Candidates who make a good initial impression and are as competent and effective as they look.

- *False Positives:* Candidates who make good initial impressions but prove to be neither competent nor effective.

- *False Negatives:* Consultants who make a less than memorable initial impression but really are both competent and effective.

- *True Negatives:* Consultants who neither look nor sound good and are neither competent nor effective.

Agents must develop a set of selection criteria that includes the minimum acceptable requirements for the candidates' consulting philosophy, competence, and personal characteristics. In this chapter we focus exclusively on the criteria against which agents may evaluate your underlying *consulting philosophy*. In the next chapter we will examine how they might assess your competence and personal characteristics.

After sixty years of combined experience as practitioners and trainers of many hundreds of consultants in the discipline of OD, the authors are convinced that there are eight philosophical beliefs and values that truly competent OD consultants share.

We have constructed a questionnaire to test whether or not you share our philosophy. The questionnaire is designed to be taken twice—once before you read our explanations and once afterward. It may be interesting for you to compare your pre-test and post-test responses, but do not look back on your pre-test answers while you are filling out the post-test. First, make some copies of Exhibit 4.1. Use one for the pre-test and save the other for the post-test. Take the pre-test now by checking whether you agree or disagree with each statement of a consulting philosophy in Exhibit 4.1.

Exhibit 4.1. Consulting Philosophy Questionnaire

Philosophy	Pre-Test		Post-Test	
	Agree	Disagree	Agree	Disagree
1. The purpose of consulting is *achieving organizational effectiveness* by maintaining a balanced focus between (a) changing behaviors and attitudes of people and (b) changing the organization's sociotechnical systems.				
2. When consulting, one should treat the entire organization or subsystem, rather than any given individual or group as "the client."				
3. Consulting involves focusing on the underlying root causes of persistent issues, rather than on their symptoms.				

Exhibit 4.1. Consulting Philosophy Questionnaire, Cont'd

	Pre-Test		Post-Test	
Philosophy	**Agree**	**Disagree**	**Agree**	**Disagree**
4. Consultants should intervene at the level of the client system's strategic mission, rather than offering quick fixes.				
5. Identifying, developing, and utilizing the client organization's internal resources and competencies is a primary purpose of consulting.				
6. Enabling leaders, managers, and members of the organization to achieve the degree of self-determination necessary for them to help themselves in the future is a primary purpose of consulting.				
7. Dealing with the client organization's immediate, real-life, practical realities is a primary focus of a consultation.				
8. Consultants should use a holistic "helicopter" perspective as the basis for intervening at a comprehensive, systemic level.				

As an OD consultant, you should find it useful to review and consider the philosophies listed in Exhibit 4.1 and see how each could be seen by the agents and leaders of a prospective client organization who are assessing you. Even though we advocate making the process of matching your philosophy and the client's explicit and transparent, be aware that questions of philosophy and values are rarely acknowledged or consciously used in selecting consultants. So why bring up the subject? Philosophical issues are always present and operative, usually at implicit, nonconscious levels. If you are not tuned in to your own values and beliefs, you may make short-sighted decisions based on transitory issues, such as making enough money to pay your mortgage or based on expediency. You could regret this later.

Also, if you are not attuned to indicators of your prospective client's values and belief systems, you may make some fatal assumptions. For example, you could think, "This organization and its leaders operate on the same code of conduct as similar companies in the same industry" or "This British company has the same values and priorities as that French company that it is about to acquire."

Each of the eight consulting philosophies from the exhibit is discussed in more detail below.

Achieving Organizational Effectiveness

There are three key components to this philosophy: (a) organizational effectiveness; (b) changing individual attitudes or behavior; and (c) changing the sociotechnical system. The first, organizational effectiveness, brings forth a recurring and valid complaint about OD consultants who are reluctant or unable to discuss organizational effectiveness in terms of "hard" data. Anyone calling himself or herself an OD consultant must be able to understand, appreciate, and communicate ways in which his or her consultation will result in concrete, meaningful, measurable improvements in the outputs of the client organization. You must be prepared to provide agents with a definition of what organizational effectiveness means to you that clearly addresses their concerns for obtaining desirable organizational results from your services.

There is no single definition of organizational effectiveness other than that it must be linked to the mission and business plan as measured by the outputs produced or created by the client organization. We believe that organizational effectiveness is a multidimensional factor, so we offer the agents of our prospective client systems a checklist of potential outcomes, including revenues, market share, quality, waste, profitability, productivity, innovations/inventions, cycle time, customer satisfaction, management of knowledge, organizational learning, employee loyalty and morale, turnover, environmental impact, corporate citizenship (relations with surrounding communities), social justice, leadership development, and the like (see Exhibit 4.2).

Exhibit 4.2. Organizational Effectiveness Checklist

Instructions: Feel free to add to this list. Then ask the client system's agents (representatives) to specify the particular dimensions of "organizational effectiveness" about which they are particularly concerned. They may simply check off the dimensions that they believe they need, or you may invite them to use the A, B, C approach to establishing priorities. "A" implies "must do right now," "B" implies "must do soon," and "C" implies "should do some time."

Dimension	Priority A	Priority B	Priority C	Comments
Revenues				
Market Share				
Quality				
Waste				
Profitability				
Productivity				
Innovations/Inventions				
Cycle Time				
Customer Satisfaction				
Management of Knowledge				
Organizational Learning				
Employee Loyalty and Morale				
Turnover				
Environmental Impact				
Corporate Citizenship				
Social Justice				
Management/Leadership Development				
Organizational Learning				
Other:				

In our experience, agents may not tell you which of these outcomes they are looking for. In fact, they may not have thought about it until we bring it up in preliminary discussions. When we ask what they are looking for in terms of outcomes or results, they tend to think first about actions to take ("solutions") that address obvious symptoms and only secondarily in terms of the outcomes that the actions are intended or are likely to achieve. When we ask for expected or required "results" but receive answers about preferred "solutions," we have to help agents to clarify their thinking and be more specific. For example, we might ask, "If we were successful in implementing this solution, what difference do you think it would make? How would your organization operate differently? How would the solution affect your productivity, cycle time, customer satisfaction, and so forth?"

It is valuable for all involved parties to clarify and specify the results that your prospective client systems need or want *in detail.* Only when you are clear about the ends can you begin to focus clearly and effectively on the means. Agents are likely to have strong opinions regarding the *means* for achieving their vague or implicit desired or required results. They may not be consciously aware of these opinions until you suggest something that violates them. It is important to help agents surface their implicit opinions and preferences and make them explicit. Then you will have to decide whether your own opinion about a viable strategy is compatible or in conflict.

Changing Individual Attitudes or Behaviors. Organization development consultants tend to hold one of two opinions or assumptions about how to change organizations and achieve organizational effectiveness (Beckhard & Prichard, 1992). The first may have evolved from clinical psychology and training and development belief systems. Here the consultant strives to induce individuals to change their perspectives, attitudes, values, beliefs, and/or interpersonal styles and skills. The assumption is that as individuals become aware of their feelings and enhance their interpersonal competencies, they will strive to make their interpersonal relations, teams, subsystems, and organizations less defensive, more open, more responsible, and more willing to take risks. It is presumed that this will result in greater productivity, innovation, and mutual satisfaction (Argyris, 1964, 1990). Implicitly, this assumption suggests that there is at least one thing about people that is deficient, inadequate, or defective. Thus, corrective interventions are called for, such as some combination of coaching, performance counseling, interpersonal confrontation, team building, and/or technical or behavioral skill training.

Changing Sociotechnical Systems. An alternative opinion about how to improve suboptimal or dysfunctional performance is to change the system within which individuals operate and then assist organizational members as they adapt. This entails a focus on such organizational elements as structure (authority), roles (responsibilities and accountabilities), systems (management information and performance management systems), work flow, rules, regulations, policies, procedures, and processes. The underlying assumption is that, to reduce cognitive dissonance (Festinger, Schachter, & Back, 1950) and/or in response to social pressure (Asch, 1956), people will adapt and modify their behavior to accommodate altered organizational conditions. There is little need to adopt a deficit orientation with regard to individuals. There is even less reason to dig around in people's minds searching for their counterproductive attitudes. Rather, sociotechnical systems interventions can provoke organizational members' awareness of their need to add to their existing capabilities in order to adapt to changing conditions and to let go of anachronistic business practices. Their behavior will change; changed attitudes and beliefs will follow.

You may ask, "Which of these two opinions is more valid?" We must answer, "Yes!" That is, evidence to support both opinions can be and usually is found in most complex systems change efforts. Therefore, interventions should focus on *both* individuals and sociotechnical systems. It is the consultant's role to operate on *both* of these "channels" in parallel and to shift frequently and quickly between the two as the change efforts impact and cause shifts in the client systems' organizational dynamics.

Treating the Entire Organization

Organizations are entities that tend to outlive their founders, leaders, managers, and members. Consultants are hired and paid by organizations, not by individuals. Thus, the primary goal of any consulting effort should be to improve organizational conditions. If the needs of the individual agents or leaders who engage consultants are in line with their organizations' needs, no problem. But when consultants promote an individual's preferences or a group's interests at the expense of the larger organization's best interests, problems occur.

Many consultants unquestionably accept the notion that their "clients" are the senior persons who speak in behalf of the organization or with whom they negotiate their consulting contracts or who authorize payment of their fees. Such consultants often feel obligated to satisfy these individual agents. As a result they orient their work around the agents' perceptions, beliefs, values, interests, and opinions. Consequently, consultants may ignore or discount the validity or relevance of the perceptions and interests of other key individuals, populations of constituents, subsystems within the organizations, or external stakeholders (such as suppliers, customers, financiers, regulators, and stockholders or owners).

In all fairness, not all consultants share this conception of who the client is. Nevertheless, we believe it is more accurate and productive to view the larger organization or total subsystem as the client.

Focusing on Causes, Not on Symptoms

It is not unusual for agents to have preconceived ideas of what they want consultants to do. It is very common for agents' preferred solutions to be based more on the observable symptoms than on their more obscure or hidden root causes. It is a part of a consultant's responsibility to help agents to re-examine their conclusions and help them to shift their orientations from needing what they want to wanting what they need.

▶ CASE IN POINT

One of the authors was recently called in by the HR director of a large manufacturing company to "discuss performance problems." Immediately after a brief "Hello, nice to meet you," the HR director said, "We want you to design and install a performance management system for us!"

The author made several attempts to probe into what the HR director meant by a "performance management system" and why, specifically, he felt his organization needed one. Apparently, these attempts to seek clarity made the HR director quite uncomfortable because he blurted out, "Look, we want a performance management system! Can you give us one or not!?"

The author explained to the HR director that he was more than willing to help them with a "performance management system" if that really was what was needed to deal with the organization's performance problems. However, before he could begin designing such a system, the author wanted to spend enough time in the organization to identify (1) the most serious performance problems and (2) their primary causes. Then he would recommend an intervention designed specifically to help the client system to reduce or eliminate the underlying causes.

The HR director blew up: "It's clear you don't want this job. I'll find someone else who is willing to listen to me. Thank you for your time!"

And, of course, the HR director was able to find a consulting firm willing to provide him with a "performance management system." Predictably, that system had little, if any, positive impact on organizational performance because it addressed the symptoms of the organization's performance problems but few, if any, of the root causes of those symptoms. ◄

When agents say that they want the prospective consultant to execute a specific "solution" based on their own or management's subjective diagnoses, not supported by comprehensive, objective data, they may be "testing" the consultant's competence, courage, and/or experience. Consultants who readily offer to satisfy their agents' requests without a challenge may be unreliable. Effective OD consultants should be prudent enough to say something like, "Before I take any action based on your perspective, I want a more comprehensive picture. Do you have any problems with my talking with some of the people in those subsystems that are directly involved in or are impacted by these issues?" In this way, you either pass the agent's test or you test the agent's openness to new approaches.

Again, your job is not necessarily to give your client system what it thinks it wants. Rather, it is to make sure that the organization gets what it really needs!

Intervening at the Strategic Level, Rather Than Offering a Quick Fix

A primary task for OD consultants is to help client systems to function effectively in the long term, not just the short run. Unfortunately, many consultants focus too much on grappling with critical current issues and ignore or defer efforts to prevent future issues. In addition, consultants often fail to make sure that the manner in which they deal with the current situation is aligned with and contributes to the realization of their system's strategic vision, mission, and business plan.

This oversight is all too easy to make in the midst of crises when the pervasive sense of urgency combines with fast-moving events. This leads to a loss of perspective and objectivity. Consultants can easily become "infected" by leaders' intense anxiety and develop their own "tunnel vision."

Even when dealing with a crisis, much of your attention should focus on helping the system to avoid a recurrence of this problem. When a client system has a history of dealing with one crisis after another over an extended period of time,

OD consultants should be particularly alert to indications of *symptom substitution.* Each crisis is probably characterized by one or more prominent issues, for example, on-the-job accidents resulting in lost time. Such issues capture the attention of leaders and managers. They find a quick fix and return to business as usual. However, time passes and a new symptom emerges and has to be dealt with, perhaps unusually high employee turnover. It is entirely possible that these issues are actually different symptoms of the same underlying root causes. The symptoms effectively hide or distort the root cause so leaders and members easily ignore or overlook them. However, until the root causes are uncovered, defined, and corrected, the organization will be plagued by periodic or irregularly occurring crises.

► CASE in POINT

One of the authors was recently asked to help the senior management team of a large chain of retail stores to "improve organizational performance." This firm had spent a fortune on training interventions over the past ten years, including customer service training, total quality management (TQM), and performance management. These interventions proved to have little impact on the organization's bottom line (profitability was the CEO's single-dimension definition of effectiveness).

In individual interviews, the author asked the firm's executives, "What is the single greatest cause of reduced performance in this organization?" Each and every executive gave the same answer: "Our purchasing department is worthless." When the consultant asked, "What have you done about this?" The answer was also universal: "Nothing." Not one intervention that was implemented over the past ten years was directed toward purchasing!

The author probed to find out why obvious problems in purchasing had not been addressed. The answers varied from, "It is too difficult to get all of the head buyers together at one time" to "They have all been with the firm a long time and we are certain that they won't change." When the author probed further, he found that the head of the purchasing function was very well-liked by everyone, apparently despite having been promoted far beyond his level of competence. The executives, it seemed, were colluding in maintaining a "public secret." They were unwilling to risk being seen as "bad guys" by firing the purchasing director! "After all," said one executive, "He'll be retiring in five years anyway." ◄

Effective OD consultants should be prepared to help leaders and members understand that interventions that create enduring results require more time, attention, and resources than quick-fix, symptomatic interventions, but the former interventions typically yield the greatest long-term, strategic payoff.

Identifying, Developing, and Utilizing Client Resources

There are very few situations in which your prospective client systems are going to be totally lacking in people who have the competencies necessary to deal with their critical issues. The challenge is in identifying precisely what competencies are needed, locating those who have these competencies, developing a collaborative relationship with them, and, if necessary, enabling them to gain sufficient credibility within the organization to be used appropriately and when needed. Of course, this suggests how important it is to set the stage for developing collaborative partnerships with prospective client systems' internal resources.

Too many consultants are more concerned with their consulting contracts than with exploring the possibility that their client systems may not require their costly services. Many consulting engagements would prove to be unnecessary if leaders could identify and utilize their existing internal resources. Some consultants may assume that merely talking with agents who are receptive and desire consulting services is evidence that the organization does not have the internal competencies it needs. This convenient assumption seems to relieve many consultants of the responsibility for exploring the possibility that the organization does not need their services. We do not want OD consultants to commit similar self-serving errors of omission.

You should be able and eager to help agents and leaders to evaluate the use of internal resources, as described in Chapter 2 (Exhibit 2.3), and the conditions under which external consultant resources should be used (Chapter 3).

Paying explicit attention to these two issues will give you an opportunity to build an enormous amount of respect, trust, and credibility. You can push agents and leaders to consider whether or not they really need consultative services of any kind or type—including your own. If the need for consultation does exist, you can push them to consider the minimal level they need.

▶ CASE IN POINT

During an OD consulting assignment with a large manufacturing firm, one of the authors was asked to help make drastic changes in the organization's structure so it would become more responsive to the needs of its customers and to changes in its highly competitive environment.

Rather than take a techspert approach and recommend a new structure, the author suggested that mid- and senior-level managers should be actively involved in designing the organization's new structure. His rationale was simple. These people knew the most about how the current structure was helping and hindering responsiveness. They would be the people to be most impacted by the new structure. They would most likely resist the new structure if it was imposed and they did not like it. And they would most likely support it if they did like it. Management agreed.

The author gathered all senior managers together for a five-day, in-residence planning session. In his introduction, the firm's highly regarded CEO reminded participants that, "It is no secret that we are in serious financial difficulty. We must take immediate action to survive." During the five-day session, the managers were introduced to a fictitious company called "XYZ Manufacturing," a company virtually identical to the participants' own company in that it manufactured the same products, had similar facilities and equipment, was located in the same social and economic environment, and had a similar customer base. Participants were told that they were to play the roles of consultants who had been hired by XYZ. Their assignment was to develop what they, as a team, thought the best possible structure would be for XYZ. The only restrictions were that the structure (1) had to help the "fictional" firm overcome its current financial crisis *and* (2) serve as a foundation for improving its responsiveness to technological and market changes in the future.

The participants engaged in this role play with great enthusiasm. They generated a list of viable options that they converted into a set of recommendations. On the following Monday, representatives of this group of managers presented these recommendations to their senior management team. By the time the presentation was completed, the senior executives were in a state of positive shock. The new structure far exceeded even their most optimistic expectations and, as a result, the recommendations were accepted with only minor adjustments. All involved parties felt strongly committed to and supportive of the implementation. The "fictional" became "real." ◄

Whether leaders accept your suggestions to involve their members or not, you will have added to your image as an ethical, conscientious OD consultant who tries to enable your client systems to become self-reliant. This is because you will have provided the leaders with previously unrecognized options that enable them to make informed, forward-looking, *strategic* decisions rather than knee-jerk reactions.

Enabling Self-Determination for the Future

We have spoken of our belief that OD consultants have an ethical obligation to work themselves out of a job. That is, you should negotiate explicit agreements with client systems stating that one of your goals is to transfer relevant information, skills, techniques, and knowledge from you to designated members of the client system. In fact, most OD consulting agreements should explicitly state that you will work with organizational members, simultaneously, along two dimensions:

- Helping the organization to achieve the intended results of the consulting effort, and

- Enabling organizational members to achieve the same kinds of results by themselves, in the future.

Transferring your OD consulting competencies to members of your client systems not only empowers these people, it also increases the organization's potential to become self-reliant. Perhaps most important, the organization's future dependence on expensive external consultants is significantly reduced.

Dealing with Immediate, Real-Life Realities

At various times, each of the authors has been labeled an "enemy" of training. To some degree, this is accurate. Despite the fact that—or perhaps because—we started our careers as training/educational specialists, we both strongly oppose training activities that utilize artificial, metaphoric, or synthetic experiences, such as pre-packaged case studies, exercises, and simulations in situations in which there is plenty of "reality" to be used. We also strongly disagree with the simplistic assumption that what participants acquire in a classroom will automatically and easily be translated and imported to their respective workplaces.

For example, a common approach to teaching team skills is to send selected managers to public training programs that are open to participants from many different organizations. Because participants may be the only representatives from their organizations or subsystems, they usually lack support when they re-enter their organizations and attempt to apply their newly learned skills. Between six to nine months after the training, they lose most of whatever skill proficiencies they may have acquired (Freedman, 1963).

A far better approach is to organize *internal* courses in which training/educational specialists partner with OD consultants to provide participants with concepts, skills, and techniques that are truly relevant to their own "real worlds." We call this process "facili-training" (Freedman, unpublished).

First, we work only with intact work teams so that people who work together also train together. Then, we start consultation-training workshops by having participants identify the actual issues with which they are currently attempting to deal in their workplaces. Participants focus on working on these issues while we, in the role of facili-trainers, observe and facilitate their work processes. If and as they exhibit clear needs for either information, conceptual models, or skill acquisition at the personal-interpersonal, group dynamics, teamwork methodologies, or boundary management levels, we intervene and provide just-in-time training. Participants quickly learn that these competencies are relevant to their actual work experiences. They leave facili-training workshops feeling competent, comfortable, committed, and confident in their ability to utilize their new competencies. And, because they work in intact teams, they share a common language, concepts, techniques, and skills. Therefore, they are likely to cooperate with and support one another in applying their learnings after they complete the program.

Using a Holistic "Helicopter" Perspective

Organizations are complex sociotechnical systems. Changes in one part of an organizational system have unexpected, often surprising, adverse effects on other parts of the organization. We call this the "clothesline effect." Imagine a long clothesline filled with freshly washed clothes hanging up to dry. Each garment is "independent" in the sense that it is separated from the other pieces of clothing—just like the different units in an organization appear to be independent. The garments are tied together by the clothesline, just as organizational units and functions are bound together by their organizational structure, the work flow or business processes, various management information reporting systems, and human resource management systems.

If you pull on one of the socks on the clothesline, the jockey shorts down the line will jump. The items of clothing on the line are *interdependent*, just as departments, regions, product groups, and functions within an organization are interdependent. Significant changes in one subsystem cannot be made without precipitating a "clothesline effect" in other subsystems or elements. The same is true for an organization in relation to its external stakeholders and constituencies, such as suppliers, owners, customers, and regulators. If the "socks" in the external environment are pulled, the "jockey shorts" inside the organization will jump.

Part of your job as a responsible OD consultant is to ensure that your client systems' leaders and members anticipate unexpected side effects and emerging issues. You can help them to adopt and keep a "helicopter perspective" over their entire organization and its transactions with its external environment. Some of these folks will prove to be quite sophisticated systemic thinkers. Many will not. You will have to discern who is which. Then your best strategy will be to "preach to the converted." Because egos are on the line, this can be a sensitive issue.

The need for a helicopter perspective is especially important for, but often neglected by, techspert consultants. They often focus exclusively on subsystems or business processes about which they are concerned and ignore or trivialize the relevance of others, even though they are bound together by a set of complex interdependencies. As a result, they may recommend a new software system platform without adequately considering the secondary and tertiary effects that the operationalized system will have on the individuals who have to use it and on the social fabric of the organization in which it is used. Or they may recommend changing the structure without adequately considering the impact that it might have on the client system's goals, strategies, values, employee/customer relationships, morale, and so forth. Techsperts are often concerned primarily with the technical elegance of their solutions. Of course, this favors the idea of forging partnerships between techsperts and OD consultants.

By maintaining a comprehensive, system-wide helicopter perspective, both leaders and any types of consultants will be better able to anticipate which subsystems are most likely to be affected by the changes being considering. Organization development consultants, in particular, should also be better able to predict what these impacts will be and consider what might be done to minimize possible negative effects and optimize the mutually desirable results of the change.

A systemic helicopter perspective also makes it easier to identify which subsystems are critical to the change effort, that is, who, if "inconvenienced" by or uncommitted to the planned changes, is likely to obstruct the implementation. This will suggest which subsystems to include early in a complex systems change process.

Summary

We have described eight distinct philosophies to which OD consultants may adhere. Some but not all of these are shared by other types of consultants (see Table 4.1). The different philosophies need not be seen as mutually exclusive, and they may overlap. They were presented as they were merely to differentiate among various types of consultants. Table 4.1 shows which type of consultant is likely to espouse each of the philosophies.

Table 4.1. A Comparison of Consultant Philosophies

Philosophy	OD Consultants	Techsperts	Training/ Educational Specialists	Extra-Pairs-of-Hands
1. Assuming that organizational effectiveness (however defined) can be best achieved by maintaining an appropriate balance between (a) changing the behaviors and attitudes of organizational leaders and members and (b) changing the sociotechnical system of the client organization.	Yes	No (focus is on changing the socio-technical system)	No (focus is on changing the skills, attitudes, and behaviors of individuals)	No
2. Treating the organizational system or subsystem, rather than individuals or groups.	Yes	Occasionally	Seldom	No
3. Focusing on the underlying root causes of persistent issues, rather than on their symptoms.	Yes	Yes (mostly technical)	At Times	No
4. Intervening at the level of the client system's strategic vision and mission, rather than offering quick fixes.	Yes	At Times	At Times	No
5. Identifying, developing, and utilizing the client organization's internal resources and competencies.	Yes	At Times (to get "representation")	No	No

Table 4.1. A Comparison of Consultant Philosophies, Cont'd

Philosophy	OD Consultants	Techsperts	Training/ Educational Specialists	Extra-Pairs-of-Hands
6. Enabling leaders, managers, and individual members of the organization to help themselves in the future, perhaps by helping them to redesign their enterprise as a learning organization.	Yes	No	Yes	No
7. Dealing with the client organization's immediate, real-life, practical realities.	Yes	Yes	Possibly	Yes
8. Using a holistic "helicopter" perspective as the basis for intervening at a comprehensive, systemic level.	Yes	No	Rarely	No

Philosophies are belief systems that exert extremely strong influences on all consultants' choices of intervention strategies and activities. These philosophies have significant consequences for what consultants pay attention to, their priorities, and their preferred modes of operating. The eight philosophical beliefs and values may differentiate between OD and other consultants. However, in combination, these beliefs and values define a way of consulting that is not limited to any kind or type of consultant. Perhaps we are describing the consultant of the future.

Many consultants are not consciously aware that they have a philosophy or what that philosophy is. To the extent that this is true of you, you may have been unaware of your beliefs and preferences (your philosophy) and the consequences of holding them. Absent awareness, you cannot make a conscious, informed decision to modify your philosophy in order to realize greater effectiveness in your consulting practice.

Now respond to the questionnaire in Exhibit 4.1 again. This is the post-test. Pay attention to any differences when you compare your post-test results with your pre-test. How do you account for the differences?

Consultant Competence

WE DEFINE CONSULTANT COMPETENCE in terms of mastery of all pertinent information, knowledge of theory and research, strategies and methods, and behavioral skills. *Mastery* refers to good judgment in determining what should be done in any given situation and proficiency to apply pertinent competencies to that situation properly. *Pertinent* refers to all competencies necessary to fulfill one's role responsibilities as a consultant in the specific situation.

Four Competencies

Four sets of competencies are required of truly skilled, fully qualified consultants of any type:

- Interpersonal competence;
- Technical competence;
- Consulting competence; and
- Self-management competence.

Unfortunately, agents of prospective client systems are not likely to begin their selection interviews by stating, "These are my criteria for assessing the competence of prospective consultants. I need to know how well you measure up." One way to tease out agents' implicit criteria is to listen carefully to the questions that they ask of you. Look for the *unasked* questions. For example, they may ask about your most recent client organizations. The unasked question may be, "Does this person have recent experience with other companies in our industry?" The significance of such an implicit criterion varies. Agents may be operating on their untested underlying assumption that qualified consultants should be intimately familiar with their industry's current issues. Or they may be very interested to know whether you have current information about their competitors' strategies. To elicit the significance of such ambiguous questions, we sometimes say, "That's an interesting question. Why do you ask?" More frequently than you might imagine, the agents tell us—straight away! You should also listen for questions that they should but do not ask. For example, if they do not ask us about our consulting philosophy, we will find a time and a way of introducing that point (see Chapter 4).

Another rather disarming way to make it easy for agents to reveal their selection criteria is to ask them two simple questions: First, "What do you look for in consultants whom you hire?" and second, "How do you know when you are talking with a consultant who has the knowledge and skills that your organization needs?" Most often, agents find these questions refreshing and respond in a forthright manner. Guarded responses are a warning that future relationships are likely to be troublesome.

Interpersonal Competence

Most consulting assignments demand that the consultant be competent in managing relationships and interpersonal transactions with client system leaders, members, and agents, as well as with other types of consultants. Depending on the requirements of the assignment, consultants may also need to be competent in helping leaders and members to manage their relationships with one another more effectively. Typically, this is an arena in which we would expect OD consultants to excel. The most essential interpersonal competencies required of a consultant follow.

Confrontation Skills. At times it is necessary for a consultant to say things to leaders or members that may be perceived as "unpleasant," for example, telling a CEO that her management style is a primary contributor to the problems that you have been helping the organization to solve.

Although this may seem like an obvious part of the OD consultant's role, we frequently encounter situations in which consultants—even OD consultants—are unwilling to confront leaders or influential members with uncomfortable truths. Perhaps they fear that such confrontations will result in losing their consulting contracts.

Risk-Taking Ability. An element of risk is almost always inherent in situations involving organizational change. For leaders and members, the perceived risks may include the fear of the consequences of venturing too far from familiar, comfortable ground; the fear that some influential stakeholder or constituent might feel hurt or embarrassed if the consultant brings up sensitive issues; or the fear of being seen by influential people within the organization as being flawed.

For consultants, the perceived risks might include fear of the secondary impacts of making unpopular recommendations, fear of confronting powerful managers who see themselves as infallible, and so forth.

Organization development consultants must not allow themselves to be paralyzed by their own fears or by those of leaders or members with whom they are consulting. They know that such fears are natural and normal and, more importantly, that they must acknowledge and manage their fears appropriately as a significant part of their consulting role. They should also know that *courage* is doing what has to be done—even though they are aware of and fear potential adverse consequences.

During initial meetings with agents, it is important to clarify your personal attitudes toward risk taking, making certain that what you consider to be an acceptable risk is also acceptable to the leaders. Directly ask agents and, if possible, the leaders, "What would you consider to be an unacceptable risk for this engagement?" Again, it is essential for your sense of tolerable risk and that of the leaders of your client systems to be compatible.

Collaboration Skills. Effective consultation, especially OD consultation, cannot be done in isolation. Rather, it is a collaborative process involving the leaders and members of the client system and, increasingly, the organization's external stakeholders. such as regulators, owners or stockholders, customers, and suppliers. You will also find it mutually advantageous to collaborate with other types of consultants, both internal and external, who may also be working within your client system on the same or related change initiatives.

Consultants who have difficulty collaborating quickly find that they have little positive and, possibly, a great deal of negative impact on the organization.

Collaborative consultants actively identify the significant parties (individuals and subsystems) who have vested interests at stake in their consulting situations. They try to specify those interests and to enable involved parties to obtain satisfaction for their needs and preferences. Such consultants clearly demonstrate their willingness to share control and power with leaders, members, consulting colleagues, and other involved parties. However, "collaborative" does not necessarily mean compliant! Most collaborative consultants do not sacrifice their integrity out of fear or in exchange for others' tolerance or indulgence.

Because agents will certainly have differing expectations about collaboration, we strongly recommend that you determine—as quickly as possible—what level of collaboration the agents expect from the consultants they engage.

Ability to Manage Conflict. Some people equate conflict with "quarrels," "feuds," "disputes," or "arguments." We believe that conflict itself is neutral; it is neither good nor bad. We define conflict as what occurs when two or more "things" try to occupy the same space at the same time; for example, conflict occurs when the goals, methods, priorities, roles, interests, needs, methods, positions, preferences, and/or desires of one individual or group differ from those of another individual or group. In other words, conflicts may be as insignificant as two people needing to use the same computer terminal at the same time or as serious as two vice presidents sabotaging one another's strategic initiatives in order to become the next CEO.

Our experience is that organizational conflict is both natural and inevitable. Further, we believe that conflict generates essential energy. It can be *directed* toward creating innovative alternatives that can satisfy most of the involved parties' interests and, at the same time, benefit the organization, if it is managed properly. Thus, we prefer to *manage* and *utilize* conflicts actively, rather than to try to *resolve* them.

You should be skilled in managing at least two types of conflict situations. The first is one in which you are personally involved in the conflict, for example, if influential persons demand that you act in ways that you consider to be ineffective or unethical. The second type of situation is one in which you are called in as a neutral, objective, unbiased "third party" to help individual members, groups, or subsystems to surface and manage their legitimate differences. We expect all types of consultants to be capable of dealing with the former situation. However, we have seen many dysfunctional relationships between consultants and their client system leaders and members. We are dismayed when consultants with inadequate or insufficient competence attempt to tackle the latter types of conflict.

You, in collaboration with leaders and agents, have to determine which sequence or combination of the following alternative strategies you will apply when faced with actual or potential conflict situations. You must decide jointly whether you will attempt to: (1) compromise, (2) dominate and overpower the opposition, (3) avoid conflict, (4) accommodate, or (5) manage and utilize conflict. This is definitely not an issue of one "right" strategy and four "wrong" strategies for managing and utilizing conflict. Depending on the situation, each strategy can be used appropriately and effectively. Problems usually occur when one strategy is overused and the others are underused. So be sure that your client system members understand and accept your use of a balanced repertoire of strategies and methods.

Relationship Building. Consultants' effectiveness is often dependent on their ability to establish and maintain *authentic* and *trusting* relationships with the management and members of their client organizations. Although relationship building is essential in any type of consulting effort, it is especially important as you work with leaders to formulate the goals or direction and strategy for the consulting project and as you gather diagnostic data. The less the leaders and members trust you, the less likely they are to open up and reveal the range and depth of information that you need to help them deal effectively with relevant organizational issues.

By *authentic* we mean saying what you think without distortions, that is, neither misinforming nor disinforming. By *trust* we mean that agents, leaders, and members have reason to believe that you will do what you say—in other words, they know that you are *reliable*. However, trust cannot simply be given; it has to be earned. Without a track record, agents and leaders cannot determine in advance whether you are trustworthy. The most that agents can learn from their first encounter with you are some provisional answers to such questions as:

- Do you respond to questions in a direct manner, or do you avoid them by changing the subject?

- Do you express your ideas in ways that makes sense to them, or do you answer with obscure references and arcane jargon?

- Do they feel reasonably comfortable when discussing sensitive issues and renegotiating unplanned changes in the scope of the work, strategies, methods, fees, and schedules?

Your challenge is to ensure that agents arrive at positive responses to each of these questions.

Technical Competence

The problems agents have in judging whether or not their consultant candidates possess the requisite technical competencies are made even more complex because the kinds of technical skills expected from one type of consultant differ significantly from those expected from others. Organization development consultants should know enough about the other types of consultants to help agents to differentiate among consultants and firms that are competing for credibility and the agents' trust.

Organization development consultants should be experts in stakeholder, organizational, intergroup, group, interpersonal, and personal dynamics. They should be proficient in enabling client system leaders and members to diagnose *issues* (problems to solve, opportunities to exploit, and dilemmas to manage) within technical areas and to plan and facilitate the implementation of desirable organizational changes effectively.

Academically, an OD consultant should have a master's or doctoral degree in organization development or a related applied behavioral science. Many excellent OD consultants have moved into the field in mid-career. These folks usually have technical or business undergraduate or graduate degrees and many years of experience as individual contributors and/or as line managers before they take additional training, such as a certificate program in OD.

Agents are usually aware that a solid education behind any type of consultant is fine, as far as it goes, but they should also understand that people who are either academically knowledgeable or skilled individual contributors by virtue of years of experience are not necessarily effective practitioners.

Helping Agents to Assess Technical Competence of Consultants. As far as we know, there are no easy, foolproof methods for assessing a consultant's technical competence. However, the following five techniques can help you deal with agents.

1. Particularly if you are a highly placed internal person, you should strive to take an active role as the selection process is being planned. If you have earned the organization's leaders' credibility, you may ask their permission to convene all involved parties and engage them in a discussion of two questions.

   - "Given what you want to accomplish, what specific skill sets should fully qualified consultants have to help you with your specific issues?" (Your job is to make sure they consider all relevant kinds and types of consultants.)

- "Do any of your permanent employees have these necessary competencies?" (The organization may or may not have the required number of qualified people with the necessary competencies.)

The answer given by the involved parties may be the explicit standards against which agents will assess you and other consultant candidates.

2. In addition to assessing internal capabilities, agents should ask prospective consultants the following questions:

   - "What do you think we should do about our current situation?" After the candidate explains, follow up by asking, "What competencies would a fully qualified consultant need to provide this kind of help?"

   - "To what degree do you, personally, possess each of these competencies?"

   - "How can we know with certainty that you do, in fact, have the competencies that you claim to possess?"

3. Agents may request consultant candidates, including you, to provide references from specific individuals who can verify claims of competence. (Be careful here! All involved parties should understand that, because of the threat of litigation, previous client systems' agents may have learned to say only that candidates were hired for such-and-such a purpose and from these-to-those dates.)

4. Very sophisticated agents may ask you and other candidate consultants to suggest—spontaneously, without an opportunity to seek advice or do secondary research—a design for a pilot activity from which they could assess some of your competencies and effectiveness. Your design would include scope, goals, strategy, and action plans. You should also be prepared to show how your proposal augments and is aligned with the mission or business plans of the target subsystem and the larger organization. Agents would listen carefully to your recommended test project and assess whether or not it seems to them to be realistic or doable.

   If you are convincing and if the agents have the authority, they might offer you a limited contract to try your recommended pilot activity or project. If they don't like the limited project's results, they can simply choose not to extend the consulting agreement and look for other consultants.

5. Agents may pose two or three hypothetical problem situations and then ask you questions similar to those in number 2 above.

Keep in mind that none of these techniques guarantees that agents will obtain positive proof that you or competing consultants do or do not have the competencies they believe are required. But using these techniques should increase their odds. Finding the right consultant is very important. Agents are concerned with avoiding errors and are likely to be averse to risk. They may not be familiar with OD consultation and are, therefore, likely to be biased in favor of more familiar techspert or training/educational consultation.

As an OD consultant, you must have sufficient skill to establish rapport and evoke feelings of comfort and confidence in your prospective client systems' agents before talking about terms and conditions in an authentic, ethical manner.

Consulting Competence

Neither interpersonal nor technical competence is enough to ensure that consultants will actually provide the requested services at the requisite levels of quality and effectiveness. It is one thing to be proficient in the necessary interpersonal and technical competencies. It is quite another to use those competencies properly and effectively when consulting with, facilitating, and/or developing others.

The four basic consulting competencies that are most often required, except perhaps for an extra-pair-of-hands, include the following:

Analysis and Diagnosis. This skill set includes proficiency in converting data into useful information. It starts with selecting sources of and methods for gathering data from those who are closest to and most familiar with the issues to be dealt with. Then, that data must be sorted and analyzed. It also includes the persistence, curiosity, interest, and wisdom to distinguish between symptoms and root causes.

Strategic and Implementation Planning. This skill set includes proficiency in helping leaders to formulate an achievable, compelling "desired state" and to select viable strategies for reaching that state. It also requires proficiency in developing implementation (or action) plans for achieving the desired state by applying the change strategies, creating action steps, assigning responsible parties, establishing start and due dates (scheduling), specifying essential resources, developing budgets, and creating mechanisms for monitoring progress and dealing with identifying unexpected side effects.

Change Management. Consultants (other than extra-pairs-of-hands) are engaged to change some aspects of their client systems and to help their leaders and members to support and adapt to that change. Therefore, effective consultants must be experts at effectively executing implementation plans, understanding change dynamics and their impact on people, facilitating change, and effectively managing resistance to change.

Evaluation. Consultants (other than extra-pairs-of-hands) should be capable of developing and using practical mechanisms and valid methods to assess progress, unexpected emerging issues, and the degree to which the intended results of the change effort have been realized. Comprehensive evaluations require using multiple methods of collecting data from multiple sources. Thus, evaluators would conduct interviews, administer questionnaires, and collect objective data about such measures of effectiveness as quality and time to delivery of goods and services from people or subsystems that have different perspectives but common interests, such as customers. Because of the potential for bias, we believe that evaluations should not be done by consultants working on the change effort or by members of client organizations. Rather, independent external consultants with expertise in evaluating progress and results are preferable.

Self-Management Competence

Although it is important to consider consultants' interpersonal, technical, and consulting competencies, it is equally important to consider consultants as persons. We strongly believe that the four essential self-management competencies are (1) ability to manage personal core values, (2) self-confidence, (3) self-awareness, and (4) personal style preferences.

Core Values

It is critical for all consultants to examine their personal core values before committing to a consulting engagement. Consider what might happen if you have strong egalitarian values and are engaged by leaders whose hidden agenda is to centralize power at the top of their organization using a rigid, command-and-control technocracy or bureaucratic hierarchy.

Skilled OD consultants realize that their "effective use of self" is a critical success factor in their consulting. This means an investment of sufficient time, energy, and commitment to explore and get in touch with your own core values, beliefs, and assumptions—both as an individual and as an OD consultant. You may also have to confront yourself around the thorny questions of your willingness to say what you think and do what you say.

To "walk the talk," consider whether or not your core values are congruent with those that are embedded in your client system's culture. Consider an early exit strategy from consulting engagements during which you discover insurmountable, irreconcilable differences between your core values and those of a client system's senior management.

Self-Confidence

Consultants who lack self-confidence have a hard time "selling" their ideas. On the other hand, overly confident consultants often come across as patronizing. This facade usually provokes resentment and increases resistance to their recommendations.

We have seen many inexperienced consultant candidates who compensate for short resumes by affecting self-confidence. Such self-presentations, like balloons, are easily punctured. Alternatively, we know many highly competent consultants who are quite conservative and even humble in presenting their qualifications. They should probably learn to brag a little.

You cannot rely on agents to help you to manage your prospecting approach and style. That is your job! So we advise no false modesty, no extravagant claims, and especially no unsolicited war stories. Use succinct, declarative statements such as, "Yes, we can do that." Let the agents take responsibility for exploring and eliciting details from you. They might ask, "What makes you think that you have the qualifications and capacity to fulfill our expectations?" They are entitled to a straight, concise, honest answer, even if your answer is, "I don't know right now. I'll have to think about it, make a few phone calls, and get back to you. Will next Tuesday morning work for you?"

Self-Awareness

Agents have the right to expect prospective consultants to be aware of and able to manage their strengths, weaknesses, and limitations. In addition to understanding your own core values, there are four specific areas for which we consider a high degree of self-awareness to be especially important for OD consultants.

Control and Influence Needs. People have varying needs to influence, if not control, the events and the people in their lives. Consultants with high control needs quickly fall into the trap of trying to "take over." Think of control needs as covering a continuum from "high" to "low." High control needs may be essential for some kinds of consultants. For example, at one extreme, techspert consultants in the nuclear power industry insist on verbatim compliance to established procedures by such client system members as control room operators. This high degree of control is justified by the Nuclear Regulatory Commission's safety concerns. NASA projects are also appropriate examples. Conversely, consultants with low needs to influence or control others make it easy for people to ignore or trivialize their legitimate concerns. Such consultants are often rather ineffective.

Effective OD consultants probably fall somewhere in the middle of this continuum, one hopes with the capacity to move comfortably in either direction, as required. For example, you would be more controlling when *guiding* leaders and members through unfamiliar processes, especially during a crisis, and less controlling when following them as they gain proficiency in applying new processes to their work after the crisis has been brought under control.

Need for Personal Contact. The need for contact with others can also be thought of as a continuum. At one extreme, consultants with very high needs for close personal contact are not likely to take risks that could endanger their relationships with leaders and members. They may deliberately refrain from raising critical but politically or socially sensitive issues. At the other extreme, consultants with very low needs for close personal contact may have difficulty developing rapport and the types of open, communicative relationships necessary to function effectively. They may appear cool, distant, aloof, disdainful, or inaccessible. As a result, people who could benefit from their contributions may not be willing to initiate contact for fear of being rejected.

Effective OD consultants probably fall somewhere in the middle. However, our experiences suggest that it is more functional to have lower level needs to maintain their marginality and emotional distance within client organizations.

Need to Belong. Again, think of this dimension as a continuum. This is a difficult personal need for many OD consultants to master. Your effectiveness stems, to a large extent, from knowing you must work with, but avoid becoming a part of, your client systems. Being "part of" an organization implies a co-dependent relationship (Margulies, 1984). For example, it is not unusual for consultants to feel secure, powerful, respected, appreciated, and even loved as a direct result of their work with their client systems. This is natural and acceptable—up to the point at which you may become unwilling to take the risks that are inherent to the practice of OD. For example, if you are excessively concerned about the possibility of losing your affiliations with a client system, you may choose to avoid confronting some vital but politically or socially "sensitive" issues.

Need for Prominence. Some consultants have very strong needs to be highly visible and prominent. They may exhibit this by dominating, pre-empting, or cutting off both their colleagues and leaders and members, or they may always have a "better way" of saying or doing anything. Leaders and members may expect and accept this behavior, but we often find such consultants to be self-satisfied, arrogant, unhelpful, intrusive—even boring. Yet, strong needs for prominence may be useful for techsperts and, at times, for OD consultants. For example, to learn new ways to achieve desired results, leaders and members might choose to subordinate themselves to the consultant's more sophisticated judgments. (We hope this would be an explicit, informed choice.)

The critical issue is the extent to which consultants gain prominence at the *expense* of leaders and members. For example, during early phases of an engagement, you may take a high-profile role and dominate members as you guide them through complex, unfamiliar problem-solving or decision-making processes. However, as they gain familiarity, competence, confidence, and comfort, you should shift into a less prominent role and encourage leaders to take more visible roles. If you refuse to make this shift when required, your needs for prominence will have become excessive and intrusive, preventing the growth and development of leaders and members. Of course, at the other extreme, maintaining too low a level of prominence or prematurely making a shift from higher to lower levels of prominence can be misconstrued.

▶ CASE IN POINT

One of the authors had a potentially career-damaging experience awhile ago when he partnered with a brand new internal director of OD. She needed to establish visibility and credibility for herself. However, the Engineering Department was experiencing a major techno-structural crisis. The author was working on a different project in another part of the organization. Being well-known and trusted by senior management, he was asked to help the new OD director with her first major internal consulting assignment.

The OD director was reasonably competent and experienced, but was unfamiliar with the system and more oriented to individual than to sociotechnical systems change. Her predispositions did not quite fit the demand characteristics of the situation. However, she was willing to accept guidance from the author, and they were very effective in implementing a joint organizational diagnosis of the Engineering Department and its inter-dependent stakeholder subsystems.

During the ensuing data feedback and problem-solving meetings, the OD director and the author agreed that she should take the prominent position. The author assumed an escort role, helping her to prepare for the critical meetings, observing and intervening only occasionally during the meetings, and providing her with feedback and planning next steps with her after each meeting.

The entire engagement was extremely effective, so the author was extremely surprised—and disturbed—when, on returning to his primary engagement, he was confronted by a senior vice president who had received feedback on the author's perceived contributions from the leaders of the Engineering Department. He was upset and angry: "I sent you over there to help out, but I hear that all you did was sit in on the meetings and didn't contribute very much at all."

The vice president was accustomed to seeing competent people competing with one another, not seeking or accepting low-profile positions. The only folks he was used to seeing who avoided the spotlight were incompetent. It took a considerable amount of explanation from the author and the very grateful OD director before the senior vice president understood and accepted our strategy. Actually, he was amazed, as he had never been exposed to this kind of partnership before. ◄

Personal Style Preference

Personal style preferences are the elements of a "set" or "pattern" of behaviors that people prefer to display when interacting with others. For example, some people seem to be very friendly, approachable, and informal. Others are seen as structured, formal, and aloof. There is no single "best" interpersonal style for OD or any other type of consultant.

However, certain styles are more—and some are less—viable in specific situations and with particular individuals. Therein lie the causes of, and solutions for, many interpersonal and intergroup conflicts.

Approaches to Self-Awareness. There are many ways to explore, understand, manage, and improve the impact of your personal style preferences. We have found it useful to gain insight into our own preferences and their implications by using such instruments as the "Big Five" personality factors (Costa & McRrae, 1992), Myers-Briggs Type Inventory (Kroeger & Thuesen, 1992), Interpersonal Dynamics Inventory (Zackrison, 1997), and Element-B (Schutz, 1994).

We have also found the NTL Institute's Management Work Conferences useful for beginning OD consultants in starting their journey toward self-awareness. NTL's Holding-On and Letting-Go and Self-Differentiation Workshops are also excellent, but more appropriate for advanced OD consultants.

Fit Between Consultant's Preferred Style and Client System's Cultural Norms. Your distinctive preferred personal style may or may not match the cultural norms of your prospective client systems. You may choose to act natural and just be yourself in all settings, regardless of the situation. If so, we suspect that you will probably fit in pretty well with 25 percent of your prospective client systems and their agents. You will probably get along reasonably well with another 25 percent. But you are likely to experience chronic tension and strained relations with 25 percent and run into major personality clashes with the last 25 percent.

On the other hand, you might try to increase the odds of a fit, first by assessing the predominant personal styles of the agents and leaders and, second (assuming your assessment is accurate), by trying to adapt to and meet their interpersonal needs for relatively brief periods. However, sustained, extended contact with people with quite different and discomforting styles will cause you to feel increasingly tense and cramped. Although you may be "successful," you will pay a price, some of which will be your level of effectiveness as an OD consultant.

Your Unsatisfied Personal Needs. You are entitled to have personal needs. All of us have these needs to a greater or lesser extent, and we have no doubt that it is legitimate for you to expect to derive gratification from your work. However, we believe that you have no business using your client systems as the primary sources of satisfaction for your personal needs. Such behavior is intrusive and unethical. It can easily result in situations that reduce or destroy the positive effects of your consulting efforts. You must satisfy your personal needs in your personal life—not through your client systems. This may be more difficult than it sounds. We have seen many consultants succumb to the temptation and exploit their privileged roles in client organizations because their private lives were impoverished. The classic example is, of course, inappropriate fraternization.

We also believe that OD consultants are responsible for being continuously aware of their own mental, emotional, and physical states, including their capacity to manage these states (and take appropriate action) when they get out of balance. If your life is so skewed in the direction of your consulting work that you have little or no personal life, you must re-establish balance. In extreme cases, this may involve taking a leave of absence from work to give yourself an opportunity to reassess your priorities.

In addition to the necessary competencies, consultants also need to be able to take advantage of cutting-edge communication tools.

The Web. The World Wide Web can be a valuable source of background information about prospective client systems. You can scan many companies' web pages quickly, particularly if you use a metasearch engine. (See a compendium of usable metasearch engines at <http://www.searchiq.com/directory/multi.htm>.)

You can also use the Web to do real-time or asynchronous assessment, feedback, and multivoting with clients. Group decision support freeware is available through such sites as <http://www.barrettsaunders.com/> and <http://artus.wiwi.uni bielefeld.de/index.html>. Groupware enables scattered decision makers to do real-time brainstorming, needs assessment, feedback, and participative action planning. Scenario building or simulation building enables users to create scenarios of desired futures and then act them out online or on the Web. See, for instance, <http://www.powersim.no/demo/tooldemo.htm>.

You can also use the Web to do the following:

- Establish a website to provide information about your consulting firm;
- Post your latest article or white paper; and/or
- Exchange information with client system agents, leaders, and members in real time.

E-Mail. Most businesspeople use e-mail to exchange information and documents. E-mail permits a rapid exchange of information. You can use it to discuss ideas, poll populations of respondents to reach quick decisions, send out surveys to be compiled rapidly, and build consensus around decisions or actions. For example, the Delphi Technique can be easily and quickly applied through e-mail or the Web (Delbecq, Van de Ven, & Gustafson, 1975).

Through communication network analysis, e-mail exchanges can be analyzed to determine what kind of information is exchanged, from whom and to whom, how frequently, and which persons or subsystems are excluded. You may also use e-mail to do the following:

- Keep in touch with professional colleagues about breaking developments;
- Network with other consultants to help you with your consulting projects;
- Send capability statements, proposals, invoices, reports, and other information to client system agents and leaders;
- Make virtual presentations through PowerPoint presentations sent as e-mail attachments;
- Assess progress and evaluate the results of your OD interventions; and/or
- Collect testimonial data for subsequent use to secure other clients.

However, words alone—without inflection and without facial expressions and gestures—account for less than 30 percent of the *meaning* of a message. That explains the mounting complaints about disrespect and pomposity of e-mail correspondents. Therefore, we encourage people to abide by Freedman's Rule: "E-mail is to be used only to *confirm* and *elaborate on* face-to-face interactions."

Telephony. Cell phones can be carried everywhere. Speaker phones and audio-conferencing technology enable you to discuss common issues with groups of individuals, regardless of their location. They also permit representatives of many subsystems to work together, assisted by facilitators who can keep meetings on target and members involved. You can also use telephony to do the following:

- Develop action plans with all involved parties, regardless of their location, and agree who will do what by when;
- Conduct coaching sessions with distant clients "on demand";
- Market your services ("telemarketing"); and/or
- Conduct timely follow-up sessions.

Videoconferencing. Color videocameras can be mounted on personal computers so you can conduct face-to-face videoconferencing from your computer in real time from any location. You can use videoconferencing to do the following:

- Substitute for expensive travel for routine meetings; and/or
- Provide emergency meeting capabilities.

Don't Confuse Experience with Competence

Experience is an extremely important variable that agents use to select consultants, but consultants' capacity to *learn* from their experiences may be far more important than the experience itself. Very often, highly experienced consultants become complacent and rely on formulas and methods they developed in the past for different people and different organizations that were operating under different conditions. Bright, interested, curious, intuitive consultants with five years of experience may be more effective than highly experienced but complacent consultants with one year of experience that was repeated twenty times. Further, most people learn most from their "failures." They tend to take their "successes" for granted and do not bother to assess what they did "right." So they just keep on doing what they have always done. They do not spend much time learning to do *better* or to do *more*.

Three Types of Consulting Experience

Agents are likely to consider any one of three distinct types of experience in developing their consultant selection criteria. They will ask; you must be prepared to respond.

Experience Dealing with Similar Issues. Agents may try to determine the specific relevance of your past experiences to their organization's current issues. For example, they may believe that you should have considerable experience in managing transactional conflicts between different organizational subsystems. Or they may believe it is essential for you to have extensive experience in managing specific inter-group conflicts between, say, marketing and production departments or between labor and management.

A deep but narrow range of past experiences can bias consultants so that they see only what those experiences have prepared them to see, rather than being able to observe from a "naive" perspective and perceive unique patterns that reflect obscure root causes.

Experience at a Specific Organizational Level. If you have not worked with the executive management of a large organization, you may lack an appreciation of executives' perspectives (for example, organizational politics, global economics, governmental regulations, competitive strategies, media scrutiny, technological innovations, and stockholders' expectations). You may also lack the (realistic) self-confidence needed to assert yourself and gain their confidence so they will allow you to help them to plan, organize, and lead enterprise-wide sociotechnical/structural changes. If your experience is based on working with lower-level workers, supervisors, and middle managers, you may be able to offer senior executives useful, possibly refreshing perspectives on how mid- and lower-level employees may perceive and react to possible complex system changes. Unfortunately, you may not achieve sufficient credibility with many executive leaders without having worked with people at their level. So beginning OD consultants face the paradox of "no work without experience; no experience without work."

One way to manage this dilemma is for well-trained but inexperienced consultants to initiate invitations to link up with more experienced consultants to co-facilitate selective pieces of work. Many people who, because of age and experience, are seen as "senior consultants" may be gratified to have younger colleagues show an interest in learning by working with them.

Experience with Similar Organizations or Industries. This can be a huge stumbling block. Agents often believe that their consultants must be intimately familiar with organizations that are similar to their own. However, we have seen many consultants with lots of "industry experience" miss critical pieces of unique information because they assumed that the underlying root causes of observed conditions in their current client system were the same as those that they had seen when consulting with similar client systems.

Agents may devalue consultants with little relevant industry experience because agents are afraid they may take too much valuable time asking "dumb" questions and learning the business. In fact, dumb questions may be extremely helpful in enabling leaders and members to investigate and to gain clarity and specificity. It is often amazing how, in responding to a naive consultant's dumb question, organizational leaders with lots of experience discover holes in their assumptions about how their organizations really work and their beliefs about how they should facilitate complex change within those organizations. They also discover that their colleagues have been operating on totally different beliefs and assumptions for years and that this kind of disconnect explains a lot about their common history of confusion and tension.

When preparing to discuss your experience with an agent, you can use the form provided in Exhibit 5.1 to record your consulting experience.

OD consultants have a unique advantage relative to other types of consultants. Your greatest strength is the core technology of OD: The *Action Research Method.* The greater your skill in applying the Action Research Method, the more confident and competent you will be in applying this comprehensive systems approach to conducting organizational diagnoses. You will also feel confident in your ability to

Exhibit 5.1. Consulting Experience Checklist

Client System:					Agent (Title):

Types of Experience	Amount of Experience				Examples
	A Lot	Some	Little	None	
Similar Issues • Strategic Planning • Restructuring • Labor Relations • Mergers & Acquisitions • TQM • BPR • ERP • CRM • • •					
Similar Level • Individual Contributors • Supervisors • Middle Managers • Senior Managers • Executives • Board of Directors • • •					
Similar Organizations • Size • Structure • • •					
Same Industry					
Same Sector • Public • Private • Government • Military • Nonprofit					

help your client systems' leaders and members to illuminate and specify not only the technical issues, but also the social context and culture that have probably exacerbated the technical issues. To a great extent, your confidence will be based on your conviction that high-involvement, highly participative processes will evoke and sustain considerable emotional investment in and commitment to support self-generated strategies and implementation plans.

Summary

We have discussed each of four basic sets of consulting competencies: interpersonal, technical, consulting, and self-management. Not all assignments require consultants who are competent in all four. It is up to agents and leaders to determine the kinds and levels of competence required of different types of consultants in specific situations. You can enhance your credibility by helping agents and leaders use these categories to make their consultant selection and deployment decisions.

Although technical competence is important, we are equally concerned about consultants' self-management competence. Thus, we emphasize the importance of gaining sufficient self-awareness to satisfy your personal needs in your personal life so that those needs do not inappropriately intrude into your consulting practice.

Many agents and leaders seem to place more faith in the self-regulating power of the consulting marketplace than we do. Unhappily, we know of many consultants who survive despite their ineffectiveness. No person or agency has the authority to monitor and control the flow of people into the various consulting practice areas. There are no barriers for any person or firm to enter any consulting area. We believe that, at present, the only regulators whose opinions determine what quality and types of consultants are hired are the agents and leaders of the consultants' client systems. To enable agents and leaders to make informed selection decisions, some form of consumer education is essential (Zackrison & Freedman, 2000). You can help by using or adapting our ideas in serving as a consumer advocate who educates the agents of your prospective client systems.

Finally, we believe that consultants of all kinds and types should get wired up. Cutting-edge communication technologies will increasingly become essential consulting tools. Among the most interesting and useful technological innovations may be virtual teamwork using websites, groupware, electronic mail, cell phones, conference calls, and videoconferencing (Rothwell, 2000).

The Selection Interview

ON THIS CHAPTER we focus on how OD consultants might approach and handle themselves during selection interviews. We examine: (1) how you can help agents and leaders to avoid mistaking you for other types of consultants; (2) how to do a self-assessment; (3) how to prepare for selection interviews; (4) what to tell, ask, and look for during the interview; and (5) what to do and expect after the interview. But first, let's consider the context for these interviews.

If you were invited, the agents and leaders undoubtedly have something in mind already. You have to help them to talk; you have to understand them as they want to be understood.

If you asked for the meeting, you are probably on a fishing expedition. However, agents probably would not agree to meet with you unless they had *some* interest in you and your services. Presumably, they know whether the fish are ready to bite. Your job is to help them to reveal the location and species of fish.

Avoiding Mistaken Identity

Let's say it is one hour before your initial meeting. You are asking yourself, "How shall I present myself?" "How should I describe who I am and what I do?" You want to differentiate yourself from other types and kinds of consultants, but you must not disparage other consultants. Your purpose is to ensure a mutually beneficial match between your interests, values, and competencies and the prospective client system's needs and preferences. Therefore, it is in your enlightened self-interest to help the agents to make informed decisions regarding what, if any, types of consultation the organization needs.

During selection interviews, be prepared to help agents understand enough about OD theory, strategy, and methods to make some distinctions. Then you must show that your OD services can add value, not by offering solutions but by helping them to utilize their existing internal resources to develop and gain widespread commitment to their own effective solutions. You must help agents identify appropriate opportunities for your services. You must also demonstrate that you are fully qualified to deliver those services.

You can help agents to specify their organizations' needs and to match various types of consultants' capabilities with these needs. In doing this, you can demonstrate the value of your OD methods. You will enhance your credibility by enabling agents to understand that competent and ethical OD consultants neither claim nor encourage agents to expect that they can fulfill *all* of their needs. Rather, you can help them to choose the most appropriate consultants for their situation. This will be an unusual experience for most agents, who are not used to having consultant candidates *disclaim* allusions to being omnipotent.

Even if you help agents to rule out your OD services for the issues at hand, you will enhance the probability that they will call on you in the future when your OD competencies *are* relevant for other issues.

Doing Continuous Self-Assessment

A periodic self-awareness checkup is a means of ensuring that you are ready, willing, and able to perform effectively as an OD consultant at all times. At a minimum, you should be well aware of your current: (1) consulting philosophy, (2) interpersonal competencies, (3) technical competencies, (4) consulting competencies, and (5) self-management competencies.

We recommend that you use the eleven questions in Exhibit 6.1 to monitor your own professional development or periodic renewal. When answering each question, take some time to reflect on the consulting work that you have done over the past six to twelve months. Do you see any patterns or themes? Are there things that you do all the time, invariably, no matter what the assignment? Are there things that you consistently avoid doing?

Exhibit 6.1. Self-Assessment Questionnaire

1. Of all the information that is available within your client systems, what do you actually look and listen for?

2. Of all that you might perceive, what is likely to register as having significance for making a diagnosis?

3. To what extent are you a proponent of "one size fits all" solutions?

4. To what degree are you concerned with "playing it safe"?

5. Do you recognize and manage the differences between consulting under crisis conditions and consulting under steady state conditions?

Exhibit 6.1. Self-Assessment Questionnaire, Cont'd

6. To what extent do you stress relationships and process-oriented interventions, as opposed to task-related activities?

7. To what degree do you recommend or rely on training/educational activities in support of, rather than as a substitute for, OD consulting work?

8. Do you work collaboratively and effectively with other consultants within the same or in different disciplines? Do you manage other consultants effectively? Are you willing to be managed by peers?

9. To what extent are you open to critical feedback from teammates and from leaders and members of your client systems?

10. Are you able and willing to acknowledge your own personal confusion and uncertainty, whether or not you feel comfortable about doing so?

11. Do you have sufficient courage to point out that "the emperor has no clothes"?

The following discussion of the questions from Exhibit 6.1 considers the implications of each in some detail.

Of All the Information Available Within Your Client Systems, What Do You Actually Look and Listen For?

Competent consultants of all types generally use some form of diagnostic model as a "radar screen" to make sense out of complex, continually shifting organizational situations. Most diagnostic models tend to emphasize some variables while ignoring others.

In our experience, the most useful diagnostic or mental models include at least the following five basic elements:

Culture and Climate. *Culture* refers to the organization's prevailing norms and values, including long-standing traditions, myths, legends, rituals, norms, practices, taboos, and the like. *Climate* refers to the current, usually temporary, emotional atmosphere. For example, if members feel they are in the midst of a crisis, they may feel fearful, lethargic, or excited and energized.

Inputs. Resources, such as raw materials, components, people, market information, funds, governmental regulations, technology, and so forth, that are brought into the organization by various suppliers or agencies.

Throughputs. What members do to or with resources as they progress through the system's work flow processes, that is, the ways in which the resources are applied, altered, combined, manipulated, and used up or destroyed to add value to the organization's processes for producing its goods and services.

Outputs. What the system delivers to its environment or customers in terms of finished goods, services, waste products, returns on investment, reports to regulators, and the like.

Feedback Mechanisms. How organizations gain information from both their internal subsystems and external environments to inform leaders whether what they are doing is achieving the desired results and whether their interdependent subsystems are properly and effectively integrated and aligned with the organization's mission, business plans, and values.

The five elements and their interrelationships form an "open systems model," as shown in Figure 6.1.

Figure 6.1. Open Systems Model

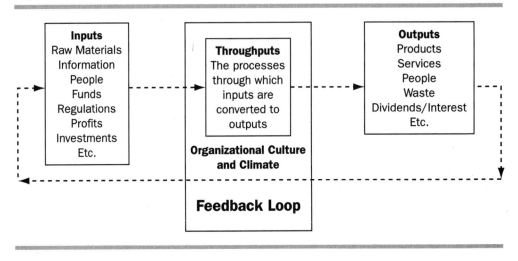

Using an explicit diagnostic model, you should be able to conceptualize what is happening within a client organization. You should also be prepared to present and explain your diagnostic models in a manner that is easily recognized, understood, and accepted by agents, leaders, and members. Because many techspert and other types of consultants tend not to use explicit organizational models, this may distinguish you from them.

Of All That You Might Perceive, What Is Likely to Register as Having Significance for Making a Diagnosis?

All too often, consultants see what they are predisposed to see. Everything else is likely to be excluded from their conscious awareness. Is it surprising that what they are predisposed to see "just happens" to be directly related to the services that they are prepared to offer?

▶ CASE IN POINT

Imagine this scene: A group of respected techspert consultants, each representing different disciplines, was given the same description of an organizational problem situation and asked what they would do to improve it. A techspert in public relations and communications saw it as a "communications problem" and recommended a series of communication skills workshops for the management team members of all major organizational subsystems. A techspert in performance management saw the problem as the result of "vague, nonspecific goals" and recommended a goal-setting workshop for executive management. A techspert in employee relations was certain that middle managers were responding to their "lack of empowerment" and recommended a change in the structure that decentralized and pushed decision making down in the hierarchy. Who was correct? Whose assessment was comprehensive? ◄

Reflect back on the consulting work that you have done over the last couple of years. If your organizational diagnoses and interventions were basically similar, you should challenge yourself by asking what indicators you used in deciding which type of intervention to use in each case. You might also ask yourself what clues would have convinced you that some type of intervention *other than those in which are an expert* would have been more appropriate in each case.

Ethical OD consultants do not overstate the relevance or applicability of their services. Your credibility is on the line. You can build credibility by clearly distinguishing between those consultative services that you can deliver effectively from those for which you have insufficient skills.

To What Extent Are You a Proponent of "One Size Fits All" Solutions?

Many consultants seem to believe that any client system will benefit from their pre-packaged solutions. They ignore or trivialize their client systems' unique purposes, qualities, conditions, or situations. If they acknowledged the significant of such variables, they would have to customize their services, leading to higher costs and more effort. Or they would have to acknowledge that they did not have the competence to deliver the services that are required. The "one size fits all" philosophy is common among naive and mass market oriented consultants. For example, we know some consultants who typically suggest that most organizational problems can be solved by simply investing in their version of total quality management (TQM) or business process re-engineering (BPR) programs. Although these may be beneficial in many circumstances, we categorically reject the idea that introducing TQM or BPR is *always* best. In fact, we believe that an over-reliance on *any* single change strategy is usually insufficient to enable organizations to achieve optimal levels of effectiveness.

Reflect back over your own recent consulting work. To what degree have you consistently recommended the same or similar interventions? To what degree have you been open to the possibility that another type of intervention—or some other type of consultant—might have been more appropriate?

To What Degree Are You Concerned with "Playing It Safe"?

Competent consultants have little need to restrict themselves to safe, narrow areas of specialization, methodologies, or issues with which they are already familiar, proficient, and comfortable. Effective consultants are aware of their limitations and invite their client systems' members to explore uncharted organizational territories jointly, that is, they actively seek creative ways to collaborate with the organization's own people to take some risks, get "out of the box," map out, and deal with unfamiliar, complex, multidimensional situations. This is the action research approach. It is not unusual for such consultants to respond to agents' requests by saying, "I don't know how you should deal with this issue, but I think I can work with you and your people to find out. Are you willing to join me in an effort?"

In your selection interviews, you may find agents who are conservative, traditional, and risk-averse. They want proven solutions; they don't like the idea of being guinea pigs. Your challenge is to nudge them out of their comfort zones and help them to experience some success as they take small risks. (Just to nudge may be another risk.)

In your review of your consulting assignments, how many and what types of risks have you taken? To what extent do you believe that these were warranted? How many opportunities to take a risk did you avoid? Why? More important, to what extent did you encourage agents, leaders, and members to take risks, rather than supporting their risk-avoiding habitual patterns?

Do You Recognize and Manage the Differences Between Consulting Under Crisis and Consulting Under Steady State Conditions?

There are significant differences between consulting under *crisis* conditions versus *steady state* conditions (Freedman, 1995). They are two ends of a continuum. You must be able to function effectively across the entire spectrum of conditions. Crisis conditions often call for "front-line combat consulting." The situation requires you to be:

- Fast-paced, attentive to both strategic and tactical issues, and clearly results oriented;
- Proactive;
- Continually scanning both internal and external environments for emerging issues and impediments to effective implementation of plans for organizational change;
- Actively seeking appropriate, high-leverage intervention opportunities; and
- Ready to intervene on *evident* needs that may not be recognized by leaders, members or stakeholders.

You must understand how individuals and groups are likely to feel and act under crisis conditions. You must realize that emotional responses interfere with "normal" group and intergroup relations and transactions. You must feel realistically confident that you can help leaders and members to understand, accept, and work through their "normal" reactions to "crazy" conditions. You have to help people regain a sense of control over the situation and feel proud of themselves for doing that.

Steady state conditions require operational consulting, that is, an operational, process-oriented, more responsive consulting style. You should still focus on issues and results, but allow members more time to explore, experiment with, and discover what they and their organization need and, most important, focus on helping them to learn from their collective experiences.

Systems-oriented OD consultants also understand that too many changes at one time under steady state conditions will cause work overload, stress, confusion, and uncertainty. Remember that no matter how beneficial each of them might be, too many changes all at once will be strongly resisted. Therefore, encourage leaders to keep the number of significant changes to no more than two or three at a time, even during steady state conditions.

How Often Do You Stress Relationships and Process-Oriented Interventions, as Opposed to Task-Related Activities?

Consultants of every type choose between emphasizing the importance of either a technostructural orientation that highlights technological, structural, procedural, task, and content issues *or* a sociotechnical orientation that focuses attention on stakeholder involvement, participative problem solving, rapport, work relationships, and emotional issues. *Technostructural* interventions focus on tasks; *sociotechnical* interventions focus on both relationships and tasks. Unfortunately, many consultants act as if they are unaware of how vital it is to *balance* task-related issues with work relationships.

One-sided technostructural approaches usually ignore the significance of participative approaches. Consultants who use them may consciously avoid difficult relationship situations. Perhaps they do not know how to deal with the possible emergence of intense feelings. They may truly believe that by changing the system, organizational members will adapt and change their attitudes, beliefs, and values.

Usually, we find it beneficial to focus on task-related issues *first*. As members struggle with the task, problematic relationship issues may emerge. If you can show how such issues interfere with effective task performance, leaders and members will usually make sufficient time available to deal with them.

To What Extent Do You Recommend or Rely on Training/Educational Interventions?

When people do not perform as their leaders expect, it is convenient to assume that these people simply do not know what to do—or they know *what* to do but not *how* or *when* to do it. This assumption is often false. Agents may ask you to provide training or educational solutions, but you often must challenge their assumptions.

Sometimes, people do need training because they don't know what to do or how to do it. More often they do know how, but feel constrained from applying what they know because of rules, procedures, or cultural norms. When we focus on tasks and discover that people do not know what or how, we have proof that they need training or education. Otherwise, they need to examine and change elements of their sociotechnical systems.

To differentiate yourself from other consultants, you must be prepared to explain the benefits and limitations of each type of consulting (see Chapter 2) and present a realistic perspective that enables agents to understand that this is not an either/or choice. Remember that beneficial synergies can be created by *working together* with other consultants.

Do You Work Collaboratively and Effectively with Other Consultants?

Agents may or may not express explicit interest in the notion that different types of consultants could or should be working together. Be prepared to respond if agents raise the issue or if the scope of the engagement suggests that the consultation will require more than a single person or single discipline.

Organization development consultants tend to work alone more often than techsperts and other types of consultants. When the demands of a consulting engagement require the services of a team of consultants, a potential problem is created. To work as a member of a consulting team means that you will have to subordinate or sacrifice some of your preferred strategies in the service of the team effort. This is essential for all team members if they are to stay "attuned" and "aligned." Naturally, a certain amount of conflict and debate is to be expected and must be managed.

Managing teams of consultants requires a different set of skills. Sooner or later, consulting teams must accept the formal or informal leadership of one or two members. The designation "leader" may be arbitrary, as any qualified team member may serve in this role. In many cases, project leadership roles go to the more senior, more experienced, or most respected team members.

We have had many experiences as members of multidisciplinary consulting teams in which the designated leaders were the most experienced and most expert of the techspert consultants. Some of these folks were effective as team leaders, but most were not. Their greatest difficulty was their inability to utilize the diverse contributions that different team members offered. They lacked the interpersonal and teamwork skills needed to identify and utilize the resources of all team members. Assuming that you are proficient in these skills, it is logical that you might assume team leader roles. However, because you probably lack competence in the technical aspects of the engagements, you may lack sufficient credibility in the eyes of either your techspert colleagues or your client system's leaders.

In our experience, you can generate credibility in two ways: (1) by providing informal process facilitation for the team as a "good" team member and (2) by providing a sociotechnical systems perspective, in which case you will enlarge the scope and improve the quality of your team's effectiveness.

Are You Open to Critical Feedback?

Openness to negative feedback is a critical element. During an engagement, you may make "mistakes" or your strategies or methods may evoke troubling emotional responses from others. Critical feedback may be about your strategies, methods, or specific actions. The feedback is often rather paradoxical, for example, "Continue to facilitate the attitudinal and behavioral changes that we need, but stop upsetting my people."

Even if you have valid objections to the feedback or direction that you receive, it is vital to demonstrate your sincere interest, willingness to listen, and careful consideration of the feedback you receive. You must remember that feedback is information. It often says as much—or more—about the provider of the feedback as it does about you.

Are You Able and Willing to Acknowledge Your Confusion and Uncertainty?

Although agents are unlikely to ask this question during selection interviews, we guarantee that this issue will come up frequently during your OD consultation engagements. No consultant can be totally certain about everything all the time! In fact, confusion can be an advantage. Confucius said something like: "To be certain is to be closed to learning." Some consultants feel it is necessary to appear in total control all the time, continuously demonstrating that they know *precisely* what should be done, why, how, when, and by whom in every conceivable situation. This can be extremely disconcerting, especially when members are feeling the opposite. Someone once said, "If you can keep your mind when everyone around you is losing theirs, perhaps you don't have an adequate grasp of the situation."

Consultants often master a facade of stoicism and certainty. But consider this: Some OD consultants are very effective in acknowledging and using their confusion and uncertainty to benefit their client systems, its members, and themselves. By admitting to your confusion you can model the fact that uncertainty is a *natural* emotional state that is a consequence of confusion, that is, being temporarily unable to make sense of the immediate situation. Your authenticity and courage can stimulate a collaborative clarification effort, often by simply saying, "Hey! I'm a bit confused. Can you help me to understand just what is going on here?" Even though members may want to rely on you as an heroic consultant who pulls them through chaotic situations, they can benefit more when they discover that you do not have a magical solution. You can be more useful to them by guiding them through an effective process that enables them to discover and develop their own way to deal with their own organizational issues. This typically produces long-term benefits in terms of members' increased self-reliance and an enhanced appreciation of the value of joint discovery and participatory problem-solving processes. Tolerance for and comfort with uncertainty and ambiguity also increases, along with pride and self-esteem.

Do You Have the Courage to Point Out that "the Emperor Has No Clothes"?

You are probably familiar with crisis situations in which almost everyone in an organization "knows" something that is considered to be so politically or socially "sensitive" that no one is willing to take the risk of speaking about it in public. Different people seem to know different aspects of such things; no one person has the total picture. But the result is that vital issues are avoided or ignored. Over time, the adverse consequences of ignored and avoided issues may accumulate to the point at which the organization is confronted by very real threats to its continued existence.

Considerable *courage* is required for persons who value their membership in an organization to take the risk of pointing out a "dead moose" and to test whether or not their fantasies about the "awful consequences" they anticipate are valid. Few leaders, and fewer agents, are willing to acknowledge and explore the existence of public secrets during selection interviews. The most you can expect are subtle indicators of discomfort and avoidance as you approach sensitive issues.

You can serve as a model for taking calculated risks in surfacing sensitive issues or you can play it safe and avoid testing the real or imagined risks. If you choose the first option, you can provide an invaluable service by helping leaders and members to confront vital issues and enable them to eliminate or reduce the power of counterproductive cultural norms. If you choose the latter option, you may inadvertently collude with members who pretend there are no critical issues.

Preparing for the Interview

We strongly recommend that you lay out a *flexible* plan before going into a meeting with agents or leaders, especially selection interviews. A functional plan for such meetings should consider our discussion in Chapter 2 and include, but not be limited to, the answers to the questions listed in Exhibit 6.2. Use this format and add your own items as needed as you make plans to meet agents and leaders.

Exhibit 6.2. Sample Plan for a Selection Meeting

Elements of Your Plan	Comments, Details

Elements of Your Plan

In what businesses are the prospective client systems engaged? How much do you know about the organization's size, structure, financial condition, and current challenges? What do you know about the system's industry?

Who are the agents of your prospective client systems? What are their normal roles within their organizations? How high up in the organizational hierarchy do they sit? What level of discretionary authority do they have for making selection decisions? Are they, for example, purchasing or procurement agents, human resource management specialists, or leaders of their organizations (or one of the major subsystems)?

What, specifically, are your goals for the interview? What do you want to have learned and/or accomplished by the time you conclude the interview?

How, specifically, are you going to ensure that you will achieve these goals? What questions are you going to ask? What must the agents do or say to convince you that you want to consult with this organization? What will you be looking and listening for? How will you know when you have seen or heard "it"?

Exhibit 6.2. Sample Plan for a Selection Meeting, Cont'd

Elements of Your Plan	Comments, Details
Who, in addition to you and the agents, should participate? How might you involve these other persons? What roles do you want them to play? Are they aware of, have they accepted, and are they comfortable in this role? Do they prefer a different role? Can you modify the roles to assure everyone's satisfaction before the interviews begin?	
Where should the interview be conducted? In your office? In the agents' conference room? In some other location? What are the advantages and disadvantages of alternative interview sites?	
What materials should you have with you to help you to describe your services and their possible relation to the prospective client system's issues? How do you intend to present these materials?	
What media support will you need? An overhead projector, flip-chart easel, marking pens, or masking tape? Who should provide these? At whose expense?	
What are the worst things that could happen during this interview? How will you handle them if any of them do occur?	

Participating in the Selection Interview

Depending on the culture of the organization, consultants and agents may use a tremendous amount of time during their first meeting setting the climate. This is an especially important process in many non-U.S. cultures. For example, a colleague who is a frequent business traveler to Japan tells us, "Before you talk business in Tokyo, you'd better be prepared to drink a lot of green tea." However, talking about how rotten the weather has been is not climate setting (no pun intended) in most U.S. organizations. Rather, it may be a tactic to give one or all involved parties a chance to sniff around the others before getting to the meat of the meeting.

At least in the United States, you may be more effective in establishing a meaningful business climate if you start by clarifying and setting mutual goals for the meeting. We recommend that you take the initiative by asking the agents to describe what they want to accomplish by the end of the meeting in order to consider it to be "productive" or a "success." We also suggest that all parties clarify how much time they have available for this meeting right up front. (You, of course, will make as much or as little time available as the agents are willing to spare—even if that means rescheduling your flight home.) These inquiries demonstrate that you are highly interested in the agents' needs and that you respect the demands on their time. It also gives you a chance to align whatever presentation you have with the agents' expectations. Be aware, however, that this strategy can backfire in cultures in which such directness (bluntness) is considered "primitive" or "uncivilized."

If you initiated the meeting, agents may ask or expect you to describe your purposes before they talk about their own.

You must demonstrate that you are seriously interested in satisfying the prospective client system's needs (without sacrificing your own integrity). You might say something like: "My primary goals for this meeting are to better understand: (1) your current situation, (2) what you are trying to accomplish, (3) what you need to achieve your goals, and (4) whether or not I think I can offer you a meaningful contribution." These discussion points should elicit sufficient pertinent information for you to understand the context and shape your proposal. Then you might ask: "And what would you like to see as a result of this meeting?"

Once all parties present their respective interests or expectations, the next step is to clarify, agree on, and prioritize the actual objectives for your meeting. You should follow two rules:

Rule Number 1: No Smoke Screens! No Mirrors! No Games! As a candidate, your primary purpose during selection interviews is to explore and clarify the degree to which your competencies and interests match the prospective client system's needs and purposes. Do not try to guess or unearth the agents' hidden agendas. Initial interviews are not for playing guessing games. They call for open and honest communication between agents and prospective consultants. It is essential that the interests of both parties be served by employing your marketing strategies, but the strategies should be transparent.

It is not unusual, however, for agents to create serious impediments by being obscure about their major issues, needs, and goals, particularly if their organization is planning to implement major initiatives to maintain, gain, or enhance their competitive advantages over their rivals. In such cases, agents may or may not tell you that they are "not at liberty to discuss specifics." This reticence must be respected. Both parties might then discuss the project indirectly—possibly using a lot of symbolism, metaphors, or analogies. This could be a useful test of your capacity to tolerate and function in ambiguous circumstances.

Rule Number 2: Control Your "Hunger"! Regardless of your cash flow, you should not be trying to sell your services during a first meeting with agents. Rather, you should strive to *understand* the agents' primary concerns. This is essential both to establish rapport and to determine whether your competencies might be relevant. If you are more interested in contracts than in understanding and helping client systems to deal with their issues, you are probably too hungry.

There are many ways for agents to detect your interests. If you consistently display any *one* of the following indicators, you will probably be perceived to be too hungry for them.

- You use most of the available time convincing agents of your credibility. You talk a lot about yourself, your firm, and your consulting experiences. You delight in telling "war stories" about all of the marvelous work you have done for other client systems, in other locations, at other times.

- You do not focus on what is going on in the agents' organizations—right *here*, right *now*. When agents bring up a concern, you quickly jump in and say, "That reminds me of a client organization I had just last year. They had *exactly* the same problem and what we did for them was. . . ."

- You redirect agents' attention away from what they are trying to explain to you onto something you want to tell them. You immediately link some *element* of the prospective client system's total situation to other engagements you've worked on and jump to suggest familiar, plausible, corrective action plans.

- You readily accept the agents' descriptions of their organizational issues and prescribe specific solutions.

- Once you know a little about the agents' perceptions of the organization's issues, you are very quick to offer advice, as if your credibility hinges on quickly coming up with plausible solutions.

Hungry consultants who are excessively anxious about building revenues often make poor decisions, at the expense of their client systems. If you are hungry, you may be willing to do what the agents or leaders *want* rather than confronting their desires for "magic bullet solutions."

We teach OD consultants-in-training to tell themselves: "If I am feeling hungry and anxious for work, it's time to imagine that I am independently wealthy." This challenges them to imagine how they would deal with selection interviews if they did not need the work. Invariably, they realize that they would not be so quick to offer agents what they seem to want, rather than insisting that they be given a legitimate opportunity to find out what the organization really needs. Recently, one of our more effective former trainees told us that he has confronted himself with this challenge when he felt hungry and off balance. He told us that the mantra calms him down instantly and enables him to do what he knows he *should* do, rather than to succumb to what others *want* him to do.

▶ CASE IN POINT

A couple years back one of the authors decided that it was time for a "half-sabbatical" to write, catch up on his professional reading, and generally recharge his batteries. He wanted to reduce his consulting load significantly and avoid new assignments, so he worked with only a limited number of existing clients.

Several times, the author was contacted by agents asking him to come in and talk with them about potential consulting work. Because he has a hard time saying "No" to such invitations, the author went with the intention of being so confrontational and demanding that the agents would seek assistance elsewhere. For example, the minute he sensed a "dead moose," he charged, shouting, "And what is this big stinky thing?" If the agents or leaders showed the slightest sign of trying to dodge their responsibility, the author said, "Look, if you folks aren't willing to take responsibility for your part in making this change effort necessary, I suggest you stop wasting my time."

What happened was incredible! Almost all the leaders asked him to accept contracts! The author is still trying to find time for his half-sabbatical.

Other "rules" can be found in Lippitt and Lippitt (1978) and in Chapter 4 of Rothwell, Sullivan, and McLean (1995). ◀

Your Interview Behavior Models Your Consulting Style

Treat the selection interview as if it were your first intervention in a new client system! The challenge is to demonstrate or *model* for the agents precisely what they can expect if they select you as their OD consultant. This way, agents have a realistic picture of your approach, the resources you offer to their organizations, your style, and perhaps what is important to you. Also, you will get a sample of what it might be like to consult with people in this organization.

If there is a fit, you will probably be invited to take the next step. If not, there's no harm done to either party.

▶ CASE ɪɴ POINT

One of the authors was asked to meet with an agent to discuss the possibility of serving as a coach to a number of physicians at the Very High Prestige Medical Center (VHPMC).

The agent was an internal labor relations techspert consultant within VHPMC's Human Resources Department. The following is a reconstruction of the discussion:

She: You were recommended by Bob Templeton. He thought you could help us with some executive coaching. We're talking with several potential coaches. And I guess the first question is, how would you describe the approach that you would take if we selected you?

Author: My approach depends on the situation and the people involved. For example, will these physicians be voluntary or involuntary recipients?

She: Involuntary. Definitely not voluntary.

Author: That could be a problem. If they don't want coaching, they will probably be defensive, if not outright resistant.

She: I think you could count on that.

Author: Exactly who are the persons who would be the coaching recipients?

She: Physicians. They are pretty arrogant and insensitive in dealing with other staff. There have been a lot of complaints by people whom the physicians think of as *subordinate.* They have been complaining to VHPMC's administration about the way the physicians treat them: nurses, lab technicians, and the like.

Author: How many of the medical staff are we talking about?

She: Just about 10 percent of 187 physicians. Most of the physicians have not had complaints made against them.

Author: Has anyone in VHPMC's administration confronted the physicians in question?

She: Yes, each of them has been warned at least once, but they either minimize the significance of the complaints or they don't see anything wrong with their behavior or attitude. They've been trained to believe that they are the elite, they are the ones who should be in complete control, and that their staff should be compliant and accommodating.

Author: What is the logic behind selecting coaching as the intervention of choice? What makes you or VHPMC's administration believe it would be effective?

She: Well, we're really taking a chance. We don't have any reason to think it will be completely effective by itself. But it does seem like a reasonable way to start because it would be a relatively low-threat initiative.

Author: That sounds like you have considered some other alternatives. What were those?

She: We thought about holding some grievance hearings that could result in firing a couple of the physicians. We thought that would send a message to the others. We may still do that. We also thought about some "sensitivity training" to show the physicians what the impact of their behavior was on their subordinate staff. And we may do that, too.

Author: How about having their service and department heads monitor these behaviors and holding them accountable?

She: Yes, we thought about that, but the service heads are mostly not physicians. We're afraid our M.D.s would not respond to them. The heads of relevant departments are, of course, M.D.s, but they are more concerned with quality of services and don't want to get into what they call "relationships" or "disciplinary issues."

Author: OK, so some of those options might be parts of a multiple strategy? [Yes.] If I were going to help with the coaching, I would need some reliable, solid data that describes the *behavior* of these physicians to use as a baseline. Is that kind of information available?

She: Yes, we have a file on every physician about whom complaints have been made. We could make that available.

Author: Good. I would also need to be properly positioned with respect to these physicians. Do you have any idea how they are likely to respond to a sixty-year-old psychologist?

She: Well, they usually don't listen to anyone who is not an M.D., but they have had some good experiences with our staff psychologists. And you're about the same age as their department heads, and they seem to accept guidance and assistance from them. Yes, I think your age would be at least a non-factor, and may even be a significant plus.

Author: Good. Now we would need VHPMC's administration to become actively involved with this. First, I would need them to explain the coaching program to the physicians in question. Its origins and why this was decided on. Second, I'd need the administration to introduce me and explain my background and my functions. Third, the administration would have to insist that the selected physicians' participation is mandatory, no exceptions. Would they have any trouble with any of that?

She: No, I don't think so. What you are saying sounds very reasonable and pragmatic.

Author: Good, because without VHPMC's administrative active and visible support, the physicians would probably find all kinds of reasons to avoid participation, such as convenient patient emergencies.

She: *Absolutely!*

Author: You sound kind of angry. Are you angry with these physicians?

She: Yes, I am! My job is keeping this hospital out of employee relations trouble. These physicians are perpetuating an issue that should not exist.

Author: I can understand that. So the idea of the coaching would be to help these physicians to become aware of their behavior and its adverse consequences and then to somehow induce them to change the nature and quality of their interpersonal relations with the staff associates?

She: *Precisely!*

Author: OK, I would also need some way to get some independent perceptions of any progress that the physicians might be making. Is that possible?

She: Yes, I think we could get feedback from the staff—probably the same staff members who made the original complaints.

Author: Well, that could be a problem. The staff are unlikely to be disinterested parties. If they are vindictive, they could continue to provide very critical feedback, regardless of what the physicians do or not do.

She: Yes, I see what you mean. We would have to find a way to deal with that. I have a different question. How long do you think a series of coaching would take?

Author: There's no way to tell in advance. Some people simply need to be confronted in a sort of "Come to Jesus" meeting. They see that this is a more serious situation than they thought, they quickly recognize what they need to do, and they adapt. Two or three sessions. For others, we may be dealing with the equivalent of addictive behavior. They will rationalize and deny the allegations. That will require considerable persistence. If VHPMC's administration doesn't keep the pressure on, some people may simply wait it out, hoping they will get tired and drop the issue. Then, it's back to business as usual. It may also be that VHPMC's philosophy or performance management system unintentionally allows—maybe even encourages—the kinds of discriminatory behavior we're talking about. To determine if that is so, those organizational elements—and the meanings they convey to the medical staff—should be studied. So it's hard to say how long the effort would take, even for one physician.

She: I understand. Let me ask you, also, how you would open a session with one of these physicians?

Author: Well, assuming that I already had some specific, behavioral descriptions of VHPMC administration's version of expected behavior, I guess I would frame the coaching sessions in as much of a win-win context as possible. That is, I assume I would have something like a file on each person that details his or her unacceptable behavior.

She: *His* behavior. They're all men. Young men.

Author: None of the female physicians—young or more mature—exhibit this undesirable behavior at all?

She: As far as we know, that's correct.

Author: OK, I would go over the data with the physicians to make sure that they recognize themselves in the complaints. I may have to deal with their denial or rationalizations. I would then remind them of the desirable behavior that VHPMC's administration expects of them. Then I would guide them through a process to help them clarify and make explicit why it is important for them to behave as desired. This would reveal the drivers. For example, if you were one of these physicians and I asked you that question, what would you say, assuming you were willing to be truthful?

She: Oh, I see how it would work. OK, I would say it is important for me to adopt the prescribed behavior to reduce friction with the staff, improve the quality of work life for everyone, increase efficiency, improve the quality of service to patients, avoid receiving poor performance ratings, and create a spirit of cooperation among the entire staff. Is that what you mean?

Author: Precisely, but it may be that what the physicians come up with is not compelling enough to motivate and sustain movement in the desired direction. If that were the case, we'd have to consider adding more powerful drivers, such as making acceptable relationships with colleagues a significant part of VHPMC's formal performance management system. Then I would guide them through a parallel process to help them to clarify why it would be difficult for them to achieve that state. This would reveal the obstacles and impediments. So, again, if you were one of them, how would you respond?

She: OK, I might say that this kind of dominating, abusive relationship is traditional; it's what I was taught. It's consistent with the idea that physicians always have to be in control of all aspects of patient care. I believe that my subordinate staff should just accept it and not make such a big deal about it. They should be more concerned with the high quality of care I'm providing to our patients. Stuff like that? That's interesting. All the obstacles have nothing to do with me as a physician. It's all about *other* people or about *tradition*. None of it is my fault.

Author: Exactly, so this would be the guts of the coaching process. I would have to help each of the physicians to figure out how *they,* by themselves or with each other, can eliminate or control the adverse *affects* of these restraining factors, even those that are part of their training, other people's attitudes, or ingrained aspects of the VHPMC's culture. They have to see that there is a tangible, meaningful payoff for them to make changes in their interpersonal behavior. They need to realize that their individual decisions to change are based on their own enlightened self-interests. Ideally, the physicians, staff, the hospital—and even patients—can gain in tangible ways from the process. However, as we've been talking, I've come up with a related concern. That is, the kind and quality of the coaching we've been discussing sounds very much like what these physicians' line managers should be doing. Don't you agree?

She: Yes, I've been thinking along those lines myself. What do you think we should do?

Author: It might be more productive to begin by working with the line managers—the department directors and service chiefs—to find out why they have such difficulty with these "relationships" and "disciplinary issues." Once we get some clarity on that we could plan some next steps.

She: That's fine—and an interesting twist. I guess I have enough information to think about for now. Can you send me a brochure or flier that describes your background and services?

Author: Of course. Let's try another shift. OK? How did I do?

She: Great. So far everyone else I've talked with has recommended 360-degree feedback instruments and psychological tests for every physician. They proposed three or four sessions with each physician. They all seemed very mechanistic, like a production line. You've come across as much less formal and much more human. You seem to be recommending a sort of evolutionary process that takes each of the individual physicians and their supervisors into consideration, rather than one size fits all. If its OK with you, we'll make some preliminary selection decisions and get back to you next week. ◄

What OD Consultants Need to Know

It is not easy to determine in advance how much information agents will—or can—divulge to candidate OD consultants. After all, you are an unknown entity at this point. If they divulge too much, agents may tell consultants more about their business than is prudent. Rejected consultants could become sources of information for the prospective client system's competitors. On the other hand, if they divulge too little, agents deny you essential information about their organizational operations, its issues, its needs, and the leaders' perspectives and concerns. With insufficient information, you are unable to determine accurately whether you can or want to be of assistance.

Opening Line

If you have initiated the interview with the agent, no later than one day before the initial meeting think of an opening line that explains why you are calling. Keep in mind that *the closing line* you want to be able to say is, "Thank you for this most interesting discussion; I'll have a summary of our meeting and a provisional proposal for the work we discussed sent to you in a day or two." Extensive background research will prove useful.

If you are an internal OD consultant, your opening line might be, "I've wanted to meet you and begin to understand how things are going in your part of the organization" (the subsystem, department, product group, or region). You can drop by from time to time and ask one or two more questions, each time delving deeper into what is going well and what is not so good. Building a relationship gradually is likely to lead to increasing openness and to the discovery of something about which you can offer to help. Then you will have gained some traction—some tangible issues that match your competencies and interests! When time passes and leaders of these subsystems discover that they haven't gotten any pressure from their bosses, they will gradually realize that you are not a spy for senior management, that you are not serving as a conduit of information. As a result, their trust in you will grow, and they will become increasingly transparent in your meetings.

If you are an external OD consultant making a cold call, however, something more substantive is called for. You may not have the budget or time to just drop by over an extended period. You need to be focused, yet nonintrusive, and without a big appetite! An opening line might be, "Hi, I heard you were the project director of an installation of an ERP platform system from PeopleSoft and that you are about six months along. I am doing some informal research on change management in ERP projects, so I'd like to drop by. We could get to know one another and I could tell you what I've learned so far. Perhaps you could tell me how things have been going, thus far, for you." By the way, a claim of doing research or having something of value to offer must be truthful. False claims are deadly!

Of course, it's very difficult to formulate an opening line when you have no idea at all about what is or is not going on within a prospective client system. It might be a good exercise for you and some colleagues or friends to experiment and test some opening lines for such situations.

Beyond the Opening Line

If you ask about their "problems," many agents will see you as just another consultant with a solution searching for a problem. Instead, ask questions that let them emphasize positive achievements and give them a chance to express pride in themselves as competent and effective leaders and managers. For example, you might ask, "What has been working *well* for you and your people?" "What do you see as your organization's *strengths*?" "What are your people particularly *proud* of?" This will help you to establish some rapport while simultaneously obtaining some useful indicators for some follow-up questions during this or for follow-up meetings. For example, consider what they are *not* talking about.

You should now have established a relational foundation that can support more specific information. A summary of pertinent questions is listed in Exhibit 6.3.

If you do not ask for this information, you may be perceived as soft, naive, anxious to please, or hungry. Also, agents may pay close attention to the particular topics about which you *do not* ask follow-up questions. This kind of omission may be perceived as tunnel vision or as your attempts to avoid revealing weaknesses.

Exhibit 6.3. What Consultants Need to Know

Questions to Ask	Agents'/Leaders' Responses
What are the primary issues (problems, improvement opportunities, or dilemmas) in the organization, as agents see them?	

Exhibit 6.3. What Consultants Need to Know, Cont'd

Questions to Ask	Agents'/Leaders' Responses

Questions to Ask

How important are these issues? To whom are they important? What are the probable consequences of not addressing or dealing with them? How might the organization be affected if the issues are not resolved?

Who are the key stakeholders? What personal stake do they have in these issues?

What have the organizations already done to try to deal with their key issues? What were the results?

What do the agents and their leaders expect from OD consultants? What roles do agents imagine OD consultants would play in helping the organization to deal with the identified issues?

How many of what other kinds of consultants would be involved in the consultation project being discussed? What are their roles expected to be? How will the activities and contributions of the various kinds of consultants be integrated and coordinated? How will the project be led and managed?

What previous experiences does the organization have with what types of consultants? Which types of consultants seem to have worked well or less well? What organizational dynamics or factors do the agents think contributed to the positive or negative results obtained?

Do these experiences suggest that they know what OD consultants like yourself actually do? Do they seem to understand and feel comfortable with how you generally work?

Exhibit 6.3. What Consultants Need to Know, Cont'd

Questions to Ask	**Agents'/Leaders' Responses**

How will the decision to select and engage some kind or type of consultant be made? By whom? When?

In addition to the issues that agents have been discussing with you, what other major events, circumstances, or activities are currently taking place in the organization? How might any of these affect (1) the agents, personally; (2) other significant parties who would be involved; (3) the availability of resources for this assignment; (4) the expected results of this assignment?

How might these concurrent events, circumstances, or activities be affected by the proposed consultation project? Test the degree of interaction and interdependency between the proposed consultation and prevailing organizational conditions. Remember that organizations do not have infinite resources. If too many change initiatives are being implemented at the same time, operational performance will suffer.

How much support will executive management and other influential organizational members be able and willing to commit for this consulting assignment? How much time, energy, resources, and budget is the organization willing to invest?

What criteria are the agents and their leaders using to select consultants for this engagement?

Submission of a Summary

One of the most powerful ways to ensure that you have differentiated yourself from other consultants is to submit to the agents a "Discovery Agreement" within twenty-four hours of the selection interview (Wilson, personal communication). This should be a summary of your impressions and perceptions of the organization gleaned from the selection interview. Even if the agents do not ask for this kind of a document, you should tell them to expect it.

Before you sit down to produce the first draft, it is useful to evaluate the results of your initial meeting with the agents. We ask ourselves a number of questions (shown in Exhibit 6.4), both from our own perspective and, as an exercise in empathy, from the agents' perspective.

Exhibit 6.4. Evaluation of Initial Meeting

Instructions: Use the following questions to evaluate the results of your selection interviews.

1. Did the agents or leaders meet the goals they had for this meeting?

2. What changes are currently taking place in this organization?

3. What do the agents or leaders see as their major organizational issues?

4. To what extent do these issues fit your OD consulting capabilities and interests?

5. How do these changes affect organizational leaders and other members whom you will need to involve in your consulting activities?

6. What kinds and types of consultants are currently working on these changes? What other consultants are expected to be involved in the near future?

7. Which of these consultants are internal and which are external?

8. How will the organization's commitments to support these consultants affect the availability of resources that you will need?

9. To what extent do the agents or leaders see the other consultants as being collaborative or competitive with your OD efforts?

Exhibit 6.4. Evaluation of Initial Meeting, Cont'd

10. What indications did you receive that the agents or leaders, as individuals, are part of the root causes of these issues, as opposed to being a part of their management?

11. Did the agents or leaders seem to be aware of the amount of time, energy, budget, and other resources that will be necessary?

12. Were they willing to commit these resources?

13. Does the organization have these resources to commit?

14. Do the agents or leaders have the authority to commit these resources?

15. Do you think you can establish an effective relationship with the agents or leaders? Why or why not?

16. What are the agents' or leaders' greatest concerns about accepting help from a consultant?

17. What are the significant "taboos" in this organization?

18. Have the agents or leaders of the organization had prior experience with OD consultants?

19. What was the nature of the consultation, and what were the results of this experience?

20. How often and for what purposes has the organization used consultants?

21. Who decides whether or not to use consultants in this organization? Does the agent have discretionary authority or must the agent submit recommendations to leaders for their decision?

22. What are the decision makers' criteria for evaluating and selecting consultants?

23. How did the agents or leaders perceive you as an individual?

24. How did the agents or leaders perceive your consulting skills?

25. How did the agents or leaders perceive the department or firm that you represent?

26. Is this a voluntary or nonvoluntary search for a consultant?

At a minimum, your Discovery Agreement should contain the following information.

- Your understanding of the organization's major current issues, including a summary of what you learned about its relevant strengths and weaknesses;

- A summary of additional information that you will need before submitting a formal proposal, including a tentative plan for gathering and organizing data that would confirm, clarify, or redefine the nature of the issues;

- A summary of your consulting philosophy and approach, with an emphasis on those factors that make you uniquely appropriate as OD consultant for this assignment; and

- A list of organizations for which you have recently consulted, the nature of the work you did, and names and telephone numbers of key persons in those organizations who can be contacted as references.

The Discovery Agreement should be written to convey the message: "It is important for me to have a clear understanding about your organization and its current situation before I submit a proposal."

Data gained during the selection interview, together with a thoughtful review of your Discovery Agreement, should enable agents to make *informed choices* about what kind and type of consultants the organization needs, as well as how you stack up against your competition. You might want to add a statement that whatever you have learned will remain confidential. We think this statement should be the first thing the reader sees.

Summary

We believe that all consultants should be prepared prior to setting foot in an agent's office. We do *not* mean that you should be ready to show the agent a huge Power-Point slide presentation in living color. Rather, you should feel grounded, balanced, and just a little anxious. One way that we prepare ourselves to manage initial meetings is to use the items in Exhibit 6.5 as a checklist before and during the interview. Although we have memorized this list, we still look it over before every meeting to remind us that we cannot rely on "gut" feelings alone.

Exhibit 6.5. Checklist for Managing Initial Meetings

1. *Determine Your Goals:* What, specifically, do you want to accomplish during this interview?

2. *Plan Your Strategy:* What, specifically, can you do to increase your chances of reaching your goals?

3. *Prepare in Advance:* Do your homework, including a scan of the recent business press reports on this organization. Look for industry and market trends that may create problems, opportunities, and dilemmas for this organization. Scan their website. Surf the Internet. Write down the most important questions that you think you should ask.

4. *Set the Climate:* Conduct the interview in an environment that is free from unnecessary distractions and interruptions; find a setting that is conducive to making contact and developing an open, unfiltered dialogue.

5. *Check Expectations:* Ask about the agent's expectations and goals for this interview.

6. *Clarify Concerns:* Ask the agent about any doubts, concerns, or reservations he or she might have about the interview process and/or your role.

7. *State Your Goals:* Clarify your goals for the interview with the agent.

8. *Clarify Limitations:* Openly discuss factors that may constrain the interview process, especially the amount of time that is available and confidentiality.

9. *Establish Contact:* Take the time to establish and maintain a rapport through personal contact with the agent, even asking for permission to interview the agent.

10. *Ask Open-Ended Questions:* Make it as easy as possible for the agent to respond openly and freely to your questions. Avoid yes/no and multiple-choice questions.

11. *Listen Actively:* Demonstrate that you understand the agent as he or she wishes to be understood. Paraphrase.

12. *Wait for Responses:* Don't rush. Give the agent time to think about and formulate answers to any questions that you might ask.

13. *Take Notes:* Don't trust your memory, especially if the interview involves a lot of details or technical information. Take verbatim notes. Much of the agent's technical jargon may not make much sense to you now, but it will later. Make sure that you ask for permission.

14. *Keep Track of Time:* Use the time that is available wisely. Do not let time run out before asking your most important questions.

Exhibit 6.5. Checklist for Managing Initial Meetings, Cont'd

15. *Check for Understanding:* Take the time to verify your understanding of what the agent says, especially if he or she uses a lot of jargon, tends to be vague or cryptic, or rambles.

16. *Do Not Debate:* Do not get trapped in arguments, childish games, and the like—especially if they are win/lose in nature. If you feel tempted to argue, *do not respond.* Sit quietly and pay attention.

17. *Check Progress:* Take time to check your progress against the goals to which you and the agent have agreed.

18. *Summarize:* From time to time, summarize your understanding of the most significant points covered. Give the agent a chance to agree, disagree, correct, or modify your summary. Give a general summary at the end of the interview.

During selection interviews, OD consultants should be prepared to help agents and leaders to avoid mistaking them for other types of consultants. We strongly recommend that you make sufficient time to conduct periodic self-assessments to prepare yourself to function effectively, both in selection interviews and in consulting settings. Review the eleven questions on the checklist in Exhibit 6.5 that we have developed for this purpose. Your responses will help to distinguish you from other consultants and reveal your unique value. You also must have a plan for preparing for selection interviews. We have provided a format for such a plan, but you must have a good idea about what you will say, ask, and look for during the interview. Remember to prepare a Discovery Agreement for the agent's review as soon as possible after the interview, prior to developing a proposal.

Of course, you must guard against being so overly prepared that you develop tunnel vision and miss the unexpected twists and turns that will emerge during these interviews. We are always ready to discard our carefully prepared plans for initial interviews when something comes up that is totally unexpected and interesting.

We have found it useful to review the contents of Exhibit 6.6 just before entering a selection interview. Use it as a quick reminder of both what to do and what not to do.

Exhibit 6.6. Dos and Don'ts for First Meetings

Do	Do Not
Make an appointment	Just drop in, uninvited
Deal with agents who represent the leaders of the organization or one of its subsystems	Deal with anyone so low in the organization that he/she is not authorized to use discretionary funds
Use as much local language as you can	Use OD jargon
Adopt an attitude of intense interest and curiosity	Display your credentials
Actively *listen!*	Tell them about all of your capabilities (Of course, if they ask for any of this information, give it to them.)
Probe for details	Gossip
Understand the speaker as he/she wants to be understood	Tell them you can solve their problems
Consider your assumptions as hypotheses to be tested for validity	Act on untested assumptions
Paraphrase what you think you are hearing	Try to sell a service
Listen some more!	Promote yourself
Take reasonable risks	Prostitute yourself
Preserve your integrity	Denigrate other consultants—of any kind or type
Provide examples of your work if asked.	Use real names of people or organizations.

Consulting Proposals and Contracts

WHEN A CONSULTANT has made a good impression during a selection interview, agents often ask him or her to submit a proposal for doing the work. If the agents like your proposal, it will serve as the basis for developing a legal contract. Thus, proposals and contracts are related documents. The difference between them is the purposes for which each is written.

Proposals

Consulting proposals are written so that agents and leaders can review and evaluate the candidates' respective strategies, styles, and fees. Contracts are legally binding documents that formalize the terms of the proposal. Both provide a framework for developing a working agreement between the client system and the selected consultant. Both should include the following elements.

A Description of the Organizational Situation. Your proposal should reveal the extent to which you have heard, understood, and appreciated the agents' views of their current organizational situation and its root causes. You should be familiar with Lewin's Force-Field Analysis (Freedman, 1993) and reflect this in your proposals. Proposals should contain your *current* understanding of:

- The desired state, including the anticipated advantages and disadvantages that agents and leaders expect from reaching that desired state.

- The current state of the prospective client organization or subsystems that are relevant to the consulting engagement, including the primary sources of the system's strengths and weaknesses or vulnerabilities and its environment's threats and opportunities.

- The driving and restraining forces currently acting on the current state, that is, factors that make it important to reach the desired state and factors that make it difficult to achieve it.

Your proposal might also reference what agents have told you about the strategies, initiatives, or action plans that their organization employed in previous efforts to deal with the current issues—and the results. Include the reactions of leaders and members to any efforts that have been made but that did not achieve the desired state. These could have affected the current organizational climate, for example, pervasive complacency or cynicism and probable resistance or persistent optimism and dedication. You will want to make a point of connecting climate to the ease or difficulty of helping the client system to reach its desired state.

Also acknowledge any other actions that leaders may have considered and include a discussion of the reasons these actions were not implemented. Of course, if you don't have this or any needed information, add to your proposal a process through which you can obtain it.

Do not restrict your description of the current situation to repeating the information that agents have provided. Supplement their perceptions with your own, including any incongruencies or holes in the picture that they may have presented. This may demonstrate your added value—or it may prove to be threatening or embarrassing to your sources of information. It is a risky choice.

Also point out that your descriptions of current situations are *provisional.* Until you have had an opportunity to verify, clarify, or add to agents' perceptions by interviewing leaders, members, and significant stakeholders, you have seen the issues only from the agents' point of view.

The Specific Goals of Your Proposed Effort. The key word here is "specific." You should provide descriptive statements of the specific results you expect from your efforts in terms that are clear, concise, and measurable. Show how these results will contribute to the realization of their desired states. Write the goals in a way that provides clear, nonambiguous direction and context for all involved parties, for example, "Where we are going" (direction) and "How achieving these goals will help the organization to realize its ultimate strategic mission, business plans, and goals" (context). This will describe "hard," observable targets against which progress and results can be measured and assessed.

There are many "formulas" for setting goals that can be used. Our favorite is the "S.M.A.R.T." format. It specifies five criteria on the basis of which leaders can evaluate your precision:

- *"S" = Specific.* The goal is stated in sufficiently precise terms to enable all parties to understand exactly what is to be accomplished.
- *"M" = Measurable.* The goal must be described in tangible terms so that everyone can recognize when they have been reached. What will they be able to see, hear, feel, taste, or smell to know that they have (or have not) reached their desired state? (Client system members who are infatuated with the term "metrics," currently in vogue, will appreciate this.)
- *"A" = Achievable.* Each goal must be seen as being within the reach of the individuals and groups who will be responsible for reaching them. But to actually *grasp* the goal, the involved parties must *stretch.*
- *"R" = Realistic.* The parties must be both able and willing to invest the requisite time and energy. They must believe that they have—or can acquire—the skills they need to execute the implementation plans. The leaders must commit themselves to provide sufficient support in the form of such scarce resources as people, training, facilities, equipment, encouragement, rewards, and recognition.
- *"T" = Time-Bound.* Exactly when people are expected to achieve each milestone and how much overall elapsed time will be required before leaders can expect to reach their ultimate desired state.

You must write these goals in language that is clear enough and familiar enough for agents to recognize that they are addressing the root causes of the problem situations, not merely the symptoms.

A Recommended Action or Implementation Plan. Your proposals should contain descriptions of your recommended integrated action steps that clearly show how you intend to deal with the specific issues. These plans should include the following key elements:

- *An Organizational Diagnosis.* A process through which you collect valid data about what is and is not contributing to the achievement of the established goals. The sources of this data should include the people who are closest to and most familiar with the issues, their root causes, and their consequences and implications. Obviously, these people are unlikely to serve as the agents with whom you have been talking. This information will enable you to validate, clarify, or modify agents' perceptions of their organizations' current state.

- *A Process to Convert Data into Useful Information.* How you will organize the data, sort it into relevant categories, and make it both understandable and meaningful. Or how you intend to help organizational members to perform this function.

- *A Data-Feedback Process.* How you will feed the organized information back to the leaders and members. Describe how you will enable leaders and members to do the following:

  - Derive their own conclusions from your findings;

  - Establish priorities among these conclusions;

  - Set their own change goals; and

  - Choose a change philosophy.

- *An Action-Planning Process.* Describe the process through which you will guide leaders and members to create their own action or implementation plans. Describe how you will help them to identify who should be expected to participate. You should also specify your role.

Specification of Responsibilities. Consider the following issues:

- For what specific responsibilities will various, specific leaders, managers, and members be held accountable during the change project?

- For what specific responsibilities will you be accountable?

- For what responsibilities may other involved parties or subsystems be accountable, for example, human resources, information technology, or other consultants?

A Strategy for Achieving the Desired State. Your proposal should recommend the change strategies through which leaders and members will achieve their desired state. This assumes that the desired changes will be achieved only if a critical mass of influential parties is willing to commit to support the purposes of the change effort and the execution of its implementation plans. We recommend the use of permutations of eight change strategies through which leaders can induce members to accept and support the change. These change strategies include: (1) fellowship, membership, or inclusion; (2) political influence; (3) economic inducements; (4) intellectual logic; (5) redesigning the structure or work environment or work processes to which people will have to adapt; (6) confrontation of resistant or uncooperative individuals; (7) physical force; and (8) high-involvement, high-participation methodologies and processes (the first seven are from Olmosk, 1972).

A "change strategy" is what leaders, usually implicitly, believe is necessary and sufficient to induce their people to commit to and support the change effort. Too many leaders and consultants believe that anyone will do virtually anything for money and rely on "economic inducements" exclusively. However, some combination or permutation of all eight strategies is necessary to win the hearts and minds of a critical mass of significant persons within an organization. Of course, the specific elements of your recommended mix of strategies must fit the unique situational conditions. A rich mix of strategies is usually most effective. A single strategy usually does not reach the target.

Your Fees, Terms, and Conditions. Your proposals should include fairly accurate estimates of the costs associated with the assessment stage of the consulting effort, including gathering, analyzing, organizing or summarizing, and feeding back assessment results. However, until the high-priority issues and their root causes have been identified, you cannot specify what you might do beyond the initial diagnosis and data-feedback process, how much time it will take, and what it will cost to design implementation plans to address the issues. Sophisticated agents avoid consultants who tell them exactly how much a "solution" will cost before the issues have been thoroughly assessed and their root causes analyzed. We refer to such consultants as "hammer salesmen." All they have to sell are "hammers," so they try to make all issues look like "nails."

Unfortunately, many naive agents tend to find this approach appealing. While hammer salesmen say, "This is what you need and this is what it will cost," the authors say, "We cannot say what it will cost until we see what the diagnostic reveals." Only then can we identify and discuss our options. When we agree on a specific course of action, then we can determine costs with a fair degree of precision.

Types of Consulting Fees. Sooner or later, you must address the issue of your consulting fees with agents. Consultants use one of two basic fee structures: time and expense (T&E) or fixed price (FP). Each has unique advantages and disadvantages.

Propose a T&E structure only if you are well-known to the organization and have earned both credibility and the confidence of the leaders and members by consistently demonstrating your competence, ethics, and fiscal integrity.

In effect, a T&E contract gives you considerable discretion to function as an intrapreneur. The leaders are permitting you to do whatever you believe is needed to help them to deal with their issues—presumably within the scope of your contract.

You must, however, use clear, practical controls to establish limits to your intrapreneurial efforts. One effective control is to use a specific, discretionary budget under which you are not authorized to exceed certain limits without explicit review and approval. Another control mechanism is to designate a single, specific "point of contact," a manager, trusted by leaders, with whom you must negotiate all variations from your original consulting contract.

Fixed price structures are "exclusionary" in nature and intent. That is, they increase the leaders' control over your activities by limiting scope, the time or duration of the consultation, costs, and other potential "excesses." Fixed price formats can serve several useful purposes for your client systems:

Limit Organizational Exposure. In the absence of experience with specific consultants, FP contracts can protect the organization from "false positive" consultants. Fixed price formats can serve as an initial test and limit client organizations' exposure while they are determining whether your services are really useful.

▶ CASE in POINT

The vice president of human resources in a large electronics manufacturer and distributor wanted one of the authors to accept an FP consulting agreement. "Only for the first piece of work . . . until we get to know [read this as 'trust'] you." When asked if this was a standard procedure in his organization, he replied, "It has been since last year when we discovered a new consultant padding his expenses and billing us for work that he did not do." ◀

Create Choice Points. Sophisticated agents and leaders expect competent consultants to recommend an organizational diagnosis that may uncover some unexpected, additional targets for change activities. By using FP formats, leaders can create a series of natural choice points at which they can review progress to date. Then they can consider which issues have been dealt with and which remain to be addressed—and what newly identified issues should be added to the list. They can re-evaluate their priorities for existing and new issues and reassess the sequence to be followed in dealing with these unfinished items.

Prevent Aggressive Change Efforts. Fixed price structures that authorize and fund only a limited scope of activities can also serve as a "warning light" and a "brake" to prevent dysfunctional consequences of well-intended but excessively ambitious change efforts. For example, it is not unusual for complex change initiatives to require organizations to redeploy their own employees to the change project. This often has an adverse impact on routine operations.

Managing FP contracts is rather complex and often awkward for all parties. One difficulty is that FP contracts are based on the assumption that it is possible to anticipate with precision what will transpire during a specific consultative engagement. In our experience, this assumption is misleading, erroneous, and potentially dangerous for all but the most basic consulting interventions. It is almost axiomatic that any effort to change an organization will reveal nascent issues and evoke unpredictable reactions. Another difficulty is determining what is *included* and what is *excluded* from FP contracts. Wording must be *extremely precise* to avoid arguments later.

One of the authors developed the proposal shown in Exhibit 7.1 for the chief financial officer (CFO) of a company that was worth about $1.3 billion in the early 1990s. Its successful execution led to several subsequent contracts with the larger organization. A T&E structure was used because the costs were estimated, not fixed. If the costs had been fixed, it would have been an FP proposal. It is a *proposal* because it asks the CFO and his management team to make several choices, including whether or not to accept the proposal. Once the leaders made their decision, agreed to the terms and conditions, and signed it, it became a *contract.*

Exhibit 7.1. Sample Consulting Proposal

TO: Samuel F. Jones, Chief Financial Officer, The Concept Corporation

FROM: Arthur M. Freedman, QUANTUM Associates

PROPOSAL: Factors Contributing to Dissatisfaction and Low Morale

Provisional Statement of the Current State:

The members of the Finance Department's senior management team (SMT) are concerned about the low morale of its approximately seventy members. The SMT believes that this is caused in part by the interactions the members have with members of the department's clients—the major subsystems of the corporation. The SMT believes the Finance Department is held in low esteem by the rest of the corporation and that the CFO is not granted appropriate recognition in establishing corporate goals and policy. As a result, Finance Department members are treated with disrespect and feel they are unable to optimize their potential contributions to their corporation, department, division, team, and their own careers.

Goals of the Consultation:

1. Validate and specify the primary indications and root causes of low morale and dissatisfaction within the department.
2. Demonstrate that the CFO and the SMT are firmly committed to take viable actions to correct unacceptable conditions within the department and between the department and the rest of the corporation.

Phase One: Announcement

Meet with CFO to do the following:

1. Confirm (or modify) this proposed plan;
2. Determine what will be said in the CFO's announcement of his intention to move forward with this effort. This announcement should include:

   a. Indicators of dissatisfaction with current conditions in the Finance Department;

   b. The need to identify the root causes; and

   c. The CFO's commitment to take both corrective and preventive actions by either changing conditions or enabling department members to adapt and adjust to changing conditions.

Estimated Costs:

Two hours, plus expenses.

Exhibit 7.1. Sample Consulting Proposal, Cont'd

Phase Two: Organizational Diagnosis

Establish and distribute composition and schedules for ten focus group sessions.

Activities:

1. In each focus group, Finance Department members conduct self-assessments of factors that contribute to dissatisfaction and also establish the ten high-priority factors.
2. Members identify the root causes of the ten highest priority factors.
3. Each focus group selects one (or two) representatives for Phase Three.

Method:

1. Form ten focus groups to include all Finance Department members (one group for senior management team; seven accounting groups with seven or eight members, maximum; mix by function and level, one group each for tax and finance with seven members each).
2. Conduct ten focus group interviews (two hours each, fifteen-minute breaks, three per day).
3. Identify factors that contribute to current dissatisfaction; members identify and organize issues into factor clusters (self-assessments).
4. Establish priorities among factor clusters; identify the five highest priorities.
5. Present "root cause analysis" format.
6. Identify root causes for each of the five high-priority factors.
7. Prepare self-assessments for Phase Three.

Products:

1. Completed self-assessments from each of the ten focus groups.
2. One (or two) members from each focus group prepared to represent their groups.

Estimated Costs:

Three and one-half days, plus expenses.

Phase Three: Data Organization and Preparation

Activities:

Representatives from each focus group form a single team and do the following:

1. Integrate the ten sets of data; and
2. Prepare for feedback session to CFO and directors.

Exhibit 7.1. Sample Consulting Proposal, Cont'd

Method:

Management team chooses from three alternatives:

1. In private.
2. With validation by a second set of representatives from each focus group.
3. In a "fishbowl" with all other finance members invited to observe and provide input through an "empty chair."

Products:

1. Format and process for data feedback meetings are selected.
2. Root cause analysis of the current state is completed.
3. Recommendations for corrective and preventive actions are developed.

Estimated Costs:

Two days, plus expenses.

Phase Four: Data Feedback Meeting

Activities:

1. Feedback of results (prioritized issues and recommendations) to CFO and directors by team of representatives.
2. Develop criteria for determining priorities (for example, members' personal concerns, degree of control over the issue, costs incurred to make the change, time to make change, visibility of the effort, and/or alternatives and additions from management team).
3. Establish priorities among the issues.

Method:

Management team chooses from two alternatives:

1. Focus group representatives interface with CFO and directors.
2. "All hands on deck" meeting.

Products:

1. Prioritized issues are accepted by most involved parties.
2. Proposals or commitments for "next steps" are determined.

Estimated Costs:

One day, plus expenses.

Contracts

The checklist in Exhibit 7.2 can be used by both leaders and consultants to ensure that the important elements of consulting contracts have been given due consideration.

Exhibit 7.2 Checklist for Evaluating Contracts

Use the following checklist when preparing proposals or contracts. Indicate whether you agree or disagree with each of the following statements. As you respond, ask yourself, "What tells me that the answer is simply 'yes' or 'no'?" "Is there a gray area or some ambiguity here?" "Should I collect some additional information to gain additional clarity and specificity? What information? From whom?"

Contract Elements	Yes	No
1. Everyone with primary responsibility for implementing any aspect of the consulting project has had an opportunity to provide input to the final contract.	☐	☐
2. Goals for the consultation are specified. Both consultants and client system leaders are comfortable with these stated goals. Leaders and other influential members believe in these goals, feel committed to them, and are willing to support them.	☐	☐
3. Leaders have a clear and accurate understanding of what the consultant expects of them and of others in the organization and are committed to holding all parties, including themselves, accountable for fulfilling those responsibilities.	☐	☐
4. Leaders are confident that consultants are fully qualified (that is, willing and capable) to fulfill their responsibilities.	☐	☐
5. The contracts specify the resources (time, information, knowledge, budget, equipment, material, people, and so forth) that both the organization and the consultants are expected to commit to the consulting effort.	☐	☐
6. The client/consultant relationship is grounded on a foundation of mutual openness and respect.	☐	☐
7. Both leaders and consultants have identified and discussed the downside risks associated with the proposed consultation. All involved parties agree to take appropriate corrective actions should any adverse risks materialize.	☐	☐
8. The contract contains provisions for handling unforeseeable occurrences, that is, all parties accept the probability that unanticipated difficulties will, inevitably, emerge. They realize that these may deflect attention away from the main issues and delay progress, but all parties are prepared to deal with them.	☐	☐
9. The consulting contract is written in clear, precise, and mutually understood language. Although involved parties may seek legal advice in writing the contracts, they can be read and interpreted easily by nonlegal members.	☐	☐

Contract Adjustments and Cancellation Clauses

Regardless of the types of consultants or the nature of the change effort, contracts are legally binding documents. They specify the goals, work plan, schedules, required resources, costs, and roles and responsibilities of all involved parties. This can lead to a number of complex problems for consultants and leaders. In our experience, consulting contracts have to be changed or adjusted fairly often during consultation engagements. Such changes are relatively easy to make in T&E contracts, but can be troublesome in FP contracts. There are several possible reasons for changing or even canceling a contract:

- One of the involved parties has violated or does not fulfill one or more of the essential terms of the contract;

- Environmental conditions that prevailed when the contract was written have changed, for example, a dramatic downturn in the local, national, and/or global economy may cause a major change in the organization's priorities, goals, and/or opportunities to use its scarce resources;

- Leaders and consultants do not develop a satisfactory working relationship;

- The diagnosis of the current state reveals additional, previously obscure, higher priority issues;

- Consultants or members are unable to continue the assignment, for example, because of illness or redeployment to other crisis situations; or

- Agents or leaders who negotiated the original contract are replaced by persons who do not support the consultants or the consulting project as defined in the contract.

Any of the above may be valid reasons to change and/or cancel a contract. In the case of violations of contract terms, the solution is relatively straightforward—*if* mutually acceptable means of terminating the contracts were clearly defined when it was first written!

Situations in which relationships between leaders and consultants have soured mean trouble for all parties. Neither consultants nor leaders "win" by demanding the continuation of consulting assignments in which either party is dissatisfied. If they try to continue, consultants will do poor work and/or leaders will provide less than adequate support.

Before Signing the Contract

Let's assume that everything looks good so far. But before the contract is signed, you should go through the following questions together with the agents or leaders and make sure that all involved parties are making decisions with which they are willing to live.

Relationship to Other Subsystems. Assuming the focus of the consultation is a particular subsystem within the larger organization, what are the potential impacts of this consulting effort on interactions between it and other major subsystems with which it is interdependent? Should these related subsystems be involved in establishing the scope, purpose, terms, and conditions for this effort?

Acceptability. To what extent is this project acceptable to various constituent populations (for example, unions and community residents)? Have these populations been involved in determining the scope, terms, and conditions of this consulting effort?

Potential for Success. What has been done to increase the chances that this consulting effort will achieve its stated goals and the organization's desired state? What are the critical success factors that are essential for this effort to succeed? Have these factors been established? Are they addressed in the proposal and contract?

Possible Risks. What are the chances that the consulting effort will fail—either partially or completely? What factors might emerge and interfere with, obstruct, or otherwise make it difficult to realize the stated goals? Have contingency plans been developed to deal with such factors?

Indirect Effects. What indirect or secondary effects might this consulting project have on the organization's relations with its suppliers, customers, the media, governmental regulators, or owners. Will it affect the image of senior management or management's ability to implement other changes or to perform their routine job responsibilities. How will it affect management's credibility in general?

Legality. Does the project violate any regulations, laws, or industry guidelines?

Resources. Does the organization have the necessary and sufficient staff, time, facilities, information, knowledge, budget, equipment, and other resources that will be required to implement this project effectively? Are the leaders willing to sacrifice in order to make these essential resources available? What would have to be sacrificed?

Scheduling. Can the consulting project be scheduled without creating work overload that could impede other scheduled initiatives or interfere with routine operations? Can leaders and other influential members contain their impatience so that only two or three significant organizational changes are authorized at one time, postponing action on other pending issues?

Short-Run Costs. What are the immediate financial and opportunity costs of this project? By committing to *this* change effort, what other opportunities must be deferred, at least temporarily?

Long-Run Costs. What costs will be incurred if the schedule for the consulting projects has to be extended? What will be done if leaders decide that the value of the consulting efforts is less than their projected costs? What are the consequences of terminating this effort before its goals are achieved? Can leaders afford to terminate this effort if costs escalate?

Summary

We began this chapter by distinguishing between consulting *proposals* and consulting *contracts.* You should understand the six common elements that form the framework of both proposals and contracts. You have to be prepared to distinguish the advantages and disadvantages of the two basic formats for contracts: time and expense versus fixed price. You have to know when and under what conditions to negotiate adjustments to your contracts and when and how to use cancellation clauses. It is also useful to be aware of a variety of issues that could affect your execution of the contract. Not the least important of these is your attention to the indirect and unintended effects that your consultative efforts may have on the routine operations of related, interdependent subsystems, external stakeholders, and internal and external constituencies.

Management
of Change

LEADERS KNOW that they can neither run nor hide from the need to change themselves and their organizations from time to time. Some embrace and use the need to change to redirect and revitalize their organizations. Others delay the inevitable as long as they can. It is no longer a question of whether or not to change, but a question of *how much* and *how often.* Changing customer needs and preferences, globalization, population trends, competition, social trends, economic volatility, politics, governmental regulations, and technology will persist with increasing frequency and intensity. These kinds of changes create unavoidable perturbations in everyone's work life. People may ignore, trivialize, divert, or slow these perturbations for a while. However, probably sooner than later, some combination of these or other variables will affect everyone.

When their business environment changes, leaders, managers, and individual contributors must also change, at least enough to adapt to and minimize the impact of unprecedented threats and capitalize on newly created opportunities. Many of the changes that people must deal with evoke powerful emotional reactions. People alternate from feeling confident and grounded in a predictable reality to feeling off balance, confused, and uncertain as they see their neat and ordered world dissolving into unprecedented disorder and chaos. Intense emotional volatility has a decidedly adverse impact on everyone's performance in all aspects of their lives. Many leaders will deny this. However, just ask an executive how he or she did at that last corporate golf tournament. The good news is that these reactions are rather predictable and can be managed, so during turbulent times you can help leaders and members learn to cope with the changes in their personal, professional, and organizational lives.

It is your responsibility to anticipate and prepare people to cope with the inevitable emotional turbulence that is provoked by change. Of course, you also have to anticipate resistance and the self-protective defenses that leaders and members will use as they try to cope with this turmoil. It is in these areas that broad-based OD consultants should employ their unique capabilities as they assist project and client systems leaders to manage the implementation of organizational changes effectively.

Managing Implementation

We believe that a very large portion of the future practice of OD consulting will take place in the context of multidisciplinary consultation teams whose members cooperate as they work on complex technostructural change projects. If you join such teams, you and your non-OD associates will have to determine who will be *responsible* for which aspects of the design, planning, and implementation of the intended changes. You will have to determine who will have what level of *authority* for which aspects of the change initiative.

In our experience, issues of responsibility and authority are vague and confusing, particularly during the early phases of large, complex systems change initiatives. You can facilitate the clarification and specification of this area of ambiguity by introducing "responsibility charting" (Beckhard, 1969; Beckhard & Harris, 1987; Beckhard & Prichard, 1992).

Leaders usually turn to techspert consultants to guide them in designing, planning, and implementing most technostructural changes. This is not surprising. Leaders respect techspert consultants for their demonstrable technical expertise. It is only natural for these leaders to leap to the conclusion that techsperts are also expert in planning and facilitating the *implementation* of complex systems change.

This is sometimes referred to as "change management" (Bond, 1995). Unfortunately, most techspert consultants know more about designing and planning than about facilitating the execution of implementation plans (Freedman, 1997). Actual results of techspert-driven implementation of technostructural changes tend to fall far short of expectations (Buckhout, Frey, & Nemec, 1999; Fisher, 1994; Kelly & Melcher, 1994; The Standish Group website, 1999).

The vast majority of your potential client systems will continuously authorize a variety of major technostructural changes. Their leaders will continue to rely on techspert consultants to design and plan these changes. However, you may believe as we do that it is in your client system's best interests for their leaders to learn how to manage the change process for and by themselves. Your purpose should be to make sure that they learn how to take control and make themselves less dependent on external resources. Dependent leaders tend to react emotionally (fearfully) to changes in their organizations' environments; self-reliant leaders are proactive and more confident. Self-reliant leaders need not be proficient in the same technologies as their techspert consultants. However, it is essential for leaders to become proficient in the planning and facilitation of change and, by extension, in the deployment and management of the various types of consultants that they employ.

We fully agree with Larry Bossidy. When he took over as CEO of Allied Signal Corporation, he opened his first executive committee meeting by stating, "Ladies and gentlemen, our job is managing change. If we fail, we must change management!" [our paraphrase]

Change Resisters and Change Seekers

Several optimistic views about human nature say that people, by nature, are adventurous and welcome changes and that they will reinvent themselves whenever they perceive an opportunity to improve their current condition. There are also several pessimistic views that claim that people are conservative and reluctant to change and will change, kicking and screaming, only when their resistance is no longer effective. Our view is that there is some truth in both perspectives.

This kind of polarity goes back at least as far as Theory X and Theory Y (McGregor, 1985). Polarity management methodology (Johnson, 1992) can provide you with a practical tool to help leaders and members to understand and manage the tensions between these different populations (see Figure 8.1).

Figure 8.1. Polarity Map of Crusaders and Tradition Bearers

Left Pole	Right Pole
L+	**R+**
1. *Tradition Bearers* identify the upside of the present pole—that which should be maintained or preserved.	2. *Crusaders* identify the upside of the opposite pole.
PRESENT POLE	**FUTURE POLE**
3. *Crusaders* identify the downside characteristics. 5. *Crusaders* create the energy needed to shift to the upside of the opposite pole.	4. *Tradition Bearers* identify the downside of the opposite pole—the potential problems they want to avoid. 6. *Tradition Bearers* create the energy needed to preserve the upside of the present pole and to avoid the downside of the opposite pole.
L−	**R−**

Many people and many organizations seem to thrive on change and seek new opportunities, new methods, new behaviors, and the like. Other people and organizations invest most of their creative energy trying to destroy, fight against, deny, ignore, avoid, or trivialize the threats and opportunities that are inherent in change. They employ a variety of tactics that they hope will preserve and maintain the conditions with which they are most familiar and comfortable.

Change seekers and change resisters tend to hold extreme views of one another. Change seekers describe change resisters as "fossils" who are likely to drive the organization into bankruptcy because they don't respond to changing conditions in the marketplace. Change resisters describe change seekers as "loose cannons" who will destroy the very qualities and elements of the organization that made it great in the first place. Left alone, these opposing groups will sap their organization's energy, waste time, and prevent change by engaging in overt and covert win-lose conflict that, sooner or later, will degenerate into lose-lose conflict.

Rather than advocating one position or undermining another, you must engage both in an effort to enable them to plan and implement change jointly. You can help both to identify and discuss both the upsides of their own preferences and the downsides of those of their colleagues who think differently. You can facilitate a public process through which they integrate their opposing views in a "polarity map" that demonstrates both the significant benefits or advantages and risks or disadvantages for each extreme position or "polarity." Then you can help both populations to create a mechanism jointly to monitor and manage the ebb and flow of tensions between the two. First, they would have to develop indicators that reveal that one polarity is gaining ascendance and creating undesirable downside effects. Second, they have to identify who would be most likely to see evidence of these indicators. Those persons or groups can be given primary responsibility for monitoring the organization and its environment. Finally, they have to determine what steps to take to reduce the dominance of one polarity and shift the emphasis to the other intentionally.

You can use this process to help both populations develop creative means to optimize the benefits and minimize the risks of both polarities. Each side can benefit from the other's strengths and compensate for its own "blind spots" or unrealized potentialities. Specifically, change resisters can slow the change process down enough to prevent change seekers from taking impulsive, premature actions. Change seekers can provoke change resisters to lean into their zones of discomfort and respond rapidly and decisively in times of uncertainty. Such cooperation can also reduce the possibility that either will overuse their strengths and cause the implementation plans to be executed either too rapidly or too slowly.

Resistance to Change

Resistance is an inevitable part of any change initiative. Knowing how to manage resistance should be one of your critical core competencies. You cannot rely on techspert consultants, training/educational specialists, or leaders to have mastered this aspect of complex systems change. It will be your capacity to guide, model, provide advice, and coach leaders and managers in this area that will distinguish you from all other types of consultants.

Change seekers tend to respond negatively to those who resist changes that they advocate. Change seekers perceive resistance as a negative behavior and use one or more of the following oppositional strategies to deal with it (Karp, 1988):

- Breaking down resistance by threatening, coercing, selling, or aggressive reasoning;
- Avoiding resistance through deflection or attempting to induce compliance through guilt or shame; or

- Discounting resistance by labeling it as unimportant, by devaluing resisters' perceptions and fears, or by appealing to the resisters' desire to comply with their leaders' wishes.

These tactics work to some extent, albeit temporarily and only in the very short term. However, they rarely result in enduring support for time-consuming, complex systems change efforts. They usually create problems in the long term. For example, threatening and inducing guilt or shame usually drives resistance underground, where it re-emerges in such disguises as "accidents" or "errors."

A "positive approach to resistance" (Karp, 1988) is based on two fundamental assumptions:

1. *Resistance is natural.* Consciously or not, people resist anything that they perceive as being in conflict with their best interests.

2. *Resistance must be honored.* Because resistance is a perfectly normal, predictable human response, people who resist must be treated in a respectful manner.

So a first step is to *surface the resistance* that exists within client organizations. Leaders must make it "safe" for people to express their resistance. Once change resisters realize they will not be attacked or punished for their feelings, they will talk. The best way to surface the reasons for resistance is to simply ask.

Second, *honor the resistance.* Leaders and consultants must authentically communicate their understanding that resistance is a vital source of *information* that can reveal potential design or implementation problems that could be avoidable. They must respect individuals' right to feel *whatever* they feel and actively listen to disturbing perceptions, opinions, and feelings. This also means that leaders must reinforce and reward resisters for taking the risk to state their views in public.

Third, actively *explore the causes of resistance.* However, what people *say* are the causes of their resistance may have little or nothing to do with the real *underlying causes.* Leaders and consultants must recognize that resistance behaviors are only observable symptoms. They have to probe deeper to identify the underlying root causes. For example, people may say they are opposed to decentralization because it will disrupt established work processes. Some probing may reveal that they are really worried they will not be able to learn how to perform their new responsibilities or how to cope with the demanding responsibilities that they fear will be added to their jobs if the organization decentralizes. In other words, they may fear they will be exposed as incapable of learning and less competent than required or they may be concerned about being held accountable for results that previously were the responsibilities of their centralized, senior managers.

Probing for the underlying root causes of resistance will also provide you and leaders with many opportunities to ask resisters for suggestions related to the change effort. This will give them self-enhancing opportunities to contribute to the change goals, rather than fight against them.

Fourth, all involved should *agree on actions to take* to reduce or eliminate the power of the underlying root causes of resistance. Leaders must commit themselves to support the actions—or provide credible explanations for rejecting, modifying, or deferring such actions.

Finally, *monitor the level of resistance* against the commitments that were made. This means that a credible and effective tracking and variance analysis mechanism must be created to assess whether the involved parties are actually doing what they committed themselves to do. This step is essential to ensure that all involved parties are held accountable and that no agreement slips through the cracks.

The purpose of this approach is *not* to eliminate all resistance—that is not possible. Instead, the purpose is to work with, learn from, and reduce or eliminate the involved parties' perceived need to resist.

Responses to Change Stimuli

Effective OD consultants must understand what triggers leaders' need or desire to change some aspects of their organizations. The process of change starts (Janis, 1989; Janis & Mann, 1977) when your client system's leaders:

- Receive some "challenging" information that indicates the presence of significant issues that threaten to prevent them from realizing their organizational mission or strategic goals, or that create intolerable consequences, and/or

- Become aware of opportunities to make significant improvements in the nature or quality of their work processes, working conditions, cycle time, or the like.

Even if leaders are aware of what provokes the need for change, they may not respond to any one or all of these stimuli. Assuming that you are in a position to exert some influence on leaders, help them to ask themselves the following two questions:

1. Which are greater, the risks and costs involved in continuing with "business as usual" or the risks and costs involved in changing in order to respond to the stimuli?

2. Are organizational leaders willing and able to commit the time, energy, and resources necessary to initiate and manage the change process effectively? If not, are they willing and able to deal with the consequences of not changing?

Before answering the first question, leaders must gather and evaluate information about real or potential losses that might be incurred if they continue as they have been. Then they must take a long, hard look at the risks or costs inherent in implementing a change process. This is where you can provide invaluable assistance.

As leaders assess these risks or costs, they must understand that complex systems change involves much more than just the financial costs of restructuring, reorganizing, relearning, and so forth. It also means sacrificing things that they may not want to give up. For instance, loyal staff members whose skills have become anachronistic and are no longer needed may have to be given early retirement, or cherished products that used to be profitable may have to be eliminated.

In comparing the options—maintaining the status quo or changing—it is essential for leaders to consider both objective and subjective information.

▶ CASE ɪɴ POINT

One of the authors worked with a CEO who had built his company from scratch and was faced with the choice of continuing as a relatively small firm or going public and growing rapidly to exploit a dramatically expanding market. Despite the fact that all of the objective data said "Expand!" the CEO, who was also the majority owner, chose to maintain his company's current size and scope. His primary concern was that expansion meant that he would risk the loss of the "family" feeling that permeated his company. After making sure that the CEO fully understood the potential advantages and disadvantages of each option, the author had to respect his informed decision to restrain his company's growth and retain the family atmosphere. ◀

You can help clarify the advantages and disadvantages of both alternatives by introducing client system leaders to the use of the "balance sheet grid" (Janis, 1982; Janis & Mann, 1977).

Major organizational changes do not "just happen." They *always* require intense attention, total commitment, and active (persistent and highly visible) involvement of formal and opinion leaders to support the change initiative. We find it useful to engage organizational members in two highly participative processes. First, creating a "commitment chart" (Beckhard & Prichard, 1992) to enable leaders to determine the degree to which each of them is committed to the change and, second, constructing a "readiness-capability assessment chart" that helps leaders to assess their willingness and ability to support organizational changes (Beckhard & Harris, 1987). If leaders are not amenable to joining the requisite critical mass or are unlikely to add value, they must be neutralized.

Leaders must understand that the direct and indirect costs and adverse consequences of poorly managed implementation can be far greater than those incurred by maintaining the status quo. If this means relocating or demoting reluctant or incapable managers or forcing them into early retirement, the leaders must be courageous enough to take such dramatic actions. They must understand that, whatever they choose to do or not do, they will be sending a clear message about their own commitment to the change to their organization and its stakeholders.

Plans for Complex Systems Change

No discussion of organizational change would be complete without some consideration of Kurt Lewin (Gold, 1999; Lewin, 1998; Marrow, 1969). Many of his students—and their students—became the founders and pioneers of OD. One of Lewin's most important contributions was his belief that planned change must be based on "action research," the experimental use of social sciences to advance the democratic process (Marrow, 1969). We consider his action research method to be the core technology of OD. Lewin, the practical theorist, admonished his students and associates not to conduct research unless it led to action and not to take action without first conducting valid research. So planned change interventions must be based on reliable diagnostic data, that is, an analysis of a system's current "field of forces." Lewin's Force-Field Analysis (FFA) contains four basic elements:

- *Current State:* How the situation looks right now;
- *Desired State:* How organizational leaders and members want the situation to be at some specific future time;
- *Driving Forces:* Factors that are exerting energy on the current state that move it in the direction of the desired state; and
- *Restraining Forces:* Factors that are exerting energy to keep the current state in place and resist change. These are obstacles that impede progress or actively push against the current state, away from the desired state.

Lewin's Force-Field Analysis provides a highly graphic picture of the dynamics inherent in any change situation. Skillful OD consultants can use FFA to involve all significant parties to analyze the discrepancies between their organizational current states and desired states. Force-Field Analysis provides data that all parties need to develop action plans intended to achieve the desired state. Figure 8.2 illustrates how FFA can be applied.

Figure 8.2. Sample Application of Lewin's Force-Field Analysis

CURRENT STATE: Techsperts attempt to transform organizations without OD support or guidance	DESIRED STATE: Techsperts partner with OD consultants, forming multidisciplinary teams with OD consultants providing techsperts with guidance and support
WHY IS IT IMPORTANT TO ACHIEVE THE DESIRED STATE?	WHAT MAKES IT DIFFICULT TO ACHIEVE THE DESIRED STATE?
Increased, widespread awareness that 70 percent of purely technology-driven change efforts fail or produce disappointing results	Techsperts rely on the power of their technologies to gain users' acceptance and overcome resistance
Increased "evidence" (or belief) that the major cause of failures/disapointment is neglect of human issues and organizational dynamics	Techsperts' pride (and arrogance?); they want to do it all by themselves
	Techsperts don't understand OD, how it can be applied, or how its benefits have value for them
	Techsperts believe that users will change their habitual, traditional behavior because they will see that their technology is more efficient
	Client system leaders are unwilling to add costs for OD services to budgets that are already stretched to the limit
	Use of OD strategies and methods take time and extend schedules, adding more cost

Current State   Equilibrium   Desired State

Force-Field Analysis can quickly, clearly, and succinctly reveal the following:

- If the total power of driving forces is greater than the total power of restraining forces, the equilibrium that defines the current state will be disrupted and move in the direction of the desired state.

- If the driving forces are substantially more powerful than the opposing restraining forces, change will take place rather rapidly.

- If the driving forces are only slightly more powerful, the change may be painstakingly slow.

- If, however, the collective restraining forces are stronger than the driving forces, the status quo will be maintained or the current state will move further away from the desired state.

The key to the effective use of FFA is convening people who have the information required to identify and analyze the driving and restraining forces, as well as the critical success factors for achieving the desired results. We use the following process:

1. Convene a team composed of leaders and members whose work will be affected by the prospective planned changes. These persons must be active representatives of the subsystems that will be affected by the change initiative (Freedman, 1999).

2. Have the team specifically define both the current and desired states.

3. Have the team identify and record all specific driving and restraining forces that are operating in the current state.
   - Driving forces can be revealed by asking, "Why is it important for us to achieve our desired state?"
   - Restraining forces can be revealed by asking, "What makes it difficult to achieve our desired state?"

4. After both driving and restraining forces have been specified, the team must determine the following:
   - Which driving and restraining forces do the team members and the subsystems they represent have sufficient leverage to *control*, and
   - In which of these forces they are *willing* to invest their limited resources.

5. Critical success factors are revealed by asking, "What are the necessary and sufficient actions that we must take to assure that our change efforts will

achieve our desired state? Which driving forces must we maintain or increase in power? Which restraining forces must we reduce in power or eliminate?" These questions stimulate team discussions that clearly indicate that there are no fortuitous, single-shot "magic bullets." Rather, this process usually reveals that most "solutions" are multi-faceted and that the most powerful factors are *human* and laden with *emotions.* Further, only through careful attention to the critical success factors can the team hope to achieve the desired state.

When you are facilitating the planning process for a significant complex system change, use the template in Exhibit 8.1. It will guide you in conducting participative FFAs.

Exhibit 8.1. Template for Force-Field Analysis

Current State (Specify)	Desired State (Specify)
Why Important? (Driving Forces) ⟶	⟵ Why Difficult? (Restraining Forces)

A Force-Field Analysis is an essential foundation for developing an implementation plan. It will reveal most factors that must be addressed for plans to be effective. If planning team members reach out to those stakeholders who may be affected, either by the implementation process or by the actual change, they will obtain useful information about both driving and restraining factors. Valid information about the various root causes of resistance will enhance the value of this information. For example, planners may learn that a significant number of end users of a revolutionary technology fear that they will lose their jobs because they may not be able to learn how to operate that technology. Such information alerts planners to address and assuage such anxieties.

In conducting organizational diagnoses of a client system's current state, it is usually necessary to test various hypotheses about the presence or absence of particular variables that could contribute to either driving or restraining forces. Unless you know what you should be looking for, it is quite likely that you will overlook some very significant information. In the following section, we discuss four elements of a formula for determining the degree to which the implementation of a complex systems change initiative is likely to be effective.

Formula for Facilitating Effective Change

We utilize a "formula" for planning change that we derived from David Gleicher's original concept, frequently discussed by Richard Beckhard (most recently presented in Beckhard & Prichard, 1992). This formula focuses attention on four key dynamics that are inherent in any attempt to generate organization change. The formula reads:

$$SCE = D \times V \times Sfs \times B$$

In this formula:

SCE Is the Chance for Success of a Change Effort. That is, the SCE is the likelihood that the execution of implementation plans will achieve the intended purposes of the change effort while contributing to the realization of the client system's mission or its business plans.

D Is the Degree of Dissatisfaction of All Significant Parties with the Current State. It is not uncommon for people to deny or suppress expressions of dissatisfaction with their organizations. They may think that expressions of dissatisfaction would be disruptive or be seen as implicit criticisms of their leaders. Invite people to adopt a radically different perspective. First, help them to describe the meanings that they attribute to "dissatisfaction." Once you know why expressing dissatisfaction is unacceptable for them, you can help them to understand and buy into the concept that dissatisfaction is essential and that it generates the *power* needed to drive any change initiative. They can harness the power of their dissatisfaction and direct it in ways that enable them to let go of the past and shift gears, embracing their discomfort so they can experiment, discover, learn, persist, and creatively adapt.

Further, those who will be impacted by the change effort and those who will be accountable for executing elements of the implementation plan must also feel dissatisfied with their organization's current state.

V Is the Vision of the Desired State. This is the degree to which all involved parties clearly understand and accept the focus of the change initiative on achieving mutually beneficial, attractive, and compelling desired states or visions.

As Alice wandered around Wonderland, she faced a fork in the road. She asked the Cheshire Cat, "Which road should I take?" Because she didn't know where she wanted to go, the Cheshire Cat said, "It makes no difference which road you choose."

Unless leaders have a clear vision of the desired state, they are in the same position as Alice! Far-sighted, persistent OD consultants can assist leaders to clarify, describe, and publicize their vision so that it is comprehensible, achievable, meaningful, and compelling for their managers and members. Visions enable people at all levels and in all parts of your client systems to focus their energy on the same targets and make operational decisions that actively support—rather than obstruct—their realization. Thus, it is vital for critical masses of influential members to understand, accept, and support common visions and see the change initiative as a viable means for achieving it.

Sfs Is Strategy for Taking the First Steps. The strategy must be integrated and coherent to move from the current state of dissatisfaction to the desired state (vision). The most essential component is taking the *first steps*. This strategy is not a complete, highly specified project plan.

Two common mistakes leaders often make as they plan their organizational change initiatives are:

- *Failure to change the plan when necessary.* Many leaders and consultants live by the reasonable axiom: "Plan your work and work your plan." Once they agree on a plan, they execute it like racehorses with blinders. They run straight ahead as if real life were the same as the perfectly groomed oval of a racetrack and avoid "distractions." They persist despite the fact that dealing with emergent distractions can make the difference between winning and losing the race.

- *Failure to take the first step in a timely manner.* You have undoubtedly encountered leaders who do not initiate implementation plans until they are entirely complete and/or "perfect," every step meticulously timed, costed out, and resource loaded.

Such leaders often fail to recognize that the time and effort incurred in perfecting their plans are usually much greater than the value of the expected benefits or total perfection. Demanding perfection is paradoxical, as it is absolutely certain that unexpected events will emerge during any complex implementation. Any action plan, no matter how perfect it may seem to be, requires mid-course adjustments.

You may have to help leaders to both understand and accept the fact that it is simply not possible to create perfect, fail-safe plans.

B **Is the Degree to Which Key Members Believe that the Change Effort Will Produce Desired Results.** Large-scale organizational change is nothing new to the leaders and members of most organizations. They have probably experienced various complex changes during their careers. Unfortunately, many of them have learned that the advertised benefits and the assurances of simplicity, low costs, and short time requirements seldom live up to their advance publicity. Understandably, people are likely to be cynical about new changes. Many will doubt that proposed change initiatives will make a significant difference, so instead of investing the requisite time and energy to assure effective execution, they keep on doing what they have always done.

Cynicism evolves into self-fulfilling prophecies. Because they do not expect success, many people become bystanders and withhold or delay essential contributions just enough to assure that the change effort falls short of expectations—or fails entirely.

Any Number Multiplied by Zero Equals Zero

If you view the change formula [SCE = D x V x Sfs x B] in mathematical terms, you don't need to be a rocket scientist to realize that if the value of any element is "0," the probability that the change effort will succeed as intended is also "0." Several examples of how a value of zero in any of the four major components of the change formula will affect the chances of success for that effort follow.

Dissatisfaction = 0

If the parties whose support or participation is essential to execute a change implementation plan are not explicitly *dissatisfied* with specific aspects of the current state, they have several options: They may adopt the role of the loyal but cynical opposition and fight against it; refuse to participate or contribute; pretend to go along but actually support the status quo; subvert the change effort; keep their heads down and wait for the enthusiasm for the intervention du jour to pass; sabotage the change initiative; or distribute copies of their resumes to prospective alternative employers.

Until and unless a critical mass of significant organizational members feel as dissatisfied as their leaders, managers will merely endure what they think is meaningless participation in an irrelevant, resource-consuming process.

Be prepared to facilitate a highly participative process that enables leaders, members, and significant stakeholders to specify and consider the potential advantages and disadvantages of each of their options. We like to use the "balance sheet grid" (Janis, 1982; Janis & Mann, 1977) and "polarity management" (Johnson, 1992) for this purpose. Then you can assist them to make consensual, informed decisions. Remember that active involvement and participation in making consequential decisions usually produces high levels of emotional investment in and commitment to support those decisions.

Help leaders to illuminate the existing dissatisfaction among themselves or their members by offering various methods of surfacing nascent dissatisfaction that may be evoked by internal or external environmental perturbations.

Leaders must understand and accept the nature and scope of internal dissatisfaction. You can design and facilitate highly participative processes that enable all parties to think through and clearly define the positive and negative consequences of both options—maintaining their organization's status quo and implementing the proposed change initiative (Johnson, 1992). Leaders' and members' data may be supplemented with data derived from employee and customer opinion surveys or from information provided by relevant subsystems (Freedman, 1999).

Internal dissatisfaction is usually stimulated by external threats and opportunities. External threats may be sudden changes in customers' preferences and requirements, increased competition, new barriers to global markets, shortages in qualified employees, and the like. Dissatisfaction is the emotional consequence of assessing one's organization and determining that it lacks, for example, strategic focus, production capacity, adaptability or agility, technologies, entry-level workers, culture, a performance management system, or a flexible structure and effective, rapid-response mechanisms to cope with the threats and exploit the opportunities.

Leaders may not know what organizational elements to change or how to change them. That's why they bring in trusted techspert consultants to tell them what to do. However, most techsperts provide services only in those areas in which they specialize. But your sociotechnical systems orientation and OD competencies should enable you to help them with the question of how to help techsperts to create some important synergies.

Leaders are often advised by techspert consultants to motivate their people to support organizational changes by creating a convincing argument that there is some kind of a "burning platform" that their organizations must quickly repair or replace before the opportunity is lost. This imagery places the threat or opportunity "out there" in the external environment. The desired effect is fear of the loss of the enterprise and all of the meanings that it has for its various employees. The fear is intended to create the requisite emotional energy to drive change. External events are threats only if an organization lacks the requisite mix of internal resources to cope with them, so the message is that, although there is nothing particularly wrong inside their organizations, leaders simply have no viable option other than to adapt to changing environmental conditions.

Keep in mind that the "burning platform" device tends to exacerbate tensions between "crusaders" and "tradition bearers" (Johnson, 1992). To maintain your objectivity, remember that your purpose is to help leaders to mobilize and focus sufficient emotional energy to deal with the *common* concerns of a critical mass of all kinds of members at all levels in all of its subsystems.

Vision = 0

All too often leaders work at cross-purposes with one another. This is particularly evident when organizational visions are ambiguous or very complex. Without a specific, agreed-on target, subsystem leaders typically pursue their own versions of vague corporate visions so that, intentionally or not, their own subsystems benefit at the expense of the others. Playing politicized win-lose "games" results in self-defeating competition and conflict. When major change efforts are initiated under these circumstances, no one wins and the organization loses.

If vision is low, leaders and members probably do not have a shared strategic direction toward which to contribute individual efforts. Without a shared vision, executives, managers, and individual contributors cannot coordinate their activities, but will pursue individual purposes at the expense of the larger system.

Your function is to help mobilize a critical mass of influential opinion leaders to formulate a mutually understood and acceptable vision. For example, you may guide the executive management teams through an extensive, participative process through which they create visions of what they want their organization to be at some future time.

Most large organizations have disbanded their strategic planning departments in favor of adding strategic planning to their leaders' responsibilities. This emphasizes the need to enable organizational leaders to acquire proficiency in an arcane skill set (Making Strategy, 1997; Mintzberg, 1994). This shift also represents a tremendous opportunity for OD consultants to gain credibility as guides or facilitators of strategic planning processes. You may have to become proficient in this area (see Lipton, 1996) or use this as an opportunity to partner with techspert consultants who specialize in strategic planning. The authors have found the Applied Strategic Planning approach (Goodstein, Nolan, & Pfeiffer, 1993), with modifications, to be very useful.

To forge a consensually validated vision that quickly galvanizes collective action, we also like to use visioning or future search (Weisbord, 1992) and other large-group interventions (Bunker & Alban, 1997).

The Plan, Including First Steps = 0

Many talented techspert consultants can develop elegant, well-formulated implementation plans by themselves. Regardless of their elegance, these plans will not induce key members of an organization to support their execution, as they may be perceived as imposed and, therefore, resisted. Thus, leaders must ensure that all key members and subsystems understand and agree to accept and support the execution of the implementation plan.

If "Sfs" is low, it may be because subsystem leaders are skeptical and fearful of making significant commitments unless they have credible implementation plans and realistic schedules to follow. You will have to find out what is credible and realistic and what is unacceptable for the various parties.

Organization development consultants know that the key to commitment is involving a critical mass of influential organizational members in the design and planning processes. The consequences are high-quality, realistic plans and shared emotional investment in the implementation plan.

Such collaborative efforts will give you plenty of information about potential clashes between people with different preferences and interests, so you may advise leaders to involve affected parties and provide support for accessing the necessary resources.

Keep in mind that if a critical mass is committed to support them, even mediocre (non-elegant) plans will be successful. Committed people do not allow their plans to fail—at least not willingly.

Belief = 0

The opposite of belief is cynicism, a primary killer of organizational change initiatives (Reichers, Wanous, & Austin, 1997). Many of the targets of change initiatives are cynical about its significance and potential value. Cynicism may be a combination of pessimism about the probability of successful change and blame for inept, uncaring, or lazy leaders. Factors that contribute to cynicism include: (1) a history of previous change programs that have "failed" or have been aborted and abandoned before they were completed; (2) a lack of adequate information about the need, goals, and plans for organizational changes and their implications for involved parties like themselves; and (3) a predisposition to cynicism.

We have found that the best antidote for cynicism is successful implementation of a carefully crafted *series* of change initiatives. We prefer to start with "low-hanging fruit" (easy change projects that seem most likely to yield a visible result quickly). By stringing together a short series of quick hits, we can create a tangible track record of successful change initiatives. This produces a vivid image of effective, competent, trustworthy change leaders.

It also seems to help to acknowledge past experiences with change. Instead of explaining them away, we like to publish what we have learned from these "failures" about the proper ways to implement change and (where appropriate) to show how past change efforts actually establish a firm foundation for current and future change initiatives.

You may have to help leaders to mount a campaign to provide their followers with sufficient credible information to convince them that leaders are irrevocably committed to the change effort. Managers and members must have absolutely no doubts that their leaders will persevere and that their change initiatives will produce measurable and meaningful results. Encourage leaders to play highly visible, consistent, and convincing roles in support of their change projects. To do so, leaders may have to sacrifice some of their familiar roles. You may have to do a lot of coaching and encourage leaders to move beyond their respective comfort zones and take some risks.

You might help leaders create and present compelling images of the "burning platforms" that are the reasons for their change initiatives. Techspert consultants are good partners in creating believable technical and economic scenarios. You might also help leaders design and implement effective, multi-modal communications campaigns that include mechanisms to elicit, validate, and use members' doubts, concerns, and reservations about the change initiative. Techspert consultants who specialize in communications and public relations would be useful partners.

Summary

We believe that, to function effectively in a rapidly changing world, the management of change must be recognized as an integral component of leaders' responsibilities. The need for this function is pervasive. It is also too critical and too fundamental to be delegated or outsourced to any single kind or type of consultant. In fact, a culture of effective change management should permeate the organization from top to bottom.

In this chapter, we have surveyed many competencies that you need to facilitate the management of complex systems change initiatives. We do not have the space to cover them all in detail. However, we provide extensive references and present Exhibit 8.2 as both a summary for this chapter and as a stimulus for your continuing education and development. Use this checklist to assess your current level of knowledge and proficiency in using the concepts and methods discussed here. Check off whether you need to do more or less of each one or whether you could do it better. Then make comments for yourself. The checklist also contains a number of critical personal qualities, attributes, and characteristics that you may want to enhance or develop.

Exhibit 8.2. Checklist of Management of Change Competencies

Competence	Do More	Do Better	Do Less	Comments
Scan internal, external environments ("scouting")				
Enhance leaders' awareness of need to change				
Identify sources, nature of stimuli of change				

Exhibit 8.2. Checklist of Management of Change Competencies, Cont'd

Competence	Do More	Do Better	Do Less	Comments
Help leaders make informed decisions				
Conduct organizational diagnoses (assess current state)				
Facilitate use of Force-Field Analysis—prepare for creating implementation plans				
Use Gleicher's formula to assess probability of effective change efforts				
• Clarify sources, nature of need for change, dissatisfaction with status quo				
• Develop compelling, meaningful visions				
• Develop acceptable first steps for implementation				
• Use involvement and participation to induce emotional investment and commitment to support execution of plans				
Identify Critical Success Factors to be included in implementation plans				
Create multi-modal communication systems				
Develop partnerships with other kinds, types of consultants				
Create mechanism to monitor execution of implementation plans, identify and deal with emerging issues				

Exhibit 8.2. Checklist of Management of Change Competencies, Cont'd

Competence	Do More	Do Better	Do Less	Comments
Develop leaders' capacity to manage members' disturbing emotional reactions				
Create multidisciplinary consulting teams				
Distinguish between techno-structural and sociotechnical change				
Analysis of leaders' ability/ willingness to change				
Analysis of stakeholders' interests, positions				
Shift from competing to combining options (polarity management)				
Specify organizational values (historical timelines)				
Assess members' readiness for change				
Recognize, deal with resistance to change				
Assess intergroup relations and transactions				
Multigroup representative team building				
Supplier/customer transactions				
Endurance, stamina, persistence				
Courage to take risks				
Capacity to shift gears from steady state (responsive) to crisis (directive) modes				
Transfer OD competencies to leaders, members (work yourself out of a job)				

Consultant Ethics

WITHOUT FIRMLY ESTABLISHED ETHICAL GUIDELINES, an "occupation," "discipline," or "field of practice" such as organization development cannot be considered to be a "profession." Some practitioners use statements of ethics to define what behaviors and practices are mandated, recommended, or unacceptable. However, a discipline does not become a profession simply because some practitioners use ethics statements.

In a true *profession,* ethics statements not only guide the activities of the professionals in the field, but also serve to inform prospective recipients of the services what they can expect.

Values of OD Consultants

Underlying ethical principles are the *beliefs* and *values* that are shared by the members of the profession. These serve as the *ideals* that members are expected to strive to attain.

The OD Institute (1999, pages 59–60) proposes that OD consultants should "acknowledge the fundamental importance of the following values" both for themselves and for their discipline:

- *"Quality of life*—people being satisfied with their whole life experience;
- *"Health, human potential, empowerment, growth and excellence*—people . . . generally, doing the best they can, individually and collectively;
- *"Freedom and responsibility*—people . . . choosing how they will live their lives;
- *"Justice*—people living lives whose results are fair and right for everyone;
- *"Dignity, integrity, worth, and fundamental rights of individuals, organizations, communities, societies, and other human systems;*
- *"All-win attitudes and cooperation*—people caring about one another and about working together to achieve results that work for everyone, individually and collectively;
- *"Authenticity and openness in relationships;*
- *"Effectiveness, efficiency, and alignment*—people [who] . . . coordinate their individual energies and purposes with those of . . . the subsystems of which they are parts, and the larger system of which their subsystem is a part;
- *"Holistic, systemic view and stakeholder orientation*—understanding human behavior from the perspective of whole system(s) . . .; recognizing [and valuing] the interests that different people have in the system's results . . .; and
- *"Wide participation in system affairs, confrontation of issues leading to effective problem solving, and democratic decision making."*

These values were derived from Gellerman, Frankel, and Ladenson (1990). Various authors agree that OD is a values-driven discipline, but there is only marginal agreement about the specific values (Marshack, 1987).

Values and OD Practice

Our values influence our OD practice, and our practice influences our values. To illustrate the latter, consider how OD strategies and methods implicitly shape our values (Peters & Robinson, 1989) and differentiate OD from, for example, many techspert consultants.

In terms of approach, OD consultants are *participative*. They assume that leaders and members have the information and knowledge to cope with their discontinuous organizational issues. Organization development consultants do not consider themselves to be content experts; their work must be collaborative, involving all of the relevant stakeholders—the local experts in both content and context—in the process of planning and implementing organizational changes.

Techspert consultants, on the other hand, assume that leaders and members lack the requisite information and knowledge to solve their unprecedented organizational problems. They consider themselves to be the content experts and see participation and facilitation of stakeholders as trivial or irrelevant. They tend to work in relative isolation with minimal involvement with leaders, and even less contact with members.

In terms of strategy, OD consultants are exploratory and *experimental*. A team composed of OD consultants, leaders, and members provisionally establishes the desired state. The current state for the entire system, including its transactions with significant stakeholders, is studied. Issues are identified and prioritized by the team. Action steps are planned and taken. The effects of these exploratory action steps are evaluated and analyzed by the team. Depending on what is discovered, modifications may be made in the planned change strategy. Then next steps are planned and implemented and *their* effects are evaluated and analyzed by the team. Organization development practice evolves in any given consultation as hypotheses are generated to explain what is learned and are tested for validity with each iteration of the cyclical act-study-plan-train-act process. Each consultation is unique.

Techspert consultants adopt a different strategy. They appear to be much more *definitive, confident, and decisive* as they study the issues and create (or search for and find) specific solutions. Their solutions are often derived from their extensive database of "best practices" and "benchmarking" studies. Techsperts search their databases until they find something external that more or less fits their current client system. These are handed back to leaders in the form of recommended goals, strategies, methods, and implementation plans that are linear, narrow, and, presumably, impervious to adverse contingencies. Techsperts may or may not ask (or be asked) to execute the implementation plans. This decision is generally based on the number and kinds of resources available in the client system.

In terms of control, OD consultants work to *empower* leaders and members. Their philosophy is emancipatory in the sense that they believe that those who create and maintain organizational conditions can, and should be, the ones who also change them. If they lack the competencies needed to take control, OD consultants strive to enable client system leaders and members to gain proficiency, either directly or through third parties. Organization development consultants stimulate leaders and members to exert more and more influence as their proficiencies expand and develop. They actively encourage self-reliance.

Techsperts have a different orientation toward control. They *maintain control* and advise leaders to make specific changes in rewards, structure, technologies, and procedures that, of course, impact members working under these conditions. Techsperts advocate "rational" control based on "proven scientific principles." Because they are the acknowledged experts, leaders and members are implicitly encouraged to remain dependent on techsperts.

The ways in which our values influence our practices as OD consultants is further revealed by some opinions about the proper role of OD consultants that have recently surfaced (Nicoll, 1998; Nirenberg, 1998). These authors' raise the question of what OD consultants should do if their values conflict with those of their client systems. Specifically, should the field of OD redefine itself as "revolutionary" with OD consultants acting as *advocates* for special interest groups—or as *adversaries* against other groups. For example, should OD consultants work with or against organizations that are believed to contaminate the environment or organizations that produce nuclear weapons? Should they actively support a CEO's huge salaries and option plans; help to eliminate jobs through downsizing; tolerate treatment of women, racial, ethnic, or religious constituencies in a discriminatory manner; or add to the degradation of an organization's quality of working life by ignoring or accepting a toxic emotional culture?

We believe that this proposed shift toward advocacy is laudable and perfectly legitimate—*but* not *for OD practitioners.* Rather, we believe that OD has been and should continue to be about the democratization of society and its institutions, not about advocating special interests. We believe that the total organization, including its various internal and external stakeholders and constituencies, constitutes the OD consultant's *client system.* That means that we must help leaders to recognize the benefits of making social responsibility issues a high priority. Then we can help them to create mechanisms and processes that enable stakeholder groups and constituencies that do have special interests to gain a credible and legitimate voice in relevant policy decisions.

However, OD consultants must not advocate any special interests. For us, a holistic systems approach to OD practice encompasses *all* involved parties. We must not make one group's interests or positions appear to have greater value than any other. Rather, we must work to help all involved parties recognize and deal with the complexity of their organizational dilemmas and how any given dilemma has differential impacts on each party's vested interests.

If you have deep personal values that are in opposition with an organization's policies and practices, you have at least three options. First, you can choose to reject OD consulting engagements with such organizations. Of course, you may take an engagement before learning that the client system's ideology and practices are odious to you. If you are caught up in a values conflict, you must discuss it with senior management. If they are willing to explore alternatives that are compatible with your values, there may be a basis for continuing in your role as an OD consultant. If senior management is irrevocably committed to the ideology and practices that are unacceptable to you, you have no option. After explaining your concerns to senior management, you must leave. We and many of our respected colleagues conduct their affairs in this manner.

Second, you can advocate the special interests with which you feel strongly aligned and work against such stakeholders or constituencies with competing strategies and priorities. But this is not OD; it is issue-based community organizing (Alinsky, 1971). This must be *entirely separate from your OD practice.* To try to switch hats and expect leaders and members to accept whatever role you *say* you are playing at the moment is an irreconcilable role conflict. You would be exceedingly naive to think you could switch from one role to another and back again without repercussions.

Third, you can accept an OD consulting engagement, establish your credibility within the client system, and then—surreptitiously—work against the ideology or practices to which you object. This violates any OD consulting agreement that you may have negotiated with your client system's agents and their leaders. To us, this is a totally unethical solution.

The Ethical Dilemma

To date, the discipline of OD does not have a single set of uniform values or ethical principles that have been endorsed by a recognized association. In fact, there is no single association that is recognized and supported by all people who identify

themselves as OD consultants. There is no state or national credentialing or cer-
tifying agency for OD. Unlike most professionals (such as physicians, CPAs,
psychologists, engineers, social workers, or lawyers), no one needs to present educational credentials and pass examinations to obtain licenses that permit them to
practice OD. Further, there is no recognized review body to pass judgment on
alleged unethical practice. Therefore, there is no mechanism through which unethical practitioners can be sanctioned. Thus, there are no barriers to enter the field.

However, a *sense* of practical OD ethics is passed on from more experienced OD
consultants through at least four mechanisms:

- Master's and doctoral degree-granting university programs at places such
  as Pepperdine, Columbia, the Fielding Institute, Union Graduate School,
  American University, Case Western Reserve, University of St. Thomas, and
  Benedictine University;
- Nondegree but certificate-granting institutions such as the NTL Institute and
  various universities;
- Continuing educational seminars and workshops presented by such associ-
  ations as the OD Institute and the OD Network; and
- Specialized self-awareness and skill-development workshops presented by
  universities and institutes such as NTL.

These organizations and their faculty members teach their own versions of
desirable ethical principles. Frequently, these principles are implicit and emerge,
one by one, during classroom experiences and discussions. Unfortunately, there is
not much consistency among them.

Because there are no standards, some persons damage the discipline by their
naive, thoughtless, or exploitative and nonethical practices and some client systems
have been damaged by unethical OD interventions. Some former clients view all
OD practitioners as snake-oil salesmen. These folks also talk to their associates, who
work in companies that could otherwise be our prospective client systems.

Even qualified, ethical OD consultants are confronted with value dilemmas,
many of which stem from fundamental differences with their client systems. To
make a decision that has ethical consequences, you must take an *informed* approach
to working within whatever moral code is required to secure consulting contracts.

Having a set of ethical principles is not exactly the same as having a moral code
of conduct, although for many OD consultants there is considerable overlap. Ethical
principles are based on ideal personal and societal values that we strive to attain.

When OD consultants violate ethical standards, it is probably not because they are immoral but that they are either ignorant of the ethical standards or they choose to act in an *expedient* or *pragmatic* manner. (Of course, the latter is a specific ethical value.)

Short-term, expedient gains are often more than offset by unnecessary long-term complications when consultants violate clients' moral code or the larger society's ethical principles. Client systems' resources are wasted in cleaning up unnecessary complications. Significant intangible costs come in the form of damaged internal relationships within client systems and between the organization and its external suppliers and customers; lost credibility for OD and OD consultants; increased cynicism among members; reduced commitment to future change efforts; and so forth.

We all pay for unethical behavior. Prospective client systems that have been "burned" by unethical OD consultants may not trust any OD consultants again.

We want to believe that the majority of consultants are sincerely interested in performing both ethically *and* competently. We want to believe that their ethical oversights are the result of inexperience, naiveté, overconfidence, or excessive enthusiasm. Unfortunately, however, there are many consultants for whom the concept of ethics in consulting and in business is foreign. Far too often, some consultants adopt some sort of casino ethics, whereby any practice or any marketing strategy is acceptable as long as it contributes to their revenues.

In a way, this is understandable. Few consulting firms have built into their performance management systems a clear, explicit statement of ethics. Very few advanced degree programs dedicate much time to the study of either business or consulting ethics (Gellerman, Frankel, & Landenson, 1990; Lowman, 1998).

Professionalization

Different types of consultants have tried to professionalize their fields by forming associations that include some type of ethics advisory committees, which typically perform four functions:

- Establish a "code of ethical conduct" for the members of their association;
- Advise members on appropriate and ethical conduct in specific consulting situations;
- Execute sanctions against members whose behavior violates their association's established ethics; and
- Respond to requests from consumers of consulting services regarding the ethical behavior that they have a right to expect from their consultants.

An Integrated Code of Professional Conduct

The International Council of Management Consulting Institutes (ICMCI), an international association composed of many kinds of management consulting specialties, has established a formal code of ethics.

The Council's code of conduct is fairly comprehensive. We shall use it as the framework for our recommended code and supplement it with material provided by the OD Institute (1999) and Gellerman, Frankel, and Landenson (1990). The key points that we will cover deal with confidentiality, realistic expectations, commissions/financial interests, assignments, conflicting assignments (dual relationships), contract negotiations, recruiting, and relations with other management consultants.

Confidentiality

The ICMCI code states: "A management consultant will treat client information as *confidential* and will neither take personal advantage of privileged information gathered during the assignment, nor enable others to do so."

There are several aspects of confidentiality that should be of interest and concern to OD consultants. Gellerman, Frankel, and Ladenson (1990, pp. 174–175, 384–385) describe four of these aspects, the first two of which are discussed together below:

1. "Make limits of confidentiality clear to client [system members] and participants."

2. "Reveal information accepted in confidence only to appropriate or agreed-on recipients or authorities."

In other words, spell out the limits of confidentiality to the agents, leaders, and members of their client systems in advance. Such limits are reached when you have reason to believe that persons, teams, or subsystems are threats to their own well-being, threats to the well-being of others (or to their organization), or are unable to perform the responsibilities for which they are accountable.

If you believe you must break confidentiality for any reason, the issue is to whom to reveal your concerns. If someone breaks the law, you must inform senior management and make sure that the proper authorities are informed. If someone threatens to harm someone, you must make sure that the potential target is warned, inform senior management, and make sure that the proper authorities are informed. If someone is exhibiting serious self-destructive gestures, you must take steps to intercede. In none of these instances can you stand aside.

However, if you are asked by senior managers to provide privileged information about one of their subsystems or subordinates or if some rank-and-file members of the client system ask you to convey messages to senior management, that's different. In the former instance, you are being asked to perform the manager's job, not the consultant's. In the latter, you should help members create an effective mechanism through which they can transmit significant information upward on their own. To accept the role of spokesperson is to invite people to become dependent on you and to enable them to avoid taking responsibility. You would also be putting yourself in the unpleasant position of being between the "dog" and the "fire hydrant."

Many consultants do not distinguish between the related but distinct concepts of *confidentiality* and *anonymity*. Too many tell respondents during diagnostic interviews that the information they provide will be kept "confidential." If that were so, OD consultants could do nothing at all with such information. Most of the time, what we *really* mean is that we will use the information but we will protect informants' identities. This is "anonymity."

3. "Use information obtained during [consultations] in writings, lectures, or other public forums only with prior consent or when disguised so that it is impossible from our presentations alone to identify the individuals or systems with whom we have worked." We fully agree with this statement, but we have heard and read quite a number of "kiss and tell" stories told or written by otherwise respectable consultants.

4. "Make adequate provisions for maintaining confidentiality in the storage and disposal of records; make provisions for responsibly preserving records in the event of our retirement or disability." This should be obvious, but we know of one situation in which an organization brought a $100-million lawsuit against a techspert consulting firm on the basis of e-mail messages that had not been deleted.

The discussion of confidentiality begs another question. Almost anything that you learn from your client systems can be an advantage in future OD consulting engagements. What information can you use, *ethically*, as you move from one client system to another?

Many consultants, including OD consultants, do not see the relevance of this question. For example, we know one well-known management consulting firm that is staffed by CPA and MBA techspert consultants. This firm's stated policy is, "All information about any of this firm's client organizations is to be made available to any qualified accountant or consultant within the firm." Many of the firm's management consulting assignments come from direct referrals from CPAs who discover that some of their client systems' issues could be addressed by their management consultant colleagues, and they can get credit for the referral.

This practice of "you scratch my back, I'll scratch yours" goes far beyond one side of the firm opening the door for the other side. It normally works something like this: Let's say that the techspert management consultant, Joe Doe, is interested in gaining entry into the Global Energy Company (GEC). In preparation for his first meeting with GEC's CEO, Joe reviews his firm's client database, which has detailed information on every client organization that his firm's techspert consultants have worked with over the past five years. Here's what he finds:

- *One of the firm's CPAs has been working with GEC.* Joe calls her. That same day a messenger delivers a complete summary of the company's "confidential" financial activities for the last three years.

- *Two of the firm's CPAs have been working with other energy companies that compete with GEC.* Joe requests the information and the following day he has complete "confidential" summaries of the competitors' activities on his desk, including detailed confidential reports on the assessed strengths and weaknesses of these competing companies.

- *The summaries show that one of the firm's management consultant teams has been helping the senior managers of GEC's major competitor to develop a new vision and strategic plan.* Joe makes an appointment with the team leader for lunch. By the time they finish, Joe has a comprehensive picture of the competitor's "confidential" strategic plan for the next five years.

Thanks to the combined information from all of these reports, Joe develops a comprehensive picture of his prospective client system as well as its competitive environment. He can now conduct a "Gee Whiz" presentation that leaves GEC's agent thoroughly impressed.

We cannot help but wonder, however, how impressed the agent would be if he knew that, if Joe gets a big contract, other consultants in his firm will have full access to Joe's "confidential" data about GEC when they prepare for meetings with GEC's competitors in the future! We also wonder how GEC's competitors would feel if they knew that *their* professional secrets could be spread around so easily.

Realistic Expectations

The ICMCI guidelines also state: "A management consultant will refrain from encouraging unrealistic expectations or promising clients that benefits are certain from specific management consulting services."

This ethical issue is not explicitly addressed by either the OD Institute (1999) or by Gellerman, Frankel, and Ladenson (1990). However, it is a critical issue. We have observed and read about major management consulting firms whose techspert consultants have promised far more than they were capable of delivering—usually in order to obtain a contract (see O'Shea & Madigan, 1997, pp. 96–99 & 99–104).

▶ CASE ɪɴ POINT

The director of consulting and training for a large manufacturing company contacted one of the authors to request a proposal for a management development program for all five levels of their managers. Two weeks before the proposal was to be submitted, the author received an emotional telephone call from an extremely frustrated director.

It seems that while attending a conference, the firm's comptroller met and was impressed by another management consultant, Ms. Jones. The comptroller invited Ms. Jones in to meet the firm's CEO. Shortly after this meeting, Ms. Jones submitted a proposal stating that her consulting firm would perform a complete organizational assessment "at no fee." She asked only that the CEO give her firm "fair consideration" if he decided to implement her recommendations. He agreed.

At the completion of the assessment, which Ms. Jones claimed had taken over thirty consulting days, the CEO was presented with a report that included the consultant's "discovery" that "over 40 percent of the company's production capacity was going to waste as the direct result of ineffective supervisory skills." Needless to say, the report included a recommendation that a consulting firm be engaged to design and implement a training program for all managers. The report concluded with the amazing statement that the consultants would "guarantee" that the company "will save $4,000,000 as a direct result of [the] recommended training program." The only stipulation was that the consultants would honor their guarantee *only* if the organization followed their exacting implementation requirements and agreed that the consultants would establish and define base-line metrics for the evaluation, develop the instruments, and conduct the evaluation of the actual savings that purportedly could be attributed to the training program! ◀

There are several ethical issues involved in the above situation. First, the only way that a consulting firm could afford the costs of conducting a free, speculative, thirty-day assessment process is if they were 100 percent certain that their assessment results would enable them to recoup their sunk costs through a huge consulting contract. The only way they could be certain of that is to know in advance what their assessment was going to "reveal."

The second ethical issue relates to the "revelation" that the managers were performing their supervisory functions "below acceptable levels." The company's internal consulting staff had repeatedly called this fact to the CEO's attention. The internal consultants were convinced that there were three causes of low performance: (1) lack of supervisory skills; (2) conflicting directives from the managers' managers; and (3) an overly complex, hierarchical bureaucracy with outdated rules and regulations that conflicted with one another. More important, the internal consultants believed that supervisory skill training for managers, alone, would produce only marginal improvements if the structural and management issues were not brought into alignment. (Ms. Jones and her colleagues made no contact whatsoever with the internal consulting and training staff during their "comprehensive organizational assessment." In fact, Ms. Jones was totally unaware that the organization had internal consultants.)

The third ethical issue deals with the "guaranteed results." The only way a consulting firm can guarantee its results is if they have full control over the evaluation of those results! It is axiomatic that evaluations must not be conducted by the same people who do the work. The possibility of experimenter bias is far too great. In ethical consultations, there must be no relationship between evaluators and consultants.

Agents and leaders are vulnerable to unethical consultants who are intuitive enough to figure out what the leaders want to hear. For example, all agents want the assurance that consultants' interventions will be quick, simple, painless, and inexpensive—and that they will immediately make major, positive, bottom-line differences.

It is only natural for leaders to hope their consultants can provide them with "magic bullet" solutions to vexing problems. Unscrupulous and unethical consultants exploit this vulnerability and give *verbal* assurances (not in writing) that leaders will get what they want.

Commissions or Financial Interest

The ICMCI also recommends that "A consultant will neither accept commissions, remuneration, nor other benefits from a third party in connection with recommendations to a client without the client's knowledge and consent, nor fail to disclose any financial interest in goods or services that are to be delivered as a part of such recommendations."

This issue is not addressed either by the OD Institute or by Gellerman, Frankel, and Ladenson (1990). Perhaps this is because the American culture and legal structures consider this practice to be unacceptable. However, this ethical standard should remind all OD consultants that these kinds of arrangements can be construed as bribery or kickbacks.

The issue is more complex than it appears. Organization development consultants often use their affiliation networks to develop legitimate reciprocal relationships. These are generally not commercial transactions in the sense of marketing one another in exchange for kickbacks. In America, for consultants to initiate or accept offers of work in exchange for a "commission" is inappropriate if the broker is a member of a prospective client organization. The following case shows that shady dealings are far from nonexistent in America and Western Europe.

▶ CASE IN POINT

One of our associates, Hans, was contacted by a colleague, Phillipe, who had been consulting with a large Scandinavian manufacturing company for so many years that he was given a position on the firm's board of directors. Phillipe informed Hans that the company's CEO was seeking an external consultant to help restructure the organization and asked if Hans was interested. When Hans said that he was, Phillipe said, "Good, I can guarantee you the assignment. All I want is 5 percent of your fee in return for my services in arranging for the contract."

When Hans informed the company's CEO of the offer, the CEO's reply was, "Oh, you must have misunderstood! We have a long, extremely satisfactory relationship with Phillipe. We have total trust in him." Need we say more? ◀

Assignments

The ICMCI also says that "A consultant will only accept assignments which he/she has the skills and knowledge to perform."

Most consultants have areas of special expertise. If they demonstrate their competence in these areas, it is not unusual for leaders to ask them to take on additional responsibilities in areas that are different from but related to their original assignments. The leaders' assumption may be something like: "If the consultants are good in *this* area, they should be just as good in *that* area." Consultants may be reluctant to admit that their competencies are limited—or they may not want to "disappoint" the leaders. They may also be reluctant to sacrifice opportunities for additional, unplanned billings. So many consultants accept such assignments *hoping* they can learn enough, quickly enough, while working to perform effectively. We have seen a number of IT techspert consultants, who were asked questions by their client system members on Monday, burning up the Internet in the evening so they could offer an answer the next morning. They could have said they did not know but would find the answers. But they denied their ignorance and equivocated. We believe this is unethical.

We agree with Gellerman, Frankel, and Ladenson (1990) and the OD Institute (1999) that ethics start with explaining to leaders or agents when an assignment is outside your areas of competence. Then you should offer to assist leaders to seek properly qualified consultants for this assignment. (You could offer to help find and evaluate or screen potential candidates.) Leaders may want you to stay involved, because you know the client system and its issues and people. In such cases, you can offer to partner with qualified consultants who can *coach* you or serve as a *shadow consultant*.

Conflicting Assignments

The ICMCI guidelines state: "A member [of ICMCI] will avoid acting simultaneously in potentially conflicting situations without informing all parties in advance that this is intended."

There are at least two facets to the issue of conflict of interest. One deals with those situations in which OD consultants are working with two similar client systems—simultaneously or sequentially. The second deals with the role conflict that often occurs when the interests of the OD consultant's firm (or department) conflict with the interests of the OD consultant's client systems.

Sometimes it is easy to see when two consulting assignments are in conflict with one another. For example, if you have assisted one client system to develop a competitive strategy, it is clear, because of the ethical principles pertaining to confidentiality, that you cannot take the same kind of assignment with one of your client system's competitors. It would be impossible for you not to be influenced by the "inside" knowledge you have gained—even if your intentions were pure.

At other times, it is far more difficult to determine the degree to which two assignments are potentially conflicting.

▶ CASE in POINT

One of the authors was responsible for an extremely successful leadership development program for a large manufacturing company. Several months after the completion of the program, the author was contacted by a program participant who had recently become the president for a competing company. He wanted the consultant to "implement the same leadership development program" for his new firm to "give them a fighting chance" to compete against his previous employer.

What would *you* do? We think the answer comes in two parts. First, who owns the proprietary rights to the management development program? If you developed it for the first client system and they paid you to develop it, the program belongs to them, unless you and the agent agreed, in writing, that both parties had equal, nonrestricted rights to use the program when you completed your work. However, if you developed this program on your own and were paid only to present it to participants in your first client system, then you retain the proprietary rights and you can do whatever you like.

Second, however, if your first client system retains some proprietary rights to the program, you must inform its leaders or agents and obtain their permission before you can use it to fulfill a contract with one of their competitors. In fact, even if proprietary rights are *not* at issue, we strongly recommend that you consult with your original client system's leaders before taking action.

It is not uncommon for consulting firms to direct their employees to recommend and deliver services that enhance the firm's revenues or prestige, rather than to do what they might consider to be in the best interests of their client systems. This is called role conflict. What would you do if you were caught in this potentially career-threatening situation? We think that you should first discuss both sides of the conflict with your manager, spelling out your perceptions of the potential advantages and disadvantages of each alternative. Then, state your opinion and ask for your manager's agreement. If your manager disagrees, you have an ethical dilemma that has significant career implications. In this case, repeat the discussion with your client system's leaders. If they agree with you, they and you should return to a discussion with your manager. Of course, this may be a source of embarrassment for your manager. Because your firm may lose revenues because of your actions, you could lose your job.

If the client system leaders disagree with you or if your manager is not dissuaded, even though you are supported by your client system's leaders, your career with your firm will be in jeopardy. The only viable, ethical choice is to *disengage* from the role conflict and walk away. If you are willing to make such a sacrifice, you will establish a personal precedent that will eventually lead to adopting casino ethics—doing whatever is necessary to generate revenues and keep your job. ◄

Contract Negotiations

The ICMCI guidelines also state: "A consultant will ensure that, before accepting any engagement, a mutual understanding of the objectives, scope, workplan, and fee arrangements has been established and which any personal, financial, or other interests that might influence the conduct of the work have been disclosed."

This should be self-evident. In addition, make sure that you and the agents have included a mutually acceptable and clearly understood means for managing *exceptions* or *deviations* from the written consulting agreement. Exception clauses are particularly important for fixed price contracts.

Recruiting

In regard to recruiting, ICMCI guidelines say: "A consultant will refrain from inviting the employees of a client to consider alternative employment without prior discussion with the client." Neither the OD Institute (1999a) nor Gellerman, Frankel, and Ladenson (1990) address this issue.

Ethical OD consultants help their client systems improve their organizational effectiveness and do not decrease that effectiveness by raiding their client systems' most effective employees! Organizations have seen so many management consulting firms recruit the "best and brightest" of their employees that an increasing number have added clauses to their legally binding contracts to exclude this practice.

However, recruiting talent from client systems could be beneficial for all parties. If you are confronted by such situations, we strongly recommend our "one year rule." When employees of former client systems contact us and express their interest in joining our firm, we will consider exploring that interest only if:

1. They initiate the contact with us.

2. They contact us no earlier than one year *after* we last worked with their organization.

3. The leaders of our former client system assure us that they fully understand the nature of the contact and support our discussions with that particular employee.

Some consultants use their broad network of contacts to act, officially or unofficially, as recruiters for their client systems. The intent could be quite innocent. For example, in a conversation with a manager, you might say, "When I was consulting to XYZ Company, I met an engineer who may be just the kind of person you need. If you like, I could contact her and see if she is interested." We also apply the "one year rule" in this type of situation.

Relations with Other Consultants

The ICMCI says: "A consultant will ensure that other management consultants carrying out work on his behalf are conversant with and abide by the Code of Professional Conduct."

We believe that OD consultants have a responsibility to protect the OD discipline by ensuring the ethics of people who claim membership. This may mean openly confronting OD consultants who behave in a less than fully ethical manner. If an OD consultant continually operates in an unethical manner, every effort should be made to *correct* that behavior. The stakes are too high to ignore or trivialize unethical behavior or practices. This book is a good place to give unethical colleagues fair warning: We will take action! You should take action also!

We agree with Gellerman, Frankel, and Ladenson (1990) in that we attempt to deal with colleagues' unethical behavior at the lowest possible level. Our initial effort is to take our wandering colleague aside and give him or her specific, direct, behavioral feedback based on our perceptions and the ethical principles we are using as the basis of conclusions. Then we ask for a change in the person's behavior or practices.

However, if private discussions prove to be insufficient, we take it to a higher level. This means bringing in another colleague as a third party, treating the disagreement between us and our colleague as a "dispute." Both parties in the dispute must have mutual respect for the third party and agree with the selection. The third party would act as a mediator, not an arbitrator.

If you and your colleague belong to a consulting firm and third-party intervention does not result in a mutually acceptable outcome, the next higher level would be to present the alleged case of unethical practice to your common manager. He or she would act as a mediator or as an arbitrator. If corrective action does not ensue, you may once again be confronted by a career-changing choice point.

It would be highly desirable if such cases could be referred to the ethics committee of an association in which all parties are members, for example, the OD Institute or the OD Network. Unfortunately, these associations have no authority to take away anyone's right to practice. They are, for the most part, merely "interest groups." They are not credentialing bodies that can investigate, verify, monitor, and bring career-ending sanctions to bear with unethical members. That is, the associations have no teeth.

That leaves only one other possible action: public confrontations in which the unethical behavior is revealed to other colleagues, current and prospective client systems, potential employers, and the general public. Not everyone is willing to take ethical issues to this level. Public confrontations could take place during meetings with client system leaders, in published articles or books, newspaper articles or press releases, broadcast journalists' reports, or civil court cases (O'Shea & Madigan, 1997; Shapiro, 1995). Of course, public allegations of perceived unethical behavior may leave us vulnerable to litigation.

We have written this book in part because we believe that knowledgeable, committed, ethical OD consultants are the best—if not the *only*—way to cull out ineffective, unethical consultants, by hitting them where they are most vulnerable—in the wallet.

To us, this is a question of *accountability*. Right now, there are few, if any, formal sanctions or consequences for unethical and incompetent persons. If such ersatz consultants find that we are willing to raise and pursue valid questions about their ethics and they are unable or unwilling to answer, perhaps they will not get enough work and will leave the field.

Summary

Organization development is a values-based discipline. We have discussed the personal values that are compatible with the practice of OD and how our values influence the manner in which we practice it. We have also discussed the reciprocal, that is, how the application of OD theory and methods may influence OD consultants' values.

We believe that, to become a true profession, the practitioners of OD must develop a strong, enforceable, commonly accepted code of conduct. The code must establish minimum criteria that aspiring OD consultants must satisfy. It must establish standards of practice and effective sanctions to enforce accountability.

Whatever institutions ultimately oversee the application of this code of conduct should also take responsibility for mounting a sustained public relations initiative for the purpose of educating consumers. Our prospective client systems will be the final arbiter of the effectiveness of this initiative. For us to become truly professional, their agents and leaders must accept and use the code. We hope our suggestions for some ethical standards will make a difference.

References

Ackerman-Anderson, L. (1996). Development, transition, or transformation: Bringing change leadership into the 21st century. *OD Practitioner, 28*(4), 5–25.

Ackoff, R.L. (1999). *Re-creating the corporation: A design of organizations for the 21st century.* London: Oxford University Press.

Adams, F.T., & Hansen, G.B. (1992). *Putting democracy to work: A practical guide for starting and managing worker-owned businesses.* San Francisco: Berrett-Koehler.

Adams, J.D. (Ed.). (1984). *Transforming work: A collection of organizational transformation readings.* Alexandria, VA: Miles River Press.

Alinsky, S. (1971). *Rules for radicals: A pragmatic primer for realistic radicals.* New York: Vintage Books.

Anderson, M.C. (1999). *Fast cycle organizational development.* St. Paul, MN: International Thomson.

Anonymous. (1996, October 14). Confessions of an *ex*-consultant. *Fortune,* pp. 107–112.

Arbnor, I., & Bjerke, B. (1996). *Methodology for creating business knowledge.* Thousand Oaks, CA: Sage.

Argyris, C. (1964). *Integrating the individual and the organization.* New York: John Wiley & Sons.

Argyris, C. (1990). *Overcoming organizational defenses: Facilitating organizational learning.* Boston, MA: Allyn and Bacon.

Argyris, C. (1993). *Knowledge for action: A guide to overcoming barriers to organizational change.* San Francisco: Jossey-Bass.

Argyris, C. (1999). *On organizational learning.* London: Blackwell.

Argyris, C., Putnam, R., & Smith, D.M. (1985). *Action science: Concepts, methods, and skills for research and intervention.* San Francisco: Jossey-Bass.

Argyris, C., & Schon, D.A. (1978). *Organizational learning.* Reading, MA: Addison-Wesley.

Argyris, C., & Schon, D.A. (1995). *Organizational learning, II: Theory, method, and practice.* Reading, MA: Addison-Wesley/Longman.

Asch, S.E. (1956). Studies of independence and conformity: A minority of one against a unanimous majority. *Psychological Monographs, 70*(9), 416.

Ashkenas, R.N., Jick, T., Ulrich, D., & Paul-Chowdhury, C. (1999). *The boundaryless organization field guide: Practical tools for building the new organization.* San Francisco: Jossey-Bass.

Astrachan, J.H. (1990). *Mergers, acquisitions, and employees' anxiety: A study of separation anxiety in a corporate context.* New York: Praeger.

Barchan, M. (1998). Beyond the balance sheet: Measuring intangible assets. *Chief Executive, 139,* 66–68.

Barcus, S.W., & Wilkinson, J.W. (Eds.). (1995). *Handbook of management consulting services* (2nd ed.). New York: McGraw-Hill.

Barker, J.A. (1992). *Future edge: Discovering the new paradigms of success.* New York: William Morrow.

Barnet, R.J., & Cavanagh, J. (1994). *Global dreams: Imperial corporations and the new world order.* New York: Simon & Schuster.

Bartlett, C.A., & Ghoshal, S. (1995, Fall). Rebuilding behavioral context: Turn process reengineering into people rejuvenation. *Sloan Management Review,* pp. 11–23.

Bass, B.M. (1998). *Transformational leadership: Industry, military, and educational impact.* Mahwah, NJ: Lawrence Erlbaum.

Beckhard, R. (1969). *Organization development: Strategies and models.* Reading, MA: Addison-Wesley.

Beckhard, R., & Harris, R.T. (1987). *Organizational transitions: Managing complex change* (2nd ed.). Reading, MA: Addison-Wesley.

Beckhard, R., & Prichard, W. (1992). *Changing the essence: The art of creating and leading fundamental change in organizations.* San Francisco: Jossey-Bass.

Bennis, W.G. (1969). *Organization development: Its nature, origins, and prospects.* Reading, MA: Addison-Wesley.

Bennis, W.G. (1998). *On becoming a leader.* Reading, MA: Addison-Wesley/Longman.

Bennis, W.G. (1997). *Managing people is like herding cats.* Provo, UT: Executive Excellence.

Bennis, W.G., & Goldsmith, J. (1997). *Learning to lead: A workbook on becoming a leader.* Reading, MA: Addison-Wesley/Longman.

Bennis, W.G., & Mische, M. (1997). *The 21st century organization: Reinventing through reengineering.* San Francisco: Jossey-Bass.

Bennis, W.G., & Nanus, B. (1997). *Leaders: The strategies for taking charge/the 4 keys to effective leadership.* New York: Harper Business.

Bennis, W.G., & Townsend, R. (1995). *Reinventing leadership: Strategies to empower the organization.* New York: William Morrow.

Black, J.S., Gregersen, H.B., & Mendenhall, M.E. (1992). *Global assignments: Successfully expatriating and repatriating international managers.* San Francisco: Jossey-Bass.

Blake, R.R., & Mouton, J.S. (1969). *Building a dynamic corporation through grid organization development.* Reading, MA: Addison-Wesley.

Block, P. (1981). *Flawless consulting: A guide to getting your expertise used.* San Francisco: Jossey-Bass/Pfeiffer.

Block, P. (1988). *The empowered manager: Positive political skills at work.* San Francisco: Jossey-Bass.

Block, P. (1996). *Stewardship: Choosing service over self-interest.* San Francisco: Berrett-Koehler.

Block, P. (1999). *Flawless consulting: A guide to getting your expertise used* (2nd ed.). San Francisco: Jossey-Bass/Pfeiffer.

Blumenthal, B., & Haspeslagh, P. (1994). Toward a definition of corporate transformation. *Sloan Management Review,* pp. 101–106.

Bolman, L.G., & Deal, T.E. (1987). *Modern approaches to understanding and managing organizations.* San Francisco: Jossey-Bass.

Bond, V. (1995). Change management. In S.W. Barcus & J.W. Wilkinson (Eds.),
Handbook of management consulting services (2nd ed.). New York: McGraw-Hill.

Bray, D.W. (1991). *Working with organizations and their people: A practical guide to
human resource practice.* New York: The Guilford Press.

Bridges, W.P. (1991). *Managing transitions: Making the most of change.* Reading,
MA: Addison-Wesley/Longman.

Brown, L.D. (1983). *Managing conflict at organizational interfaces.* Reading, MA:
Addison-Wesley.

Brown, J.S., & Duguid, P. (1991). Organizational learning and communities of
practice: Toward a unified view of working, learning, and innovation. *Organization Science, 2*(1), 40–57.

Brown, S.L., & Eisenhardt, K.M. (1997). The art of continuous change: Linking
complexity theory and time-paced evolution in relentlessly shifting organizations. *Administrative Science Quarterly, 42,* 1–34.

Buckhout, S., Frey, E., & Nemec, J., Jr. (1999, Second Quarter). Making ERP succeed: Turning fear into promise. *Strategy & Business, 15,* 60–72.

Bunker, B.B., & Alban, B.T. (1997). *Large group interventions: Engaging the whole
system for rapid change.* San Francisco: Jossey-Bass.

Buono, A.F., & Bowditch, J.L. (1989). *The human side of mergers and acquisitions:
Managing collisions between people, cultures, and organizations.* San Francisco:
Jossey-Bass.

Burke, W.W. (Ed.). (1977). *Current issues and strategies in organization development.*
New York: Human Sciences Press.

Burke, W.W. (1982). *Organization development: Principles and practices.* Boston, MA:
Little, Brown.

Burke, W.W. (1993). *Organization development: A process of learning and changing.*
Reading, MA: Addison-Wesley/Longman.

Burke, W.W. (1996). *Managing organizational change.* New York: American Management Association.

Bushko, D., & Raynor, M. (1998). Knowledge management: New directions for IT (and other) consultants. *Journal of Management Consulting, 10*(2), 67.

Byrne, J.A. (1994, July 25). The craze for consultants. Retrieved January 4, 1996, from *www.businessweek.com*

Cameron, K., & Quinn, R. (1997). *Diagnosing and changing organizational culture.* San Francisco: Jossey-Bass.

Caldwell, B. (1994, June 20). Reengineering slip-ups, missteps, miscues. *Information Week,* pp. 50–60.

Cartwright, S., & Cooper, C.L. (1999). *Managing mergers, acquisitions, & strategic alliances: Integrating people and culture.* Woburn, MA: Butterworth-Heinemann.

Champy, J. (1994). *The state of reengineering report.* CSC Index.

Champy, J. (1995). *Reengineering management: The mandate for new leadership.* New York: Harper Business.

Clegg, B., & Birch, P. (1998). *Disorganization: The handbook of creative organizational change.* New York: Financial Times/Pitman.

Clegg, S.R., Hardy, C., & Nord, W.R. (Eds.). (1996). *Handbook of organizational studies.* Thousand Oaks, CA: Sage.

Clemente, M.N., & Greenspan, D.S. (1998). *Winning at mergers and acquisitions: The guide to market-focused planning and integration.* New York: John Wiley & Sons.

Coates, J.F., & Jarratt, J. (1989). *What futurists believe.* Bethesda, MD: World Future Society Books.

Coch, L., & French, J.R.P., Jr. (1948). Overcoming resistance to change. *Human Relations, 1,* 512–532.

Cohen, A.R., Fink, S.L., & Gadon, H. (1988). *Effective behavior in organizations* (4th ed.). Homewood, IL: Irwin Professional.

Cohen, A.R., & Bradford, D.L. (1990). *Influence without authority.* New York: John Wiley & Sons.

Collins, J.C. (1995, May 29). Change is good—But first, know what should never change. *Fortune,* p. 141.

Collins, J.C., & Porras, J.I. (1994). *Built to last: Successful habits of visionary companies.* New York: Harper Business.

Conger, J.A., Lawler, E.E., Jr., & Spreitzer, G.M. (1998). *The leader's change handbook: An essential guide to setting direction and taking action.* San Francisco: Jossey-Bass.

Conner, D.R. (1998). *Leading at the edge of chaos: How to create the nimble organization.* New York: John Wiley & Sons.

Connor, R.A., & Davidson, J.P. (1985). *Marketing your consulting and professional services.* New York: John Wiley & Sons.

Cook, C.W., Hunsaker, P.L., & Coffey, R.E. (1996). *Management and organizational behavior.* New York: McGraw-Hill.

Cooperrider, D.L., & Dutton, J.E. (Eds.). (1999). *Organizational dimensions of global change: No limits to cooperation.* Thousand Oaks, CA: Sage.

Costa, P.T., Jr., & McCrae, R.R. (1992). *NEO PI-R: Professional manual–Revised NEO personality inventory (NEO PI-R) and NEO five-factor inventory (NEO-FFI).* Odessa, FL: Psychological Assessment Resources.

Culbert, S.A. (1996). *Mind-set management: The heart of leadership.* London: Oxford University Press.

Cummings, T.G., & Worley, C.G. (1997). *Organization development and change* (6th ed.). Minneapolis, MN: Southwestern.

Cunningham, J.B. (1993). *Action research and organizational development.* Westport, CT: Greenwood Publishing Group.

Davidson, M. (1996). *The transformation of management.* Boston, MA: Butterworth-Heinemann.

Davis, A., Maranville, S., & Obloj, K. (1997). The paradoxical process of organizational transformation: Propositions and a case study. *Research in Organizational Change and Development, 10,* 275–314.

Davis, S.M. (1984). *Managing corporate culture.* Cambridge, MA: Ballinger.

de Geus, A. (1997). *The living company.* Boston, MA: Harvard Business School Press.

Delbecq, A.L., Van de Ven, A.H., & Gustafson, D.H. (1975). *Group techniques for program planning: A guide to nominal group and delphi processes.* Glenview, IL: Scott, Foresman.

Demarco, T., & Lister, T. (2000). *Peopleware: Productive projects and teams* (2nd ed.). New York: Dorset House.

Devane, T., & Holman, P. (1999). *The change handbook: Group methods for shaping the future.* San Francisco: Berrett-Koehler.

Dotlich, D.L., & Noel, J.L. (1998). *Action learning: How the world's top companies are re-creating their leaders and themselves.* San Francisco: Jossey-Bass.

Drucker, P.F. (1973). *Management: Tasks, responsibilities, practices.* New York: Harper & Row.

Drucker, P.F. (1992). *Managing for the future: The 1990s and beyond.* New York: Truman Talley Books/Dutton.

Drucker, P.F. (1993). *Post-capitalist society.* New York: Harper Business.

Drucker, P.F. (1999). Knowledge-worker productivity: The biggest challenge. *California Management Review, 4*(2), 79–94.

Farnham, A. (1996, October 14). In search of suckers. *Fortune,* pp. 119–126.

Feldman, M.L., & Spratt, M.F. (1999). *Five frogs on a log: A CEO's guide to accelerating the transition in mergers, acquisitions, and gut wrenching change.* New York: Harper Business.

Festinger, L., Schachter, S., & Back, K. (1950). *Social pressures in informal groups.* New York: Harper.

Finkelstein, S., & Hambrick, D.C. (1996). *Strategic leadership: Top executives and their effect on organizations.* St. Paul, MN: West Publishing Company.

Fiol, C.M., & Lyles, M.A. (1985). Organizational learning. *Academy of Management Review, 10*(1), 803–813.

Fisher, A.B. (1994, January 24). How to make a merger work. *Fortune.*

Flamholtz, E.G., & Randle, Y. (1998). *Changing the game: Organizational transformations of the first, second, and third kinds.* London: Oxford University Press.

Fournies, F.F. (1988). *Why employees don't do what they're supposed to do and what to do about it.* New York: Liberty Hall Press.

Francesco, A.M., & Gold, B.A. (1997). *International organizational behavior: Text, readings, cases, and skills.* Englewood Cliffs, NJ: Prentice Hall.

Freedman, A.M. (1963). *Changes in perceptions of on-the-job problems following laboratory training: II.* Unpublished master's thesis, Boston University, College of Business Administration, Boston, MA.

Freedman, A.M. (1982). *A four-phase process for OD consultants to work themselves out of a job.* Arlington, VA: NTL Institute.

Freedman, A.M. (1987). The swamp model: A socio-technical systems model for diagnosing organizations in relation to their environments. In A.M. Freedman (Ed.), *Diagnosing organizations with impact readings.* Alexandria, VA: NTL Institute.

Freedman, A.M. (1993). *Kurt Lewin's force-field analysis.* Chicago, IL: Quantum Associates.

Freedman, A.M. (1994). Stress management training. In W.R. Tracey (Ed.), *Human resources management & development handbook* (pp. 1063–1077). New York: AMACOM.

Freedman, A.M. (1995). The consultant's sense of urgency: Steady-state versus front-line combat OD. In J.W. Pfeiffer (Ed.), *The 1995 annual: Volume 2, consulting* (pp. 213–220). San Francisco: Jossey-Bass/Pfeiffer.

Freedman, A.M. (1997). The undiscussable sides of implementing transformational change. *Consulting Psychology Journal, 49*(1), 51–76.

Freedman, A.M. (1998). *Developing high performance teamwork: Core competencies in facilitating four critical team processes.* Chicago, IL: Quantum Associates.

Freedman, A.M. (1998). Pathways and crossroads to institutional leadership. *Consulting Psychology Journal, 50* (3), 131–151.

Freedman, A.M. (2000). Multi-group representation: Representative teams or teams of representatives. *Consulting Psychology Journal, 52*(1), 63-81.

Freedman, A.M., & Levinson, H. (1998). The symbolic meaning of change. Presented at the *Mid-Winter Conference of the Society of Psychologists in Management,* San Diego, CA.

French, W.L., & Bell, C.H., Jr. (1995). *Organization development: Behavioral science interventions for organization improvement* (5th ed.). Englewood Cliffs, NJ: Prentice Hall.

French, W.L., Bell, C.H., & Zawacki, R.A. (Eds.). (2000). *Organization development and transformation: Managing effective change.* Burr Ridge, IL: Irwin Professional.

Friedlander, F. (1999, August 25). Personal communication.

Frost, P.J., Moore, L.F., Louis, M.R., Lundberg, C.C., & Martin, J. (Eds.). (1985). *Organizational culture.* Thousand Oaks, CA: Sage.

Galbraith, J.R. (1977). *Organization design.* Reading, MA: Addison-Wesley.

Garbarro, J.J. (1987). *The dynamics of taking charge.* Boston, MA: Harvard Business School Press.

Gasparski, W.W., & Botham, D. (1998). *Action learning: Praxiology: The international annual of practical philosophy and methodology* (Vol. 6). New Brunswick, NJ: Transaction Publishers.

Geisler, E. (1997). *Managing the aftermath of radical corporate change: Reengineering, restructuring and reinvention.* Westport, CT: Greenwood Publishing Group.

Gellermann, W., Frankel, M.S., & Landenson, R.F. (1990). *Values and ethics in organization and human system development: Responding to dilemmas in professional life.* San Francisco: Jossey-Bass.

Gibson, J.L., Ivancevich, J.M., & Donnelly, J.H. (1998). *Organizations: Behavior, structure, processes.* New York: McGraw-Hill.

Gleick, J. (1987). *Chaos: Making a new science.* New York: Viking.

Glidewell, J.C. (Ed.) (1989). *Corporate cultures: Research implications for human resource development.* Alexandria, VA: American Society for Training and Development.

Gold, M. (Ed.) (1999). *The complete social scientist: A Kurt Lewin reader.* Washington, DC: American Psychological Association.

Goleman, D. (1997). *Emotional intelligence.* New York: Bantam Books.

Golembiewski, R.T. (Ed.). (1993). *Handbook of organizational behavior.* New York: Marcel Dekker.

Goodstein, L.D., Nolan, T.M., & Pfeiffer, J.W. (1993). *Applied strategic planning: A comprehensive guide.* New York: McGraw-Hill.

Gouillart, F.J., & Kelly, J.N. (1995). *Transforming the organization.* New York: McGraw-Hill.

Greenberg, J., & Baron, R.A. (1999). *Behavior in organizations: Understanding and managing the human side of work.* Englewood Cliffs, NJ: Prentice Hall.

Greenwood, R., & Hinings, C. (1996). Understanding radical organizational change: Bringing together the old and the new institutionalism. *Academy of Management Review, 21*(4), 1022–1054.

Greiner, L.E. (1972). Evolution and revolution as organizations grow. *Harvard Business Review, 50*(4), 37–46.

Greiner, L.E., & Metzger, R.O. (1983). *Consulting to management: Insights to building and managing a successful practice.* Englewood Cliffs, NJ: Prentice Hall.

Hall, E.T. (1976). *Beyond culture.* Garden City, NY: Anchor Press/Doubleday.

Hambrick, D.C., Tushman, M.L., & Nadler, D.A. (1997). *Navigating change: How CEOs, top teams, and boards steer transformation.* Boston, MA: Harvard Business School Press.

Handy, C. (1993). *Understanding organizations.* London: Oxford University Press.

Hanson, P.G., & Lubin, B. (1997). *Answers to the most frequently asked questions about organizational development.* Thousand Oaks, CA: Sage.

Hardy, R.E., & Schwartz, R. (1996). *The self-defeating organization: How smart companies can stop outsmarting themselves.* Reading, MA: Addison-Wesley.

Harrison, R. (1995). *The collected papers of Roger Harrison.* San Francisco: Jossey-Bass.

Harvey, J.B. (1988). *The Abilene paradox and other meditations on management.* Glenview, IL: Scott, Foresman.

Harvey, J.B. (1999). *How come every time I get stabbed in the back my fingerprints are on the knife?: And other meditations on management.* San Francisco: Jossey-Bass.

Hatch, M.J. (1997). *Organization theory: Modern, symbolic, and postmodern perspectives.* London: Oxford University Press.

Hellriegel, D., Slocum, J.W., & Woodman, R.W. (1997). *Organizational behavior.* St. Paul, MN: International Thomson.

Hersey, P., & Blanchard, K.H. (1988). *Management of organizational behavior: Utilizing human resources.* Englewood Cliffs, NJ: Prentice Hall.

Hesselbein, F., Beckhard, R., & Goldsmith, M. (Eds.). (1998). *The organization of the future.* San Francisco: Jossey-Bass.

Holder, R.J., & McKinney, R.N. (1993, Fall). Scouting: A process for dealing with the frontiers of an uncertain world. *OD Practitioner,* pp. 20–25.

Hofstede, G.H. (1984). *Culture's consequences.* Thousand Oaks, CA: Sage.

Hofstede, G.H. (1991). *Cultures and organizations: Software of the mind.* New York: McGraw-Hill.

Hofstede, G.H. (1994). *Uncommon sense about organizations: Cases, studies, and field observations.* Thousand Oaks, CA: Sage.

Huber, G. (1991). Organizational learning: The contributing processes and the literatures. *Organizational Science, 2*(1), 88–115.

Hunt, J.G., Schermerhorn, J.R., & Osborn, R.N. (1997). *Organizational behavior.* New York: John Wiley & Sons.

Huntington, S.P. (1996). *The clash of civilizations and the remaking of world order.* New York: Simon & Schuster.

International Council of Management Consulting Institutes. *ICMCI code of conduct.* Published on the Internet. www.icmci.com

Ivancevich, J.M., & Matteson, M.T. (1995). *Organizational behavior and management.* New York: McGraw-Hill.

Janis, I.L. (1982). *Groupthink: Psychological studies of policy decisions and fiascoes.* Boston, MA: Houghton Mifflin.

Janis, I.L. (1989). *Crucial decisions: Leadership in policymaking and crisis management.* New York: The Free Press.

Janis, I.L., & Mann, L. (1977). *Decision making: A psychological analysis of conflict, choice, and commitment.* New York: The Free Press.

Jaques, E. (1989). *Requisite organization: The CEO's guide to creative structure & leadership.* Arlington, VA: Carson Hall.

Jayaram, G.K. (1976). Open systems planning. In W.G. Bennis, K.D. Benne, R. Chin, & K.E. Corey (Eds.), *The planning of change* (3rd ed.) (pp. 275–283). New York: Holt, Rinehart & Winston.

Johann, B. (1995). *Designing cross-functional business processes.* San Francisco: Jossey-Bass.

Johns, G. (1996). *Organizational behavior: Understanding and managing life at work.* New York: HarperCollins.

Johnson, B. (1992). *Polarity management: Identifying and managing unsolvable problems.* Amherst, MA: HRD Press.

Jones, J.W. (1993). *High-speed management: Time-based strategies for managers and organizations.* San Francisco: Jossey-Bass.

Kanter, R.M., Stein, B.A., & Jick, T.D. (1992). *The challenge of organizational change: How companies experience it and leaders guide it.* New York: The Free Press.

Kaplan, R.S., & Norton, D.P. (1996). *The balanced scorecard: Translating strategy into action.* Boston, MA: Harvard Business School Press.

Karp, H.B. (1988). A positive approach to resistance. In J.W. Pfeiffer (Ed.), *The 1988 annual: Developing human resources* (pp. 143-146). San Francisco: Jossey-Bass/Pfeiffer.

Katz, D., & Kahn, R.L. (1990). *The social psychology of organizations.* New York: John Wiley & Sons.

Kelly, K., & Melcher, R.A. (1994, September 12). Mergers today, trouble tomorrow? *Business Week On Line.* www.businessweek.com Department: Top of the News.

Kernberg, O.F. (1998). *Ideology, conflict, and leadership in groups and organizations.* New Haven, CT: Yale University Press.

Kets de Vries, M. (Ed.). (1984). *The irrational executive: Psychoanalytic studies in management.* New York: International Universities Press.

Kets de Vries, M., & Miller, D. (1989). *The neurotic organization: Diagnosing and changing counterproductive styles in management.* San Francisco: Jossey-Bass.

Kets de Vries, M. (1991). *Organizations on the couch: Clinical perspectives on organizational behavior and change.* San Francisco: Jossey-Bass.

Kilburg, R.R. (Ed.). (1996). Executive coaching. *Consulting Psychology Journal: Practice and Research* (special issue), *48*(2), 57–147.

Kilmann, R.H. (1989). *Managing beyond the quick fix: A completely integrated program for creating and maintaining organizational success.* San Francisco: Jossey-Bass.

Kilmann, R.H., & Covin, T. (Eds.). (1988). *Corporate transformation: Revitalizing organizations for a competitive world.* San Francisco: Jossey-Bass.

Kilmann, R.H., Saxton, M.J., Serpa, R., & Associates. (1985). *Gaining control of the corporate culture.* San Francisco: Jossey-Bass.

Klein, D. (1969). Some notes on the dynamics of resistance to change: The defender role. In W.G. Bennis, K.D. Benne, & R. Chin (Eds.), *The planning of change* (2nd ed.) (pp. 498-507). New York: Holt, Rinehart & Winston.

Kline, P., & Saunders, B. (1993). *Ten steps to a learning organization.* Arlington, VA: Great Ocean Publishers.

Knowdell, R.L., Branstead, E., & Moravec, M. (1994). *From downsizing to recovery: Strategic transition options for organizations and individuals.* Palo Alto, CA: CPP Books.

Kolb, D.A., Rubin, I.M., & Osland, J.S. (1994). *Organizational behavior: An experiential approach.* Englewood Cliffs, NJ: Prentice Hall.

Kotter, J.P. (1996). *Leading change.* Boston, MA: Harvard Business School Press.

Kouzes, J.M., & Posner, B.Z. (1996, May/June). Envisioning your future: Imagining ideal scenarios. *The Futurist,* pp. 14–19.

Kroeger, O., with J.M. Thuesen. (1992). *Type talk at work: How the 16 personality types determine your success on the job.* New York: Delacorte.

Labovitz, G., & Rosansky, V. (1997). *The power of alignment.* New York: John Wiley & Sons.

Lajoux, A.R. (1998). *The art of M&A integration: A guide to merging resources, processes, & responsibilities.* New York: McGraw-Hill.

Lawler, E.E., Jr. (1988). *High-involvement management: Participative strategies for improving organizational performance.* San Francisco: Jossey-Bass.

Lawrence, P.R., & Lorsch, J.W. (1969). *Developing organizations: Diagnosis and action.* Reading, MA: Addison-Wesley.

Levinson, H. (1994). Why the behemoths fell: Psychological roots of corporate failure. *American Psychologist, 49*(5), 428–436.

Lewin, K. (1997). *Resolving social conflicts* (originally published in 1948) and *Field theory in social science* (originally published in 1951). Washington, DC: American Psychological Association.

Lewis, J.P. (1998). *Team-based project management.* New York: American Management Associations.

Lichtenstein, B.M. (1995). Evolution or transformation: A critique and alternative to punctuated equilibrium. *Academy of Management Journal—Best Papers Proceedings,* 291–295.

Lippitt, G., & Lippitt, R. (1978). *The consulting process in action.* San Francisco: Jossey-Bass/Pfeiffer.

Lipton, M. (1996, Summer). Demystifying the development of an organizational vision. *Sloan Management Review,* pp. 83–92.

Lowman, R.L. (1998). *The ethical practice of psychology in organizations.* Washington, DC: American Psychological Association.

Luthans, F. (1997). *Organizational behavior.* New York: McGraw-Hill.

Lynn, G.S. (1998, Summer). New product team learning: Developing and profiting from your knowledge capital. *California Management Review, 40*(4), 74–93.

Mager, R.F., & Pipe, P. (1970). *Analyzing performance problems or "you really oughta wanna."* Belmont, CA: Fearon.

Making strategy. (1997, March 1). *The Economist*, p. 65.

March, J.G. (1991). Exploration and exploitation in organizational learning. *Organization Science, 2*(1), 71–87.

Marks, M.L., & Mirvis, P.H. (1998). *Joining forces: Making one plus one equal three in mergers, acquisitions, and alliances.* San Francisco: Jossey-Bass.

Margulies, N. (1984). Notes on the marginality of the consultant's role. In R.J. Lee & A.M. Freedman (Eds.), *Consultation skills readings* (pp. 105–107). Alexandria, VA: NTL Institute.

Marquardt, M.J. (1999). *Action learning in action: Transforming problems and people for world-class organizational learning.* Palo Alto, CA: Davies-Black.

Marrow, A.J. (1969). *The practical theorist: The life and work of Kurt Lewin.* New York: Basic Books.

Marshack, R.J. (1987, February). OD values, ethics and practices. *CBODN Newsletter, 2*(2), 6–7.

Massarik, F. (Ed.). (1990). *Advances in organization development* (Vol. 1). Norwood, NJ: Ablex Publishing.

Massarik, F. (Ed.). (1993). *Advances in organization development* (Vol. 2). Norwood, NJ: Ablex Publishing.

Massarik, F. (Ed.). (1995). *Advances in organization development* (Vol. 3). Norwood, NJ: Ablex Publishing.

Masterpasqua, F., & Perna, P. (Eds.). (1997). *The psychological meaning of chaos: Translating theory into practice.* Washington, DC: American Psychological Association.

Matteson, M.T., & Ivancevich, J.M. (Eds.). (1998). *Management & organizational behavior classics.* New York: McGraw-Hill.

McGinn, D. (1995, April 17). Business by best seller. *NewsWeek*, p. 49.

McGregor, D. (1985). *The human side of enterprise* (2nd ed.). New York: McGraw-Hill.

McHugh, P., Merli, G., & Wheeler, W. (1997). *Beyond business process reengineering: Moving towards the holonic enterprise.* New York: John Wiley & Sons.

McKenna, R. (1997). *Real time: Preparing for the age of the never satisfied customer.* Boston, MA: Harvard Business School Press.

McLagan, P., & Nel, C. (1995). *The age of participation: New governance for the work place and the world.* San Francisco: Berrett-Koehler.

Merry, U., & Brown, G.I. (1990). *The neurotic behavior of organizations.* New York: Gardner.

Meyerson, D., & Martin, J. (1987). Cultural change: An integration of three different views. *Journal of Management Studies, 26*(6), 623–647.

Micklethwait, J., & Wooldridge, A. (1996). *The witch doctors: Making sense of the management gurus.* New York: Random House.

Miller, D. (1982). Evolution and revolution: A quantum view of structural change in organizations. *Journal of Management Studies, 18,* 1–26.

Miller, J.B., & Brown, P.B. (1984). *The corporate coach.* New York: Harper Business.

Mink, O.G., Mink, B.P., Owen, K.Q., & Esterhuysen, P.W. (1993). *Change at work: A comprehensive management process for transforming organizations.* San Francisco: Jossey-Bass.

Mintzberg, H. (1994). *The rise and fall of strategic planning: Reconceiving roles for planning, plans, and planners.* New York: The Free Press.

Mirvis, P.H., & Marks, M.L. (1992). *Managing the merger: Making it work.* Englewood Cliffs, NJ: Prentice Hall.

Mohrman, S., Cohen, S., & Mohrman, A., Jr. (1995). *Designing team-based organizations.* San Francisco: Jossey-Bass.

Mohrman, S., Galbraith, J., & Lawler, E. (Eds.). (1998). *Tomorrow's organization: Crafting winning capabilities in a dynamic world.* San Francisco: Jossey-Bass.

Montgomery, C.A., & Porter, M.E. (Eds.). (1991). *Strategy: Seeking and securing competitive advantage.* Boston, MA: Harvard Business School Press.

Moorehead, G., & Griffin, R.W. (1997). *Organizational behavior: Managing people and organizations.* Boston, MA: Houghton Mifflin.

Morgan, G. (1989a). *Riding the waves of change: Developing managerial competencies for a turbulent world.* San Francisco: Jossey-Bass.

Morgan, G. (1989b). *Creative organization theory: A resource book.* Thousand Oaks, CA: Sage.

Morgan, G. (1997). *Imaginization: New mindsets for seeing, organizing and managing.* Thousand Oaks, CA: Sage.

Morrisey, G.L. (1996). *A guide to strategic thinking: Building your planning foundation.* San Francisco: Jossey-Bass.

Morrison, I. (1996). *The second curve: Managing the velocity of change.* New York: Ballantine.

Moynihan, P. (1993). *Pandaemonium: Ethnicity in international politics.* London: Oxford University Press.

Muirhead, B.K., & Simon, W.L. (1998). *High velocity leadership: Managing speed and direction in the world of faster-better-cheaper.* New York: Harper Business.

Myers, P.S. (1996). *Knowledge management and organizational design.* Boston, MA: Reed Elsevier Group.

Nader, F.P., & Merten, A.G. (1998, September). Achieving breakthrough performance. *Journal of Applied Behavioral Science, 34*(3).

Nadler, D.A. (1977). *Feedback and organization development: Using data-based methods.* Reading, MA: Addison-Wesley.

Nadler, D.A. (1998). *Champions of change: How CEOs and their companies are mastering the skills of radical change.* San Francisco: Jossey-Bass.

Nadler, D.A., Gerstein, M.S., Shaw, R.B., & Associates. (1992). *Organizational architecture: Designs for changing organizations.* San Francisco: Jossey-Bass.

Nadler, D.A., Shaw, R.B., & Walton, E. (1994). *Discontinuous change: Leading organizational transformation.* San Francisco: Jossey-Bass.

Nadler, D.A., & Tushman, M.L. (1997). *Competing by design: The power of organizational architecture.* New York: Oxford University Press.

Nahavandi, A., & Malekzadeh, A.R. (1993). *Organizational culture in the management of mergers.* Westport, CT: Quorum Books.

Nahavandi, A., & Malekzadeh, A.R. (1998). *Organizational behavior: The person-organization fit.* New York: Simon & Schuster.

Naisbitt, J. (1994). *Global paradox: The bigger the world economy, the more powerful its smallest players.* New York: William Morrow.

Nanus, B. (1992). *Visionary leadership: Creating a compelling sense of direction for your organization.* San Francisco: Jossey-Bass.

Natemeyer, W.E., & Gilberg, J.S. (1990). *Classics of organizational behavior.* Danville, IL: Interstate Publishers.

Neuhauser, P.C. (1990). *Tribal warfare in organizations: Turning tribal conflict into negotiated peace.* New York: HarperCollins.

Nevis, E.C. (1987). *Organizational consulting: A gestalt approach.* New York: Gardner.

Nevis, E.C., Lancourt, J., & Vassallo, H.G. (1996). *Intentional revolutions: A seven-point strategy for transforming organizations.* San Francisco: Jossey-Bass.

Newman, K., & Nollen, S. (1998). *Managing radical organizational change.* Thousand Oaks, CA: Sage.

Newstrom, J.W., & Davis, K. (1996). *Organizational behavior: Human behavior at work.* New York: McGraw-Hill.

Nicholas, J.M. (1990). *Managing business & engineering projects: Concepts and implementation.* Englewood Cliffs, NJ: Prentice Hall.

Nicoll, D. (1998). Revolutionary OD. *OD Practitioner, 30*(1).

Nirenburg, J. (1998). Revolutionary OD. *OD Practitioner, 30*(1).

Noer, D.M. (1993). *Healing the wounds: Overcoming the trauma of layoffs and revitalizing downsized organizations.* San Francisco: Jossey-Bass.

Nohria, N., & Eccles, R.G. (Eds.). (1994). *Networks and organizations: Structure, form and action.* Boston, MA: Harvard Business School Press.

Nolan, R.L., & Croson, D.C. (1994). *Creative destruction: A six-stage process for transforming the organization.* Boston, MA: Harvard Business School Press.

Nutt, P., & Backoff, R. (1997). Transforming organizations with second-order change. *Research in Organization Change and Development, 10,* 229–274.

OD Institute (1999a). The organization development code of ethics (22nd ed., last revised December 1991). *The international registry of O.D. professionals and organization development handbook,* (pp. 59–63). Chesterland, OH: Author.

OD Institute (1999b). *The international registry of O.D. professionals and organization development handbook.* Chesterland, OH: Author.

O'Hara-Devereaux, M., & Johansen, R. (1994). *Global work: Bridging distance, culture & time.* San Francisco: Jossey-Bass.

Ohmae, K. (1982). *The mind of the strategist: The art of Japanese business.* New York: McGraw-Hill.

Ohmae, K. (1990). *The borderless world: Power and strategy in the interlinked economy.* New York: Harper Business.

Olmosk, K.E. (1972). Seven pure strategies of change. In J.W. Pfeiffer & J.E. Jones (Eds.), *The 1972 annual handbook for group facilitators.* San Francisco: Jossey-Bass/Pfeiffer.

O'Shea, J., & Madigan, C. (1997). *Dangerous company: The consulting powerhouses and the businesses they save and ruin.* New York: Random House.

Oshry, B. (1992). *The possibilities of organization.* Boston, MA: Power & Systems.

O'Toole, J. (1995). *Leading change: Overcoming the ideology of comfort and the tyranny of custom.* San Francisco: Jossey-Bass.

Ott, J.S. (1997). *Classical readings in organizational behavior.* San Diego, CA: Harcourt Brace.

Owen, H. (1987). *Spirit: Transformation and development in organizations.* Potomac, MD: Abbott Publishing.

Owen, H. (1991). *Riding the tiger: Doing business in a transforming world.* Potomac, MD: Abbott Publishing.

Parker, G.M. (2000). *Cross-functional teams: Working with allies, enemies, and other strangers.* San Francisco: Jossey-Bass.

Parker, M. (1990). *Creating shared vision.* Oslo, Norway: Dialog International.

Pascale, R.T. (1990). *Managing on the edge: How the smartest companies use conflict to stay ahead.* New York: Simon & Schuster.

Pasmore, W.A. (1994). *Creating strategic change: Designing the flexible, high-performing organization.* New York: John Wiley & Sons.

Pasternack, B.A., & Viscio, A.J. (1998). *The centerless corporation: A new model for transforming your organization for growth and prosperity.* New York: Simon & Schuster.

Pauchant, T.C., & Mitroff, I. (1992). *Transforming the crisis-prone organization: Preventing individual, organizational, and environmental tragedies.* San Francisco: Jossey-Bass.

Pepall, L., Norman, G., & Richards, D.J. (1998). *Industrial organization: Contemporary theory and practice.* St. Paul, MN: International Thomson.

Peters, M., & Robinson, V. (1989). The origins and status of action research. *The Journal of Applied Behavioral Science, 20*(2), 113–124.

Peterson, D.B., & Hicks, M.D. (1996). *The leader as coach: Strategies for coaching and developing others.* Minneapolis, MN: Personnel Decisions International.

Pfeffer, J. (1994a). *Competitive advantage through people: Unleashing the power of the work force.* Boston, MA: Harvard Business School Press.

Pfeffer, J. (1994b). *Managing with power: Politics and influence in organizations.* Boston, MA: Harvard Business School Press.

Pfeffer, J. (1997). *New directions for organizational theory: Problems and prospects.* Boston, MA: Harvard Business School Press.

Pfeffer, J. (1998b). *The human equation: Building profits by putting people first.* Boston, MA: Harvard Business School Press.

Porter, M.E. (1990). *The competitive advantage of nations.* New York: The Free Press.

Price Waterhouse Change Integration Team, The. (1996). *The paradox principles: How high-performance companies manage chaos, complexity, and contradiction to achieve superior results.* Burr Ridge, IL: Irwin Professional.

Pritchett, P., Robinson, D., & Clarkson, R. (1997). *After the merger: The authoritative guide for integration success* (rev. ed.). New York: McGraw-Hill.

Prochaska, J.O., DiClemente, C.C., & Norcross, J.C. (1992, September). In search of how people change: Applications to addictive behaviors. *The American Psychologist,* pp. 1102–1114.

Pucik, V., Tichy, N.M., & Barnett, C.K. (Eds.). (1993). *Globalizing management: Creating and leading the competitive organization.* New York: John Wiley & Sons.

Quinn, R., & Cameron, K. (Eds.). (1988). *Paradox and transformation: Toward a theory of change in organization and management.* Cambridge, MA: Ballinger.

Random House dictionary of the English language: Unabridged (2nd ed.). (1987). (p. 659). New York: Random House.

Reichers, A.E., Wanous, J.P., & Austin, J.T. (1997). Understanding and managing cynicism about organizational change. *Academy of Management Executive, 11*(1), 48–59.

Ritvo, R., Litwin, A., & Butler, L. (Eds.). (1995). *Managing in the age of change.* Burr Ridge, IL: Irwin Professional.

Robbins, S.P. (1998). *Organizational behavior: Concepts—controversies—applications.* Englewood Cliffs, NJ: Prentice Hall.

Robbins, S.P. (1999). *Essentials of organizational behavior.* Englewood Cliffs, NJ: Prentice Hall.

Robinson, D.G., & Robinson, J.C. (1995). *Performance consulting: Moving beyond training.* San Francisco: Berrett-Koehler.

Romanelli, E., & Tushman, M. (1994). Organizational transformation as punctuated equilibrium: An empirical test. *Academy of Management Journal, 37*(5), 1141–1166.

Rothman, J. (1997). *Resolving identity-based conflict in nations, organizations, and communities.* San Francisco: Jossey-Bass.

Rothwell, W.J. (1999). *The action learning guidebook: A real-time strategy for problem-solving, training design, and employee development.* San Francisco: Jossey-Bass/Pfeiffer.

Rothwell, W.J., Sullivan, R., & McLean, G.N. (Eds.). (1995). *Practicing organization development: A guide for consultants.* San Francisco: Jossey-Bass/Pfeiffer.

Rubin, I.M., Kolb, D.A., & Osland, J.S. (Eds.). (1995). *The organizational behavior reader.* Englewood Cliffs, NJ: Prentice Hall.

Ruma, S. (1974). A diagnostic model for organizational change: Where the flexible is functional. *Social Change, 4*(4).

Ryan, K.D., & Oestreich, D.K. (1991). *Driving fear out of the workplace: How to overcome the invisible barriers to quality, productivity, and innovation.* San Francisco: Jossey-Bass.

Salmon, B., & Rosenblatt, N. (1995). *Consulting really works.* Ridgefield, CT: Round Lake Publishing.

Sanchez, R., & Heene, A. (1997). *Strategic learning and knowledge management.* New York: John Wiley & Sons.

Sarvary, M. (1999). Knowledge management and competition in the consulting industry. *California Management Review, 41*(2), 95–107.

Schein, E.H. (1992). *Organizational culture and leadership* (2nd ed.). San Francisco: Jossey-Bass.

Schein, E.H. (1999). *The corporate culture survival guide: Sense and nonsense about culture change.* San Francisco: Jossey-Bass.

Schermerhorn, J.R., Hunt, J.G., & Osborn, R.N. (1996). *Organizational behavior.* New York: John Wiley & Sons.

Schoemaker, P.J.H. (1995). Scenario planning: A tool for strategic thinking. *Sloan Management Review, 36*(2), 25-40.

Schuster, J.P., Carpenter, J., & Kane, M.P. (1996). *The power of open-book management: Releasing the true potential of people's minds, hearts & hands.* New York: John Wiley & Sons.

Schutz, W. (1994). *The human element: Productivity, self-esteem and the bottom line.* San Francisco: Jossey-Bass.

Scott, C.D., Jaffe, D., & Tobr, G. (1994). *Organizational vision, values and mission: Values and mission.* Menlo Park, CA: Crisp.

Senge, P.M. (1990). *The fifth discipline: The art and practice of the learning organization.* New York: Currency/Doubleday.

Senge, P.M., Roberts, C., Ross, R.B., Smith, B.J., & Kleiner, A. (1994). *The fifth discipline fieldbook: Strategies and tools for building a learning organization.* New York: Currency/Doubleday.

Senge, P.M., Kleiner, A., Roberts, C., Ross, R., Roth, G., & Smith, B. (1999). *The dance of change: The challenges to sustaining momentum in a learning organization.* New York: Currency/Doubleday.

Shani, A.B., & Lau, J.B. (1999). *Behavior in organizations: An experiential approach.* New York: McGraw-Hill.

Shapiro, E.C. (1995). *Fad surfing in the boardroom: Reclaiming the courage to manage in the age of instant answers.* Reading, MA: Addison-Wesley.

Sherman, H., & Schultz, R. (1998). *Open boundaries: Creating business innovation through complexity.* Reading, MA: Perseus Books.

Shula, D., & Blanchard, K. (1995). *Everyone's a coach.* New York: Harper Business.

Skibbins, G.J. (1974). *Organizational evolution: A program for managing radical change.* New York: American Management Association.

Sorensen, P.F., Head, T.C., Mathys, N.J., & Cooperrider, D. (1995). *Global and international organization development.* Champaign, IL: Stipes Publishing.

Spencer, L.J. (1989). *Winning through participation: Meeting the challenge of corporate change with the technology of participation.* Dubuque, IA: Kendall/Hunt.

Srivastva, S. (1983). *The executive mind.* San Francisco: Jossey-Bass.

Srivastva, S., Cooperrider, D.L. (1990). *Appreciative management and leadership: The power of positive thought and action in organization.* San Francisco: Jossey-Bass.

Srivastva, S., & Cooperrider, D.L. (Eds.). (1997). *Organizational wisdom and executive courage.* San Francisco: Jossey-Bass.

Stacey, R.D. (1996). *Complexity and creativity in organizations.* San Francisco: Berrett-Koehler.

The Standish Group (1999). Chaos. www.standishgroup.com.

Steele, F.I. (1973). *Physical settings and organization development.* Reading, MA: Addison-Wesley.

Stein, H.F. (1987). *Developmental time, cultural space.* Norman, OK: University of Oklahoma Press.

Tannenbaum, R., Margulies, N., Massarik, F., & Associates. (1985). *Human systems development: New perspectives on people and organizations.* San Francisco: Jossey-Bass.

Tenner, E. (1996). *Why things bite back: Technology and the revenge of unintended consequences.* New York: Alfred A. Knopf.

Tichy, N.M. (1990). *Managing strategic change: Technical, political, and cultural dynamics.* New York: John Wiley & Sons.

Tichy, N.M. (1997). *The leadership engine: How winning companies build leaders at every level.* New York: Harper Business.

Tichy, N.M., & Charan, R. (1998). *Every business is a growth business: How your company can prosper year after year.* New York: Random House.

Tichy, N.M., & Devanna, M.A. (1997). *The transformational leader: The key to global competitiveness.* New York: John Wiley & Sons.

Tichy, N.M., McGill, A.R., & St. Clair, L. (Eds.). (1997). *Corporate global citizenship.* San Francisco: Jossey-Bass.

Tichy, N. M., & Sherman, S. (2000). *Control your destiny or someone else will.* New York: Harper Business.

Tobias, L.L. (1990). *Psychological consulting to management: A clinician's perspective.* New York: Brunner/Mazel.

Trompenaars, F. (1994). *Riding the waves of culture: Understanding diversity in global business.* Burr Ridge, IL: Irwin Professional.

Tuller, L.W. (1992). *Cutting edge consultants: Succeeding in today's explosive markets.* Englewood Cliffs, NJ: Prentice Hall.

Turner, A.N. (1982, September/October). Consulting is more than giving advice. *Harvard Business Review, 60*(5), 120–129.

Tushman, M., & O'Reilly C. (1996). Ambidextrous organizations: Managing evolutionary and revolutionary change. *California Management Review, 38*(4), 8–30.

Vaill, P. (1989). *Managing as a performing art: New ideas for a world of chaotic change.* San Francisco: Jossey-Bass.

Van Eynde, D.F., Hoy, J.C., & Van Eynde, D.C. (Eds.). (1997). *Organization development classics: A history of the future of change—The best of the* OD Practitioner. San Francisco: Jossey-Bass.

Van Maanen, J. (Ed.). (1998). *Qualitative studies of organizations.* Thousand Oaks, CA: Sage.

Waldman, D.A., & Atwater, L.E. (1998). *The power of 360 degree feedback: How to leverage performance evaluations for top productivity.* Houston, TX: Gulf.

Waldrop, M.M. (1992). *Complexity: The emerging science at the edge of order and chaos.* New York: Simon & Schuster.

Walton, R. (1985, March/April). From control to commitment in the workplace. *Harvard Business Review,* pp. 76–84.

Walton, R.E. (1989). *Up and running: Integrating information technology and the organization.* Boston, MA: Harvard Business School Press.

Weisbord, M.R. (1987). *Productive workplaces: Organizing and managing for dignity, meaning, and community.* San Francisco: Jossey-Bass.

Weisbord, M.R., & 35 International Coauthors. (1992). *Discovering common ground: How future search conferences bring people together to achieve breakthrough innovation, empowerment, shared vision, and collaborative action.* San Francisco: Berrett-Koehler.

Wheatley, M.J. (1992). *Leadership and the new science: Learning about organization from an orderly universe.* San Francisco: Berrett-Koehler.

White, J.B. (1997, March 3). Management consulting firms broke revenue records in 1996. *The Wall Street Journal.*

Whitmore, J. (1994). *Coaching for performance.* San Francisco: Jossey-Bass/Pfeiffer.

Wicks, A.C., & Glezen, P.L. (1998, January). In search of experts: A conception of expertise for business ethics consultation. *Business Ethics Quarterly, 8*(1).

Wind, J.Y., & Main, J. (1998). *Driving change: How the best companies are preparing for the 21st century.* New York: The Free Press.

Woodward, J. (1994). *Industrial organization: Theory and practice.* London: Oxford University Press.

Worley, C., Ross, W.L., & Hitchin, D.E. (1995). *Integrated strategic change: How organizational development builds competitive advantage.* Reading, MA: Addison Wesley/Longman.

Yates, R.E. (1995, November 24). Structural weakness from re-engineering study: Some firms are less efficient, flexible and competitive now. *Chicago Tribune.*

Yergin, D., & Gustafson, T. (1993). Scenario planning. *Russia 2010 and what it means for the world: The CERA report.* New York: Random House.

Zackrison, R.E. (1997). *Interpersonal dynamics inventory.* St. Helier, Jersey, C.I.: Effectiveness Consultants Limited.

Zackrison, R.E., & Freedman, A.M. (2000). *A corporate guide for managing consultants.* Aldershot, Hampshire, England: Gower.

About the Authors

 **A**rthur M. Freedman, Ph.D., is the Director of the American University/NTL Institute (AU/NTL) Masters degree program in Organization Development and the Personnel and Human Resource Management (PHRM) masters degree program at the School of Public Affairs, American University. The AU/NTL-PHRM programs also provide certificate programs in OD and HRM as well as contract services to business, industry, government, and non-profit organizations. He has consulted to over two hundred client systems in a wide range of industries, large and small, domestic and global, public and private. Dr. Freedman also conducts public workshops each year through the NTL Institute.

He has more than sixty publications, with more books and articles in the pipeline, and has delivered over sixty presentations at professional and trade associations. He received the *1994 RHR International Award for Excellence in Consulting*

Psychology (Division 13, American Psychological Association) and is a past president of the Society of Psychologists in Management. He received the *Consulting Psychology Journal's* award for the Most Outstanding Article of 1998 for "Pathways and Crossroads to Institutional Leadership."

Dr. Freedman received his B.S. degree in business administration and his MBA from Boston University and his Ph.D. in clinical psychology from the University of Chicago. He is a Fellow of the American Psychological Association (Consulting Psychology Division) and past-president of the Society of Psychologists in Management, American Society for Training and Development, International Society for the Psychoanalytic Study of Organizations, OD Network, OD Institute, the NTL Institute, and the Academy of Management. He has maintained his Illinois license as a clinical psychologist.

Dr. Richard Zackrison, Ph.D., is the founder and Director of Effectiveness Consultants, an international management consulting firm with over 20 consultants working out of offices in Sweden, England, Scotland, the U.S. and Zimbabwe. His formal education includes a Bachelor's degree in Management and a Master's in Education and a Doctorate in Adult Education, in addition to extensive graduate and postgraduate studies in individual and group psychology, including training in counseling.

He has served as an Associate Professor of Management, Seattle University and as an adjunct faculty member at Stockholm School of Economics, where he has been co-director of the institute's Management Consulting Course. Dr. Zackrison is a "Registered Organization Development Consultant" with the OD Institute in the U.S., a former Board Member for the Swedish Association of Management Consultants (SAMC) and former co-chairman of that SAMC's Consultant Certification Program.

His consulting experience includes over 20 years of senior level consulting experience in the areas of leadership development and organizational change and development. In addition, he is the primary designer and senior trainer for Effectiveness Consultants' Consultant Training Program, which has trained over a 1000 internal and external organizational consultants over the past 20 years.

Of special note, Dr. Zackrison was recognized by the Organization Development Institute for the Outstanding OD Application Worldwide for 1999 for his innovative work with Zimbabwe's National Breweries.

About the Editors

William J. Rothwell, Ph.D. is professor of human resource development in the College of Education at The Pennsylvania State University, University Park. He is also president of Rothwell and Associates, a private consulting firm that specializes in a broad array of organization development, human resource development, performance consulting and human resource management services.

Dr. Rothwell has authored, co-authored, edited, or co-edited numerous publications, including *Practicing Organization Development* (with R. Sullivan and G. McLean, Jossey-Bass/Pfeiffer, 1995). Dr. Rothwell's latest publications include *The ASTD Reference Guide to Workplace Learning and Performance*, 3rd ed., 2 vols. (with H. Sredi, HRD Press, 2000); *The Competency Toolkit*, 2 vols (with D. Dubois, HRD Press, 2000); *Human Performance Improvement: Building Practitioner Competence* (with C. Hohne and S. King, Gulf Publishing, 2000); *The Complete Guide to Training Delivery: A Competency-Based*

Approach (with S. King and M. King, Amacom, 2000); *Building In-House Leadership and Management Development Programs* (with H. Kazanas, Quorum Books, 1999); *The Action Learning Guidebook* (Jossey-Bass/Pfeiffer, 1999); and *Mastering the Instructional Design Process*, 2nd ed. (with H. Kazanas, Jossey-Bass/Pfeiffer, 1998).

Dr. Rothwell's consulting client list includes thirty-two companies from the *Fortune* 500.

Roland **Sullivan** has worked as an organization development (OD) pioneer with nearly eight hundred organizations in ten countries and virtually every major industry.

Mr. Sullivan specializes in the science and art of systematic and systemic change, executive team building, and facilitating Whole System Transformation Conferences—large interactive meetings with from three hundred to fifteen hundred people.

Mr. Sullivan has taught courses in OD at seven universities, and his writings on OD have been widely published. With Dr. Rothwell and Dr. McLean, he was co-editor of *Practicing OD: A Consultant's Guide* (Jossey-Bass/Pfeiffer, 1995).

For over two decades, Mr. Sullivan has served as chair of the OD Institute's Committee to Define Knowledge and Skills for Competence in OD and was a recent recipient of the Outstanding OD Consultant of the World award from the OD Institute.

Mr. Sullivan's current professional learning is available at *www.changeagent.net*.

Kristine **Quade** is an independent consultant who combines her background as an attorney with a master's degree in organization development from Pepperdine University, and years of experience as both an internal and external OD consultant.

Ms. Quade draws from experiences in guiding teams from divergent areas within corporations and across many levels of executives and employees. She has facilitated leadership alignment, culture change, support system alignment, quality process improvements, organizational redesign, and the creation of clear strategic intent that results in significant bottom-line results. A believer in whole systems change, she has developed the expertise to facilitate groups ranging in size from eight to two thousand in the same room for a three-day change process.

Recognized as the 1996 Minnesota Organization Development Practitioner of the Year, Ms. Quade teaches in the master's programs at Pepperdine University and the University of Minnesota at Mankato and the master's and doctoral programs at the University of St. Thomas in Minneapolis. She is a frequent presenter at the Organization Development National Conference and also at the International OD Congress and the International Association of Facilitators.

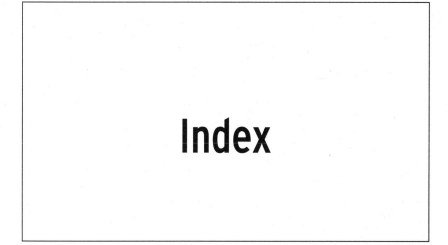

Index

Virtual teamwork, 106
Viscio, A. J., 44
Vision, 36; shared, 168, 171–172
Visioning, 172

W

Waldman, D. A., 45
Waldrop, M. M., 46
Walk the talk, 96
Walton, E., 44
Walton, R. E., 44
Wanous, J. P., 173
Weaknesses, issues seen as, 35
Websites, consultant marketing on, 11–12
Weisbord, M. R., 45, 46, 172
Wheatley, M. J., 46
Wheeler, W., 44
Whitmore, J., 45
Wilkinson, J. W., 42

Win-lose games, 171
Wind, J. Y., 45
"Wired" contracts, 13
Woodman, R. W., 47
Woodward, J., 47
Word-of-mouth advertising, 14
Work redesign, 145
World Wide Web, consulting resources on, 101
Worley, C., 44, 48
Writing: confidentiality and, 185; marketing through, 10–11

Y

Y2K problems, 42

Z

Zackrison, R. E., 48, 100, 106